WITHDRAWN

BURL

Journalism Giant and Medical Trailblazer

Jane Wolfe

Andrews McMeel
PUBLISHING®

Andrews McMeel Publishing
a division of Andrews McMeel Universal
1130 Walnut Street, Kansas City, Missouri 64106

www.andrewsmcmeel.com

22 23 24 25 26 RR2 10 9 8 7 6 5 4 3 2 1

ISBN: 978-1-5248-7179-6

Library of Congress Control Number: 2022931133

Editors: Evelyn M. Duffy, Jean Z. Lucas
Art Director: Holly Swayne
Production Editor: David Shaw
Production Manager: Carol Coe

ATTENTION: SCHOOLS AND BUSINESSES
Andrews McMeel books are available at quantity discounts with
bulk purchase for educational, business, or sales promotional use.
For information, please e-mail the Andrews McMeel Publishing
Special Sales Department: specialsales@amuniversal.com.

In 1984, as his contribution to the seventy-fifth-anniversary project of the Society of Professional Journalists, Burl addressed the topic "What a Free Press Means to America" with these words. May they continue to inspire and encourage journalists the world over.

A free press is important to America only if freedom itself is important.

Next to life itself, no value in our culture has been so cherished as freedom.

No society has long preserved its freedom without preserving the free exchange of thought.

No better prism than the press has yet been devised to communicate the competition of ideas, even unpopular ones, necessary to a democracy.

That is why the press is important—not because journalists are special people but because America is a special country. It's free, and a free press helps to keep it that way.

"Out in Texas, when we find a turtle on a fence post, we say one thing: he had a lot of help."

—Burl Osborne

Dedication

· · ·

To all working journalists today and all those who have died while covering the news to protect the freedom of the press;

to all doctors, nurses, and medical specialists who treat kidney disease and perform miraculous procedures to improve their lives;

to all the brave recipients and donors of organs and to all those doctors, nurses, and medical specialists who make transplantation happen;

and to all of Burl's colleagues from The Associated Press, *The Dallas Morning News,* and the many industry boards on which he served.

Special Dedication
David Osborne
Harry Wilder Osborne
Robert and Maureen Decherd
Lee Harris

Contents

PART II

The Dallas Morning News . . . 131

PART III

Retirement ... 255

Foreword

· · ·

Burl is a book about an exceptional person whose life story causes us to reflect deeply on the relationship between courage and accomplishment. It is also a book about ideas—ideas that define our nation and are the foundation for fairness and common decency among people of all walks of life.

Burl Osborne would never have pretended that he alone created this story. His seventy-five years were an intricate pattern of family, genuine friends, doctors, role models, mentors, mentees, competitors, and, yes, the public. Burl tended honorably to them all.

You will find in these pages several references to Burl being a presence in the room. He was He was also barely five feet, five inches tall. Some people have a physical presence that puts others at ease while at the same time conveying gravitas. Burl was one of these people, and he reinforced his persona by being careful in expression, in how he listened, and even in how he dressed.

Burl was really smart; his intellect was apparent in every way. But his distinguishing ability was to grasp a situation and quickly devise a response that galvanized the people around him. This extended from news stories he supervised to personal situations of every kind. Burl could lobby you without you realizing you were being lobbied. I've always attributed half credit for *The News'* first Pulitzer Prize run to this skill of his. Burl's newsroom won six Pulitzers in just eight years for a newsaper that, before his arrival, was not particularly well known or admired on a national level.

Burl's sense of humor amplified the confidence of people around him. At the same time, he was self-deprecating in a manner that his peers and colleagues appreciated. He was fiercely competitive, essentially at his best when leading the latest "tour de force." If you worked with or for Burl, you also knew that he didn't countenance fools or incompetents.

Burl puts in stark relief what those of us closest to him knew: he lived every day to the limit. Burl took nothing for granted and expected the rest of us to follow the same philosophy. Burl and his mother, Juanita, were medical pioneers in the field of organ transplantation—many experts called them heroes. Burl wrote moving Associated Press (AP) stories about his years of acute nephritis and the eventual failure of both kidneys in 1964. But he was more private about the kidney transplant that saved his life and empowered him to concentrate his talents on the art of journalism, preferring to discuss his extraordinary medical passage in forums that advanced the art of organ transplantation.

One of the best things about this book is that it embraces the writing style and cadence that Burl respected and perfected. It's AP standards and the AP style book in the form of a biography. He would have liked that very much.

The AP's principles defined Burl's professional life, where the ideas of freedom of speech and journalistic integrity reigned supreme. When Burl and I first discussed how best to describe what we wanted to accomplish at *The Dallas Morning News*, we always returned to the moniker "a newspaper of distinction." Of course, that characterization is in the eye of the beholder, but we agreed that it came down to a comprehensive news report and a commentary that were always balanced and fair. These themes run deep throughout *Burl*; they rely on the simple, powerful notion that tone is everything. Burl knew this from endless numbers of experiences and believed it to his core.

Burl's conviction about free speech and the effect of great journalism led him to take to the bully pulpit throughout his life. He did so with great effect because he always believed his audiences were more important than him. He was an orator at heart, and his oratory style perfectly matched his convictions. When he delivered a speech—each of which he wrote himself—or engaged in repartee, Burl projected the person he was through precise prose and an intentional, measured delivery.

For many editors, the concept of civic engagement by a newspaper runs counter to a conviction about editorial independence. Burl believed, to the contrary, that the lifeblood of a successful journalistic institution is its relationship with the communities it serves, in every way and at all levels. He made this a hallmark of his years at *The News* and in many personal endeavors.

Were he editing this biography, Burl would have gone to lengths to emphasize the roles of people who collaborated in his successes throughout his life. Foremost among these at *The News* were Jeremy Halbreich, Bill Cox, Ralph Langer, and Bob Mong. There were many more *News* stalwarts on Burl's "long list"! And Burl would have made the presence of Betty and Jonathan even more strongly felt.

Burl Osborne was loyal. Loyal to the people he loved and admired. Loyal to the institutions that gave him voice, notably the AP, the A. H. Belo Corporation, and *The Dallas Morning News*—each of which thrived because of him. Above all, throughout his life and far beyond his successes, Burl was grateful. Those of us who knew him well, and counted him as our friend, will always remember that most of all.

—Robert Decherd
Dallas, Texas
December 1, 2020

PART I

The Associated Press

1

Four Rooms and a Path

Burl Osborne—no middle name—was born on June 25, 1937, in Jenkins, Kentucky, a tiny Appalachian coal camp in the southeastern edge of the state. His sixteen-year-old mother, Juanita, gave birth with the help of a midwife in a four-room wood duplex that she shared with her twenty-one-year-old husband, Oliver. The company-owned duplex was small and austere. Its one luxury—something many people in that part of Appalachia did not have—was an indoor toilet.

Burl's father, Oliver, tall and dark haired, worked in the coal mines stringing communication and electrical lines into the interiors of mines and between the various mine shafts. The job paid little and was dangerous, exhausting work that required him to climb tall, rickety poles. But in the middle of the Great Depression, with only a second-grade education and no ability to read or write, his options were limited. (Decades later it was determined he probably had dyslexia.)

Located at the foot of the Pine Mountains, about five miles from the Virginia state line, Jenkins was not a pretty place. Most roads were unpaved, and black coal dust was everywhere. It covered the hills and the miners' clothes and their faces. Coal dust crept under the doors of the duplex and into the Osbornes' kitchen. In the winter when it snowed, Jenkins' children had to dig deep down into drifts to see fresh white snow.

"When you'd go to pick up your paycheck, you'd carry a gun," said Burl's younger brother David Osborne. "People were desperate for even a little bit of money."

Oliver was a binge drinker who was known to bet on boxing matches and gamble at the pool hall. He stayed drunk all weekend but usually managed to sober up by Monday morning when it was time to go back to work.

Juanita Smallwood Osborne had a strong will and made most of the decisions for the family. She was only about five feet tall and was five years younger than Oliver, but she was self-confident, smart, and not easily pushed around.

Juanita had spent her early childhood in Danville, Kentucky. It was a difficult upbringing. Her childhood home burned, her parents divorced, and she was sent to her father's hometown of Dorton, Kentucky, to live with his mother. Granny was a difficult woman and didn't care much for girls. Juanita was eager to get away from home. Although she met Oliver at fifteen and had Burl a year later, she graduated high school and loved the debate team.

Not long after her marriage to Oliver, Juanita had gone to her father for help. Her new husband was drinking and gambling. Her father told her that she had made her bed and she had to lie in it.

After Burl, Juanita didn't have another child for six years.

Early in 1943, Oliver decided to leave the coal mine to secure a job in the growing World War II shipbuilding operations in Michigan. Shortly after Burl's brother David was born, Oliver left his wife and his two sons in Jenkins. It wasn't long, however, before the portion of his paychecks he sent home began to decrease. Juanita assumed he was gambling away the money. She packed up baby David and left Burl with Oliver's parents. While he was with them, six-year-old Burl became so ill with a severe case of strep throat that he couldn't get out of bed for several days.

Juanita headed for Michigan with an ultimatum for her husband: she was going back to Kentucky, and if he chose to remain in Michigan rather than accompany her, he should never come home at all.

The couple returned to Kentucky. Oliver quickly found a job stringing telephone lines in Ashland, a town of 30,000 people located about 125 miles north of Jenkins on the Ohio River where the states of Kentucky, Ohio, and West Virginia converge.

They found a small four-room wood-frame house to rent. Though this house did have a kitchen sink with running water, it had a backyard outhouse in lieu of an indoor toilet. Heat came from several fireplaces and a wood-burning stove, and each room was illuminated by a single hanging light bulb.

"Affluent families had bathrooms," Burl once said. "We had four rooms and a path."

Soon, relatives moved in with them, and the bleak little two-bedroom house was home to ten people. "With so many people living in this little house, you slept wherever you could find a spot," David said. "It wasn't easy, but that's all we knew."

• • •

Ashland, Kentucky, in the 1940s had much more to offer than Jenkins did. Although small compared with the state's largest city, Louisville—which was ten times its size—Ashland was nevertheless a thriving commercial city. Ashland's two largest companies, Armco Steel and Ashland Oil, provided employment to most local people who wanted a job.

Burl thrived in school. He was an exceptional student, and his early teachers gave him much encouragement. When Burl was about eight, the family moved to Summit, not far from Ashland, but out in the country. Burl later recalled that his teacher cried when they moved because she was concerned he would fall behind at the country school and not fulfill his potential.

In Summit, Oliver and Burl raised show rabbits, many of which they entered in local contests. They often returned home with a prize and the rabbit, which Juanita cooked for dinner. The family had a milk cow, chickens that ran free in the yard, a horse, and several hogs. A third child, Rick, was born in 1946.

"If Burl or one of us wanted to go out with our friend, first we'd have to do the chores around the farm," David said. "We'd have to fix a fence post, or kill a chicken for dinner, or churn the milk, or catch one of the hogs. Burl didn't like that kind of farm work. He did it because my mother told us to, but he didn't like it at all."

On Sundays, Oliver hunted squirrels. After Juanita and the boys returned home from Baptist church in Ashland, she would cook and serve the squirrels with dumplings for Sunday lunch. "We were not rich," Burl said years later, "but neither were we hungry."

The resourceful family took advantage of the farm's natural resources. A seam of coal ran through their property. "You could dig the coal out of the ground," David said. "We would knock the coal out of there and burn the coal in the pot-bellied stove. We made do with what we had."

Burl continued to be an outstanding student. He knew about college from an early age from his grandfather, who had attended Centre College without graduating and became an engineer with the railroad. Juanita hadn't been able to attend college and encouraged Burl's academic drive along with his teachers.

On and off during his boyhood, Burl got sick as a consequence of the strep infection he had suffered. But in 1949, at the age of twelve, he became so ill that the family took him to see a doctor, who diagnosed him with acute glomerulonephritis—a progressive disease in which the kidneys become inflamed, reducing their ability to remove waste from the body's blood. The doctor gave Burl a devastating prognosis: He could become blind at any moment. He would most likely not live past his teenage years. He should forget about going to college; he wouldn't live that long. And, even if he did, college would be far too strenuous for him. The doctor's prescribed treatment? Burl should spend most of his time in bed.

At the time only a sixth grader, Burl rode his bike over to the town's public library to research his disease for himself. What little he could learn was discouraging. At that time, almost nothing could be done for ailing kidneys.

Burl's parents and brothers didn't lose hope. "At our house, we were aware that Burl had this life-threatening disease," David said. "But not that much changed, except my mother rid the house of salt."

Burl refused to take the doctor's prediction as the final word. He would not stay in bed—missing out on fishing, boating, and other water sports on the Ohio River or the Saturday Roy Rogers and Lone Ranger serials at the Paramount Theatre in downtown Ashland. He would live as normal a life as possible, he told himself.

Except for the times when his kidneys flared up, he did.

• • •

When he turned sixteen, in mid-September 1953, Burl got a job as a carhop at one of Ashland's popular drive-in restaurants, the Outpost. When he wasn't serving customers twenty-cent hotdogs and hamburgers, he was eyeing the new (and old) cars that pulled up to the curb. As was true in many American cities in the early 1950s, drive-ins were teenage hangouts, and there were two in this part of Kentucky that were heads above the rest: the Outpost and the Bluegrass.

"A typical Friday or Saturday night would have cars packed with teenagers driving back and forth all night long between the Outpost and the Bluegrass, just six miles down the road," said David. "You'd see everybody you knew." Although the carhop job didn't pay much— a nickel was the usual tip—Burl put in long hours at the Outpost, about thirty-five each week.

Burl joined a group of fellow teens who were wild about cars. They called themselves the Asphalt Angels. Burl drove a Chevy, the back end of which he altered by adding Cadillac tail fins.

But he didn't like working on cars nearly as much as he loved racing them, and he raced them as often as he could. It nearly cost him his life one day when he and best friend, John Paul Powell, were speeding along a country road and Burl flipped the car.

"Blood poured from one of Burl's ears, and for the moment he thought his ear had been cut off in the accident," said Powell's widow, Edith. "It wasn't cut off. But Burl and John Paul were lucky to have escaped alive."

One night an attractive blonde parked her car at the Outpost and introduced herself to Burl. Her name was Louella Kirk. Burl was immediately taken with her. Even though she attended Ashland High School, they had many friends in common. Louella knew Burl was editor of his high school's yearbook, had won the school's drama award, and had been voted Best All-Around Boy his junior year. She was likewise taken with him. He soon asked her out on a date.

Louella remembered her first impression of Burl. "He was very intelligent. And he had a very strong drive. You just knew when you met Burl that if he said he was going to do something, he was going to do it."

Burl got his first taste of the newspaper business in Ashland, Kentucky. In his junior and senior years at Boyd County High School, he was the manager of the baseball and basketball teams. *The Ashland Daily Independent* "needed somebody to call in, as a stringer, and I needed the twenty-five cents a game as spending money," Burl recalled.

During his senior year, in the spring of 1955, Burl became sick again and had to drop out of school for several weeks. His body lost blood, and he was constantly nauseated. His kidneys, doctors said, were becoming progressively weaker, but there was nothing that could be done for him. He did slowly improve, however, and was able to go back to school for the last few weeks before graduation.

As he waited on stage to accept his diploma, Burl couldn't stop the constant replay in his head of the doctor's words: "You probably won't live beyond your teenage years."

"The Outpost" (Credit: Tony Compton)

2

Anybody Here Want to Be a Cub Reporter?

Burl enrolled at the University of Kentucky in Lexington to study civil engineering. His grandfather said Burl should be an engineer because he was. Burl found that a compelling reason at the time, although he later grew to hate engineering. He also received an engineering scholarship from the Kentucky Department of Highways that came with a paid internship with a salary of $150 per month. On June 5, 1955, he assumed his duties with a survey crew. Burl recalled:

> But I hated it. I had a summer job with the Kentucky Department of Highways once and was entrusted to set the level of the highway that was under construction in a curve. Unfortunately, in my hometown. Well, in curves you are supposed to make the outside of the curve higher than the inside, but if you get the formula wrong, you can reverse that, which is what I did. And today there is a four-lane highway running through the middle of my hometown with a curve where you have to slow down to thirty miles an hour or you can't get around it. So that is my contribution to the engineering community in this country.

Shortly after he began the fall semester, Burl's kidneys flared up, and the sickness forced him to withdraw.

When he recovered, he enrolled in Ashland Junior College, which would later become the Ashland branch of the University of Kentucky. He declared engineering as his major and got a full-time day job at the Ben Williamson and Co. hardware store in Ashland in October 1956.

Louella and Burl continued to date. Louella—whom Burl started calling Lou, a nickname that quickly caught on with her friends and family—had been raised in modest circumstances, like Burl. Her father was a laborer, and she'd attended the Ashland city schools. She also attended the Ashland branch of the University of Kentucky and worked part-time at Ashland Oil, the city's largest employer.

"Everyone in Ashland wanted to work at Ashland Oil," she said. Even Burl applied for a job there. He was impressive—one of her bosses told Lou that he "felt very uncomfortable around Burl because he was so smart"—but he failed the company's physical exam due to his kidney disease and didn't get the job.

Two years after they first met, Burl and Louella married. They were both nineteen. Burl's father and brother made a one-room apartment for them above the garage where an enterprising Oliver Osborne housed a makeshift grocery store. The apartment was crude, with no running water for a toilet or sink and only one small light fixture. A tiny portable stove struggled to heat the room. Soon after, they were able to rent a slightly more hospitable apartment in the Ashland suburb of Westwood.

• • •

During an evening class, Burl's English professor, Nancy McClellan, asked her students, "Anybody here want to be a cub reporter?" As Burl recalled the moment: "So help me, she used that term—cub reporter. With great deliberation I asked, 'How much does it pay?' I [figured I could] con my way into a job even though I knew nothing about it. I did know $60 a week was better than $40 a week."

With McClellan's encouragement—"your prose is crisp and your use of language perfect"—Burl interviewed at *The Ashland Daily Independent* newspaper, owned by the Ashland Publishing Co., and "they gave me a chance," he said years later.

Founded in 1896, *The Independent* had a daily circulation of 17,000 and Sunday circulation of 20,000. Burl joined the staff on June 17, 1957, one week before his twentieth birthday. The newsroom was small, with only six or seven general assignment reporters. Day one on the job was unforgettable to Burl:

They did all the normal things they did in those days to cub reporters, like sending me out to look for the "type lice" and asking me to do other assorted impossible tasks. And that's how I got into the business, and I decided very quickly that that was what I wanted to do. I switched my major and continued to work at the local newspaper. Later I spent a couple of years at a television station doing reporting and photography of all things. In those days you really didn't have to have a lot of training. I think I had about twenty minutes, and after that it was just chase the fire truck. So I just chased the fire truck for a while.

Young Burl began where most reporters did—writing obituaries, "very brief little stories about those who died." But he didn't remain an obit writer for long. Soon he advanced to covering breaking news. If a fire broke out in the city, Burl raced to the editor's desk, asking to cover it.

Burl transferred to Marshall College (now Marshall University), located sixteen miles from Ashland in Huntington, West Virginia. When the managing editor of *The Independent* learned of Burl's college transfer, he suggested that Burl consider applying to The Associated Press, which had a bureau in Huntington, "because I seemed to have some aptitude for breaking news."

The Associated Press, more commonly known as the AP, was an 111-year-old cooperative organization that gathered news and sold it to member newspapers and TV stations to print or broadcast alongside its own reporting. Fast, trustworthy news obtained from around the country or the world was worth paying for, and the AP had both the news-gathering network and the technology to provide it. Newsrooms were set up with teletype machines, an automated improvement over the telegraph. These "squat, black boxes" had glass lids and "clattering keys, ringing bells and scrolling paper"[1] and received news over networks of wires—so the AP and its competitors were known as wire services. The teletype machines printed news all day and night, with the most interesting and newsworthy items coming across as bulletins that set off bells to announce their arrival. A select few stories each year warranted what was called a "flash," triggering ten to fifteen bells to mark news the AP judged to be "of transcendent importance."

Burl took his managing editor's advice and applied, but the AP told him the job required broadcast experience.

. . .

Burl took a job as a reporter and photographer for WHTN-TV, Channel 13, in Huntington to get TV experience. This new job meant exhausting eighteen-hour days: he attended classes from early morning until midafternoon each day, then worked as a reporter full time until 11:30 each night. Not exactly what his doctors had ordered, but he loved the work.

The work loved him back. He soon earned a promotion to evening news producer at the station.

According to the station's manager, Burl had a "hillbilly" accent, which was unacceptable at a young TV station trying to make a name for itself. "They sent me off to a voice coach to get rid of it," he said. Try as he might, though, he could not shake his subtle Kentucky pronunciation of certain words. "That's when I decided print was my best option," he once told a reporter.[2]

Money was tight for Burl and Lou after paying their school expenses, so Lou began working full time too. Between school and work, Burl didn't have time to be a typical husband.

His full-time job left little time for typical student life either. Other than writing an occasional story for the school newspaper, *The Parthenon*, which Burl described as a "necessary evil," he avoided all other extracurricular activities. He never attended a campus party. "It was rewarding," he said of his time at college, "but, I realized later, fairly intense. I think my grades could have been better, but I did manage to stay on the dean's list. I didn't get much of the liberal arts piece of education; I wish I had because there simply wasn't time. For the most part, I just took what I had to take."

Burl was in a hurry, eager to get a degree and a career.

One particular aspect of Burl's experience at Marshall proved invaluable. After changing his major from engineering to journalism, he enrolled in a class taught by a professor "who probably had a greater influence on what I became than any other individual." The professor's name: W. Page Pitt, founder and head of Marshall's journalism department.

Pitt had freelanced for wire services that provided stories to newspapers in Columbus, Cincinnati, and Pittsburgh and had a medical story of his own: he'd been almost blind since the age of five yet modeled for his students how this had never held him back.

By the time Burl arrived at Marshall, Pitt was a legend, known in West Virginia as "Mr. Journalism." Pitt liked to tell his students, "You are not here to learn mediocrity; you're here to learn how to excel."

"I thought he had a particular gift for explaining to young people who wanted to be journalists the importance of staying in the middle of the road. Of maintaining a balance and not getting too involved emotionally with the subject," Burl later told Dr. Ralph J. Turner, a professor in Marshall's W. Page Pitt School of Journalism in the 1990s.

"[For instance,] I was working for the TV station while still in school, and I was out after some politician," Burl said. "Page took me aside and really pounded into me for several hours the whole notion of fairness and balance. He said, 'Okay, are you really being fair?' Page also stressed the importance of detail—*accurate* detail and all of that has been very useful to me."

Burl continued:

> Page Pitt believed in the basics. He believed in nuts and bolts. He believed in writing direct sentences. He believed in simply reporting what was going on, and he wouldn't tolerate anything less.
>
> Get it right. Be fair. Make it microscopically correct and get out of the way. He would say, "This is factually correct, but it's wrong." And what he would mean by that is that, yeah, the individual facts were all correct, but the context was not correct. And it's the stuff the spinmeisters make a living at today. We didn't call it spinning the news, but that's what it was. It was using factual information but causing one to reach the wrong conclusion.
>
> Let's get down to reporting what happened. Not what you think should have happened. And that's a lesson that I think

stood me in good stead and probably would be worth repeating every now and then today.

And that's the way he taught students, by doing. And if he was teaching reporting, he caused students to go report. And if he was teaching editing, he made them edit. And so on. The instruction one got from him was a very practical, useful, applicable variety.

In essence, he practiced what he preached: He knew the language, and he treated it firmly, gently, and with respect. He wrote and he talked and he taught in clear, direct, active, exciting sentences. He taught fairness, and balance, and compassion. He cautioned against looking at the world through rose-colored glasses. It's not all peachy, and it shouldn't be. He had spent time in the business, but he had a wonderful understanding of people and how to relate and of what happens when you are honest and what happens when one is not honest.

He had a personal relationship of some kind during senior year with everyone, and it was described as a course, but it was really a seminar where he spent time every week individually with every student. So there was a lot of opportunity to discuss relative career opportunities or philosophy, which he was always eager and willing to do. Those discussions probably seemed like a waste of time then, but in hindsight, they are perhaps the most important conversations we had.

Burl graduated from Marshall in May 1960, the first member of his family to finish college. Despite that achievement, "I wasn't sure what I wanted to do," he said. "And I had an offer to work [at *The Charleston Daily Mail*] in Charleston, West Virginia, and told the interviewer, 'You know, I think I really would like to work for the AP one day. I'll just stay at the television station and see if anything develops."

3

The First Corvette

The editor in Charleston talked to the AP bureau chief there. The bureau chief then called Burl.

"They offered me the most remote, smallest, least important bureau the AP had then and, to my knowledge, has ever had," he recalled in 2008. "They said, 'We'll make you a star; we'll start you as a correspondent,' which sounded really good, but which [really] meant, 'It's a one-person bureau'!"

As a newly hired AP correspondent who was no stranger to the Allegheny and Appalachian mountain ranges, Burl felt at home when he pulled into Bluefield, West Virginia, in late July 1960.

Lou opted to stay in Ashland, over 100 miles away. She moved in with her parents so she could continue working for Ashland Oil, and she and Burl rarely saw each other. "Some weekends I would go there, or he would come to Ashland," she recalled.

Burl rented a small converted garage apartment. The only thing he baked in the tiny oven were chicken pot pies, which were cheap and easy.

Having exceeded the doctor's expectations, Burl celebrated being hired by the AP by buying himself a red Corvette. Decades later he reflected on that extravagant purchase. "When I was working in Bluefield and thought I was going to die of nephritis, I went out and purchased a Corvette with everything I had."

Turns out, his new steady paycheck covered his modest living expenses and then some. According to fellow newsman Strat Douthat: "How did Burl afford a Corvette in Bluefield? The AP paid six cents a mile and a small car stipend. Burl earned enough driving to cover stories to make his car payment."

• • •

When Burl started out at the AP in 1960, the newspaper business in the United States was robust. Reading habits were changing, new types of media commanded Americans' attention, and journalists had to craft new styles to remain relevant—but the industry proved resilient. The newspaper business' workforce was massive and growing in 1960, and the number of daily newspapers had increased at a steady rate following World War II. Consumers consistently relied more on newspaper advertisements to buy products such as furniture and televisions than ads in any other media.[3]

Once asked to briefly describe The Associated Press and how it related to newspapers, Burl gave this answer:

> We call it the AP for short, and it is an organization where newspapers go together in a cooperative to cover the news and have the news covered, and each paper pays its share of the cost of doing that. It started, oh, I guess, 140 years ago in New York when the newspapers there used to row boats out to meet the ships coming in from Europe and there was always a big boat race whenever the ships came in. . . . The publishers finally figured out they could save a lot of money if, instead of having six or eight or ten boats all running out to meet the ships, they bought one big fast boat and then all [the reporters] went out in the same boat, came back to the dock, and then raced from the dock back to their paper. . . . The race [could] occur there, instead of all over the water. So that's how that was formed. And it has grown over the years so that it now serves most of the newspapers in the United States.

Burl learned that his predecessor hadn't worked out very well in Bluefield. The *Bluefield Daily Telegraph*'s irascible managing editor, Virgil "Stubby" Currence, had frequently threatened to cancel the AP and pick up a competing news service, known as United Press International, more commonly known as UPI.

The two wire services were locked in competition for breaking news. The AP was larger, with more reporters in more places, and was owned by its members. It prided itself on accuracy. Its motto was "Get it first, but first get it right." But that meant it was also heavy on attribution, which contributed to the feeling that it was somewhat dull. UPI, on the other hand, was privately owned and a little more imaginative, a little more footloose. It allowed reporters wiggle room on the "get it right" side of the equation.

Burl instinctively knew how to handle the members of the AP's nonprofit cooperative. "Even from the beginning, part of the job in Bluefield was to try to get along with the cantankerous managing editor who ran the newsroom there," he said.

Burl settled in at the *Bluefield Daily Telegraph* newsroom, where he had a desk and typewriter. He had to use other reporters' desk phones because the AP did not give him one of his own. Long distance calls were placed through telephone company operators located half a block away. And the bureau's lifeblood—the AP teletype machine—sat in a small closet with a broken skylight.

But soon his AP boss gave him a special assignment that guaranteed the young reporter a national audience.

"Get over to Pound, Virginia," his new boss barked into the phone.

Americans had been on the edge of their seats for weeks as they read about the CIA's U-2 pilot, retired U.S. Air Force Captain F. Gary Powers, who'd been shot down over the Soviet Union on May 1. By August 19, he'd been tried, convicted of espionage, and sentenced to ten years' confinement—three to be in prison, the remainder in a labor camp.

"We need the reaction from the Powers family," his boss said. "And we need to get it first." This story would get national play.

Burl soon found himself in his Corvette on the twisty two-lane mountain roads headed for Pound, Virginia—"about one inch on the map and about one day by car to get to."

Home Town Divided on 'Reception' for Pilot
August 19, 1960
Bluefield Daily Telegraph

POUND, Va. (AP)—"He had to tell the truth ... there was nothing else the man could do," said H.C. Litton, a theater manager.

But, on the other hand …

"His testimony doesn't sound as American as I think it should be," said Johnny Jones, a college student.

Thus, in different fashion, the people in Francis Gary Powers' home town are reacting to the U2 pilot's spy trial in Moscow.

The homefolks unanimously want him to go free. Almost to a man, they don't believe the Russians will sentence him to death. They are just about sure he'll get a prison sentence — some say a short one, some say a long one.

But as to how Francis Gary Powers might be accepted were he to return today, to his home in this Southwest Virginia town, there is a variety of opinion.

Using Him

"I think they're using him for a great propaganda purpose," said Litton. "I don't think they (Russia) could hold face with the world if they put him before the firing squad. He had to tell the truth. The State Department had already admitted it (the spy charges) for him … there was nothing else the man could do."

Litton guesses Powers will be sentenced to a "minimum of 10 years."

Jones, a senior at Carson-Newman College and a major in education, guesses the sentence will be 15 to 20 years.

"He (Powers) seems to be testifying so things will go his way," said Jones. "It's hard for me to think anyone from the United States could say he was sorry (for the flight) … Powers started out higher in the esteem of his associates, but because of his testimony it may not be that way now … His testimony doesn't sound as American as I think it should be."

A housewife about 50 agreed with Jones.

Lower Opinion

"I think the opinion of the people in Pound of Powers will be lower. He's given out so much information he may be treated like a turncoat if he returns, like dirt under your feet. He is blaming our government, as much as calling us warmongers, and we're not."

But there was another lady about 55 who said she thought Powers was "doing the best he could."

"He's fighting for his life," she said. "The people here feel he was just doing a job and got caught in it. ... I feel every minute as if we're almost in war."

A service station attendant figured Powers "will get some time out of it — I don't know how much. The case is mostly against the United States. I don't think the main part of the government knew what was coming off."

Women Tense

The women in Powers' home town seem tense as they await the outcome of his trial in Moscow. The men are divided. Some regard the U2 pilot as a hero. Others don't. There is, for instance, Clarence Wright, a restaurant owner, who says he thinks "the boy (Powers) is telling the straight truth."

"He'll get what it takes to give Russia the most propaganda advantage," said Wright. "It will be the maximum sentence — or the minimum ... Russia would like to put the fear of Russia in any flier who might fly over in the future. On the other hand, they're trying to make people believe the United States is a warmongering nation."

Burl's bosses liked his humane article, as did Currence. He took a liking to Burl, giving him the nickname Buckskin. Why? Depending on the day, Currence offered two answers: one, because Burl sometimes wore a fringed tan-colored suede jacket that reminded him of the buckskin jacket Buffalo Bill wore in his legendary Wild West shows in the late 1800s or, two, because Burl was short in stature but "an absolutely aggressive reporter."

Currence began frequently hosting Burl to dinner at his home and assigned him stories the paper was too short staffed to cover. Burl took full advantage.

> The neat part was that the newspaper regarded the AP correspondent as sort of one of the staff, and so you got to do a lot of stuff: got to see a lot, got to handle a lot, got to write a lot. It was such a place—remote from folks in New York and Charleston and Richmond—that there were always interesting stories to cover, ranging from black-tie events at the historic, majestic Greenbrier resort in White Sulphur Springs to coal mine disasters in the

southern tip of the state. There was no time clock, none of that. I worked when there was work to do and played the rest of the time.

The paper's owner, Hugh Shott, was likewise drawn to Burl. He would frequently walk out of his office in the evening and over to Burl's desk. "He'd say, 'Come on. Let's go.' Then we would be off for a drive around the area to discuss events of the day or whatever else happened to come up," Burl recalled.

In an October 28, 1960, letter to General Manager Frank Starzel, the AP bureau chief in Charleston, West Virginia, Jack Davis, lobbied for a promotion of sorts for the cub reporter. He wrote, "Burl Osborne has been acting correspondent at Bluefield for three months. During that time, he has conducted himself with enterprise and tact and has been influential in bettering our relations with the Bluefield members. I recommend that the 'acting' be dropped from his title."

In late January 1961, when his probationary period drew to an end, Burl wrote a respectful letter of his own to the general manager at the AP's New York headquarters. "After six months, I am extremely happy with the AP," he wrote. "I hope the AP is happy with me."

In a March 20, 1961, letter to the bureau chief in Charleston, West Virginia, Assistant General Manager Wes Gallagher wrote, "If I recall correctly, we have had constant trouble in Bluefield until Burl Osborne arrived there because of the sensitivity of the member." Currence and Shott were happy with Burl. Gallagher wanted him to remain right where he was. Senior executives at the AP took notice.

Buckskin and Brownie

Like every reporter, Burl wanted the greatest possible exposure for his stories. Glimpses of rural American life fascinated big-city readers. Consequently, the bigger newspapers across the United States eagerly picked up and printed articles full of regional color and curiosities.

The hills and hollows of Appalachia were ripe for those types of stories. "It was a fascinating time," Burl recalled. "One of the things you do in southern West Virginia if things are dull is to go to one of the churches where part of the parishioners' faith is handling poisonous snakes. Where they let God make the decision as to whether they should live or die. That's usually enough to get you published in some of the more urban newspapers where they're not accustomed to that. And, occasionally, somebody gets bitten and dies, in which case . . . you might even get a larger headline."

One of the snake stories Burl wrote about that fall concerned Columbia Gay Hagerman, "an attractive 23-year-old divorcee who resided at Paynesville near the West Virginia-Virginia line. She was bitten by a yellow timber rattler on the right hand on Sunday night, at the Church in Jesus at the nearby town of Jolo. It was the first time that Mrs. Hagerman, mother of a nine-year-old-daughter, had handled the snakes. She died at the home of her stepfather and mother, Mr. and Mrs. Robert Elkins, without medical attention."

Mrs. Elkins said, "We stayed within steady prayer since it happened, and she prayed with us. We feel when He don't heal us he has a better purpose . . . I could have got a doctor, but I know God is God."

Burl's lifelong friend Bill Nowlin reminisced about the time he rode to a service in the red Corvette. He was along as Burl's photographer. "When we went inside, someone walked up to us and called us 'uncircumcised instruments of the devil.' Burl looked down at his pants and then back up at me and said, 'How did he know that?'" Nowlin photographed a woman with gray hair that evening. "[Suddenly] I noticed that there were two copperhead snakes moving around in her hair. I remember saying to myself, 'If she keeps coming [toward me], Burl's on his own.'"

At another such church service, Burl was jostled and pushed around until he was within a few inches of the snakes, which scared him. "They wanted him to handle the snakes, and he wouldn't handle them," Louella remembered. "He was with a state patrolman, and the patrolman wouldn't handle them either. The church folks told Burl that if he didn't handle the snakes, something bad would happen to him. On the way back home, he was going around a corner and the brakes in his car locked on him. He said it made him wonder about their prediction."

• • •

Burl's reputation for finding attention-getting stories grew within the AP. Davis wanted Burl transferred to his offices for broader exposure and administrative experience. In the fall of 1961, Davis wrote letters to Gallagher and Starzel.

Gallagher's October 6 response on behalf of Starzel was short and to the point: "I think it inadvisable to transfer Burl Osborne at this time. . . . We have difficulties in Bluefield, and if he is doing a first-rate job we want to keep him there."

Meanwhile, Burl went on with the daily business of covering murders, thefts, fires, a flash flood in the state capital, a plant explosion in Virginia. He wrote engagingly about politicians, Boy Scouts, and sporting events.

On October 28, while chasing a rabbit, a mixed-breed hound dog named Brownie fell down an abandoned mine shaft in the hamlet of Gilbert, West Virginia, some twenty miles west of Bluefield.

The lead on Burl's first story about the dog: "Brownie yelped Thursday."

The hook set, Burl then reeled his readers in. "He had reason to yelp. He has been trapped 46 days in an abandoned underground mine — given up for dead, his master reported. The three-year-old mongrel hound's feeble whine has prompted a tedious tunneling rescue effort that already has taken the better part of a month."

Burl went on to describe the heroic efforts by Brownie's twenty-one-year-old owner, Richard Hatfield ("a distant descendant of the Mingo County Hatfields of Hatfield and McCoy feud fame"), to extricate the dog from the mine. Brownie had been missing for eighteen days before Hatfield heard him whining deep in the earth below. Using a pickax and shovel, Hatfield immediately began to create a tunnel at the bottom of the mine's fault. By the time Burl arrived on the scene in mid-December, dozens of neighboring farmers had joined the rescue attempt. But the tunnel was still eighteen feet from the spot where Brownie was trapped. At that rate it could be several more weeks before Hatfield would reach the dog.

Meanwhile, Hatfield kept Brownie alive by dropping scraps of food to him. According to Currence, "Burl chased the story doggedly."

Burl filed daily reports about the rescue effort that went out on the AP wire to newspapers and TV stations throughout the United States. The response from the captivated audience far and wide was staggering. Hundreds of letters, telegrams, and offers of help poured into Hatfield's mailbox, the local post office, and even Burl's one-desk office—much of the mail addressed simply to "Brownie-The-Dog, West Virginia." The small post office was also flooded with packages containing dog food and dog bones, leashes and collars, and toys. One well-wisher suggested a club be formed, "to get Brownie out by Christmas."

Currence drew attention to Burl's personal connection to Brownie in the *Daily Telegraph*'s "Now And Then" feature dated December 17, 1961:

Little Boys Don't Forget

December 17, 1961
Bluefield Daily Telegraph

Burl Osborne of the Bluefield Associated Press Bureau and known throughout the entire AP organization as one of its top writers, is staying close to Brownie. Those heart-tugging stories you have been reading about Brownie's plight are coming from his typewriter.

"Buckskin," which is what his friends here call Burl, has been in Hampden for three days. He listens for Brownie's every whimper . . . he even pokes food down the mine "break" for the little 3-year old mongrel dog who has been a captive in a dark, wet mine for 48 days.

You see, when Buckskin was a little boy in his native Kentucky, [his grandparents] had a little mongrel dog. [When Burl walked home from their house the dog often followed him home.]

He had, that is. But one day a big passenger bus ran over and killed Buckskin's dog. His color was black, but his name was Brownie, too.

For weeks and months afterward, the little Kentucky boy threw rocks at every like bus, headed for Louisville, that passed his house.

His Brownie is gone, but Buckskin's love for dogs — especially those named Brownie — will be with him forever.

Maybe this Brownie reminds him of [the] dog [he loved]. And maybe Buckskin wants to be sure that he is at the old worked-out mine when Brownie comes out.

Burl's stories grabbed and held the nation's attention, so much so that his New York bosses told Burl to forget taking Christmas off from work. As long as the dog was trapped, they told Burl, he would stay on the job. Burl risked the wrath of his mother, who loved the holiday more than any other, but endearing human interest stories like these don't come across the wire every day.

In his next dispatch he mentioned they might need the help of a bulldozer to rescue Brownie. To Burl's surprise, six bulldozers showed up at the scene the very next day. "I came to understand the *power* of the newspaper story," Burl said. "The mere mention of the bulldozer in my story changed everything. Bulldozers appeared, and suddenly, Brownie was going to get out." Unbeknownst to Burl at the time, a man named Eddie Steele was then PR man for Bluefield Supply Company, the area's premier distributor of Rish Construction Equipment. It was he who "finally convinced [my bosses] of the publicity value of getting the dog out," Steele later told the reporter.

On the morning of December 19, a bulldozer broke into Brownie's underground prison. Burl brought his readers right into the scene.

Brownie the hound, skinny but tail wagging, was rescued Monday after spending what felt like an eternity trapped in an abandoned mine shaft.

The dog was taken from a mine break by Charles Dillon who lives in Hampden near the dog's owner, Richard Hatfield.

The dark brown hound was quiet as he darted from a crevice about 20 feet below the spot where he entered the mine Oct. 28.

The break was opened by a bulldozer, which had been working on the rugged southern West Virginia mountainside since Saturday.

Dillon crawled back under the stone shelf and located the dog on a ledge beside a pool of water. "He seemed blind at first," Dillon said, "but boy he wagged his tail when I reached through that hole and laid my hands on his head."

Hatfield was half laughing and almost crying as he carried his 3-year-old rabbit hound off the mountain.

Burl finished the story: "Long after he was out of the mine shaft and off the mountain Brownie's tail wagged. Otherwise, he was noncommittal about the whole affair. His long ears drooped from his head."

Brownie the dog was such a sensation nationally that producers of *What's My Line?* flew him to New York to appear on the show. While in Manhattan, Brownie also made it onto local news programs.

So many people had followed the story that editors and reporters in and around the *Daily Telegraph* began calling Burl by a new nickname. Now, interchangeably with "Buckskin," he was called "Brownie."

Ever the honest newsman, Burl shared a sad postscript to the story a few months after Brownie returned to West Virginia. The local sheriff shot and killed the hound dog for killing a farmer's chickens.

• • •

Burl soon received another urgent summons from AP headquarters: the Soviets had just released U-2 pilot Powers in exchange for a Soviet officer.

"When [Powers] was released and came home, I was told to find him and interview him," Burl recalled. "Eventually, we did, though not as quickly as the folks in New York would have liked. The thing that held me up was the mountains. It's a very slow drive across those mountains—or it was then. I tried to explain those roads in southwest Virginia but got no sympathy."

A Grateful Powers Gets Ovation from SW VA Folks
March 13, 1962

BIG STONE GAP, Va. (AP)—U2 pilot Francis Gary Powers, vindicated by congress and the President, received a standing ovation here Monday from his Southwest Virginia neighbors.

"I'm very thankful to all of you who had a part in this," he told some 800 Wise County residents attending the welcome home ceremonies at the National Guard Armory.

Tribute was paid the 32-year-old flyer by government officials ranging from town mayors to Rep. W. Pat Jennings, D-Va.

Talking with newsmen afterwards, Powers said he felt "a lot of people were saying a lot of words about something about which they knew nothing."

He said pictures released immediately after his capture by the Russians were said not to show the wreckage of his plane. "But the plane I saw in Moscow was the U2," he said.

Powers said both wing and tail sections were intact.

He said Monday's welcome made up for his ordeal, and added, "I hope people realize I'm a normal man who has done a job."

Oliver Powers, eyes reddened with tears, told his neighbors, "I'd like to thank everybody for this turnout to honor my son ... words cannot express how happy we are."

The senior vice commander of the Veterans of Foreign Wars in Virginia, E.K. Smith, pinned a citizenship medal on Powers, dressed in a dark suit. Powers immediately showed his mother the bronze medallion held by a red, white and blue ribbon.

"I am a pilot, not a speaker," Powers told the crowd with a grin.

The people who turned out from this mountainous area wore their Sunday best and looked proudly at a banner over the platform. "Wise County Welcomes You Home, Gary," it read.

Many brought cameras and scraps to be autographed. Francis led the clapping when the band struck up "Dixie." His parents followed suit.

Norton Mayor B.E. Ball decried those who "just attempt to cast doubts ... the people join in a genuine and joyous welcome home."

Rep. Jennings drew a loud "amen" when he quoted from the Bible: "I will lift up mine eyes to the hills from whence comest my strength."

Applause frequently interrupted the brief talk by Jennings, Milligan (Tenn.) College President Dr. D.E. Walker, mayors from Wise County communities and two members of the Virginia General Assembly.

Del. Orby L. Cantrell of Pound said, "We certainly don't envy you, but we try to be sympathetic. This is the very least we can do for you."

State Sen. M.M. Long said, "We welcome him back with open arms."

Powers talked with reporters for 20 minutes after the ceremony, then went into a side room to exchange greetings with friends.

He said he planned to spend several weeks in the Washington area before deciding on his future. He said he has not checked the possibility of returning to the Air Force, and added, "I hope to continue flying, either for pleasure or business."

5

A Little Bit of Everything

As Burl's two-year anniversary as AP's man in Bluefield approached, executives in New York finally issued orders that would transfer him to West Virginia's larger state bureau in Charleston. Davis got his wish. Strat Douthat would replace him.

In a farewell column to Burl with the headline "Good Luck, Friend," Currence wrote: "The boys in the *Daily Telegraph* news room hate to see him leave. During the 2 years he has been in Bluefield, he has been a well-liked member of the newspaper family, always willing and ready to lend a hand far beyond the call of duty."

Currence also felt compelled to send the executive editor of the AP a letter in praise of Burl, writing, "In addition to being a natural reporter, he is also a splendid writer, and we have found his copy to be most objective and always right down the middle. . . . He is a young man whose talents far surpass his age."

• • •

With its population of 85,000 in 1962, Charleston, West Virginia, was no metropolis. Nevertheless, it *was* the state capital, the Kanawha County seat, and four times larger than Bluefield.

Charleston, situated at the confluence of the Kanawha River and its tributary the Elk, also put Burl fifty-nine miles closer to his family in Ashland, Kentucky.

As he had in Bluefield, Burl rented an apartment and lived alone. Lou came down some weekends to visit him, but their marriage wasn't going well. And Burl—a workaholic—knew he needed no distractions when diving into a new job.

His apartment was a modest place in the city's South Hills community, not far from either the Kanawha River or the Kanawha State Forest. Burl bought a powerboat—a sixteen-foot Dunphy runabout that he raced up and down the Ohio River. "Just like with the Corvette, he bought the boat on time, paying just a little down," Lou recalled.

Burl threw himself into his role as desk supervisor, reporting to Davis, who had lobbied for his promotion. "He was really quite an extraordinary writer and a good editor," said Burl of his mentor. "He could take a reporter's work and, without changing the thought, without changing the idea, without changing the stream, could make it much better and usually with just a few small edits."

Before long, Burl was covering the statehouse and sports events around the state. "That's what we did in those days. *Everybody* did a little bit of *everything. And* I wrote some broadcast, finally." He quickly learned that he was expected to write the kinds of articles that made the "A-wire"—the national news wire that featured the AP's top stories.

As time went on, Burl took on an additional unofficial role as "news editor," which meant he did lots of rewriting and editing in addition to his own original reporting. He kept an eye out for curiosities that played well to the national audience. He was even able to connect one to the story of Brownie he'd written shortly before leaving Bluefield.

Mountain Music To Make Us Rich?
April 23, 1963

CHARLESTON, Va. (AP)—A one-gal task force, who traded her G-string for some mountain music and the shocking aroma of ramps, has taken it upon herself to help solve West Virginia's economic problems.

This ambitious project is being undertaken by showgirl Marlane MacLane. "In my own little way," she said Monday.

She offered her services to the West Virginia Centennial Commission to help promote the state's 100th birthday and came to Charleston to meet with centennial officials.

Miss MacLane, who at times has worked undercover for the FBI and under no cover at all as a stripper, said she has turned producer.

Mountain Music

One of the commodities she wants to produce is "mountain music" — not hillbilly, not country and western — but "mountain music."

And she wants it done in no small fashion. "Everyone in the country will go for it — it will be the thing."

No more crooning, no more rock and roll — just plain mountain music.

Everyone involved — including Miss MacLane — will make a potful of money, she said. Some West Virginia talent already is under contract, including Wheeling radio singer Bonnie Baldwin, who now is in New York for recording.

There is enough raw talent in West Virginia to, if developed, help change the state's image as a depressed area, Miss MacLane allowed.

Her image starts with a wild thatch of black hair and ends with a well-turned ankle.

Her politics are about as conservative as her hair isn't.

"I always played to the right side of the house when I was stripping," she said.

The Place To Go

"I'll make West Virginia 'the place to go' for vacationers from the east," she said. Money will follow the tourists, she reasoned, and the state will be on its way to good health.

Mechanics of her plan were a bit unclear.

But the first step would be a talent-hunting caravan touring the states, "the likes of which, Honey, New York has never seen." Next, a mountain music festival for West Virginia, tied in with nationwide success by the newly found singers.

This all will be accomplished during this year's centennial. And here it is April.

Eventually, she said, there are plans for a mountain music-type Broadway show. Currently, she's producing a play called "The Pay's Not The Thing." It's about a stripper turned barber.

"I'll make eating ramps the thing too," she said after a farmhand's helping of the onion-like plant at a weekend Rishwood ramp feed.

Ramps, for the uninformed, make an ordinary onion seem no stronger than a green bean. They're considered quite the dish in some communities. But everyone must partake — in self-defense.

Miss MacLane adopted West Virginia after she became involved in the rescue of a dog which had been trapped nearly two months inside an abandoned coal mine in southern West Virginia. The dog was saved and she befriended both hound and master.

"I like these West Virginia people," she said. "They're gutsy."

On Friday, November 22, President John F. Kennedy was assassinated in Dallas, Texas. Burl had briefly met and interviewed Kennedy, as well as his brothers and wife, on the campaign trail in West Virginia. Kennedy was killed during the fall football season, and Burl was logging hundreds of miles covering games across West Virginia. Burl recalled his whereabouts when the news broke:

> I was driving from Charleston to Morgantown to cover the West
> Virginia–Pittsburgh football game, which was to have occurred
> on that Saturday. And it just . . . everything stopped. I literally
> pulled my car off the road—to listen [to the radio] and—I'm
> trying to remember if they canceled the game. I don't remember.
> I don't even remember the game.

Toward the end of 1963, Burl sat down to reflect on what he had achieved in that year and what his goals were for the future. "In those days there were what we [at the AP] called the dream sheets," he recalled. "Everyone, every year, did a sort of self-evaluation and could also describe what they'd like to do next. I filled those out and wanted to move ahead, although I wasn't especially eager just to leave what I was doing."

One of the questions on the self-evaluation was to list the top places you'd like to work. Burl consistently put the nation's capital, Washington, at the top of his list.

• • •

Burl's colleagues didn't know that he suffered from chronic glomerulonephritis. Though the people he interacted with—some daily—never saw traces of it, Burl had been having headaches, occasional blurred vision, shortness of breath with moderate exercise, and bruises on his arms and legs.

Douthat, now in Charleston, too, remembered one evening at the "after-hours" club the newsmen retired to once the Press Club closed. Burl left the table abruptly. When he returned later on, he quietly apologized and said he had been ill, but not from drinking. It was the only time in the years he'd known Burl that Douthat gave Burl's health a thought.

Burl kept his health private with good reason. Chronic health problems in the 1960s were often viewed as personal failings or tragedies that left the people who suffered from them unable to work. And lingering social belief that "personal carelessness and imprudent lifestyle choices" caused poor health meant never knowing what judgment one's health conditions would face in the workplace.[4] The Americans with Disabilities Act, which would prohibit employment discrimination on the basis of medical conditions, was nearly three decades away from becoming law.

In early March 1964, Burl's symptoms from his kidney disease had worsened to the point that he drove the forty-four miles to Huntington for a physical. The lab results confirmed that Burl was also suffering from anemia and hypertensive cardiovascular disease.

Characteristically, Burl resumed his duties without fanfare—refusing to let his illness slow him down.

• • •

Soon Burl's colleagues and admirers across the state were bidding him farewell. Perhaps in a playful payback for Burl using his car allowance and mileage reimbursement to purchase a Corvette, headquarters granted his wish and sent him to Washington, all right. *Spokane, Washington.*

Ironically, assigning Burl to Spokane ended up saving his life.

The *Bluefield Daily Telegraph*'s Currence chronicled the move in his March 15 column.

Buckskin Climbs the AP Ladder

Burl Osborne, known sometimes by the names of Buckskin and Brownie, is going up The Associated Press ladder. Everyone who knows him knew it was sure to happen. He has been promoted to head man of the AP's important Spokane, Wash., bureau and leaves in a few days for the great Northwest.

Buckskin started his AP career in Bluefield more than 3 years ago and after nearly 2 years here he was transferred to the Charleston bureau, where he has been located since leaving Bluefield.

One of the most talented of all the AP's young men around the country, Buckskin soon made quite a reputation for himself as a fellow who could "smell news" and knew what to do with it once he hit the trail and the keys of his typewriter.

... We are sorry to see Buckskin leave this state, because W. Va. can ill afford to lose such a capable and dedicated reporter, but we are real happy to see him move up ... it's recognition due a magnificent reporter and a great boy.

"Spirit of West Virginia" (Credit: Osborne family collection)

6

Extraordinary Providence

The Seattle AP bureau chief, a World War II vet named Murlin Spencer, flew to Spokane to give Burl the keys, show him where the office was, and tell him what he was supposed to be doing. He picked Burl up at the airport, and they decided to have a drink before getting started. But then the phone rang.

The urgent call was from New York, telling Spencer of an earthquake in Alaska, part of the territory he covered. Seattle was the control point for the AP's Alaska bureau. The "Good Friday Earthquake" of March 27, 1964, struck Alaska's Prince William Sound, about 75 miles southeast of Anchorage. With a magnitude of 9.2 it was (and still is) the most powerful earthquake recorded in U.S. history. The 4-minute-38-second-long quake "wobbled" Seattle's Space Needle twelve hundred miles southeast and was registered in every state except Connecticut, Delaware, and Rhode Island. The resultant ground fissures, collapsed structures, and tsunamis caused about 130 deaths.

"Murlin said, 'I've got to go, Burl. The office is down here. Here are the keys. Be there in the morning. See you when I get back.' I didn't see him for six weeks. That's how I came to Spokane," Burl recalled.

The earthquake was an apocalyptic story, but it wasn't Burl's to tell. Burl and his team in Spokane had responsibility for the eastern half of Washington, the northern part of Idaho, and western Montana. Occasionally during the mid-'60s, they also covered "a little piece of Oregon." Because theirs was such a vast territory to cover, mostly by phone, they had a big radio obligation there and lots of splits every day.[5] But Burl went in and handled that. As he put it, the Spokane fellas "kind of rocked along, and I guess we did okay, kind of guessing our way as we went, since our leader was out of pocket."

Burl loved Spokane as soon as he arrived. Situated on the Spokane River, it was about thirty miles directly west of Coeur d'Alene, Idaho, along the Bitterroot

Range of the Rocky Mountains. As he wrote to friends back in West Virginia, it was seventy-seven degrees in early April, "but folks were skiing on the mountain just outside of town. And there are plenty of lakes." Just one hundred miles to the north was the Canadian border. With a population of about 181,000 in 1960, Spokane was more than twice the size of Charleston, West Virginia, and the second-largest city in Washington after Seattle. Spokane's economy depended on timber, mining, and agriculture, giving the city a rural, slightly Wild West feel.

Burl quickly found a house to rent and settled into a routine of hard work balanced with a little sightseeing. Burl and Louella discussed the possibility of her joining him in Spokane, but she didn't want to leave her mother and aunt.

The story that occupied Burl the better part of June was what Montana's National Guard officers called "the worst natural disaster in state history." In his June 10, 1964, article, Burl described the situation from Great Falls, Montana: "Floodwaters poured over lowlands at record levels. ... At least 30 persons were dead, dozens were missing and hundreds were homeless."

• • •

Soon, the earth shook again for Burl—not literally this time but physically.

Burl suffered a major kidney flare-up. Suddenly, he couldn't muster the strength to climb the four flights of stairs to his office. Lou arrived at the beginning of July, and three weeks later—on July 22—Burl checked into the hospital. During Burl's prior acute bouts of nephritis, he would feel terribly nauseated as his body lost blood and thoughts of imminent death crawled into his mind. After a week or two in the hospital, however, his health would inevitably improve, and he would be well enough to go home and go on with his life. This time was different. The diagnosis was end-stage renal disease.

Today, such a diagnosis means it is time to consider options for treatment. In 1964, the term meant the end, period. Tens of thousands of Americans died each year of kidney failure. Death could come in as soon as a few weeks.

Spokane was one of only a few places in the country where doctors were experimenting with chronic dialysis to treat nonacute kidney disease.

"I always said Burl had his own guardian angel," said Lou. "It turned out that we were in just the right place at that moment. If we hadn't been in Spokane, he would not have survived."

Decades later, Burl spoke of the miraculous nature of his transfer to the Pacific Northwest. "It was the most extraordinary providence of my life. I had just come from a part of the country where there was zero treatment available to a city whose name I could barely pronounce, without knowing that Spokane had one of the very, very few artificial kidney facilities in the world."

That facility was the brand-new Spokane and Inland Empire Artificial Kidney Center at Sacred Heart Hospital. Funded by the U.S. Public Health Service, it was one of only two places in the country where patients could get government-funded hemodialysis. And, with merely four beds, the center was always full. Most people who needed dialysis were turned away—and left to die. Fewer than two hundred were saved by artificial kidneys in the mid-1960s.

Because of the limited capacity of the dialysis center, a four-person committee of Sacred Heart's nephrologists determined who would receive treatment at the center and who would not.

Burl appeared before the committee and presented his case for a bed. The committee turned him down. Burl and Lou weren't surprised. "There was a long list of people waiting to get onto the machines. We hadn't been in the state of Washington that long, and there were people who had been on a list for a long time," Lou recalled.

One other option existed. Dr. Peter T. Ivanovich, who worked under Dr. Loren Gothberg, who ran the center, was both a member of the four-person committee and the medical director of the dialysis center. "This selection committee was deciding who was going to live and who was going to die. I didn't believe in excluding anybody," Ivanovich recalled. "I said, 'Train them how to do the dialysis themselves.'"

Drs. Gothberg and Ivanovich told Burl: "If you'll join this experiment and try to do this yourself, we will let you in." If Burl agreed to do it, he would be the first person the center trained in the radical new concept. They quickly agreed to it. Burl became one of a dozen people worldwide trying home dialysis. Burl and Lou had no idea what a major undertaking it would be but had no alternative. Without dialysis to remove excess water, solutes, and toxins from his blood, he would die of uremic poisoning.

• • •

Dr. Belding H. Scribner at Seattle's University of Washington first became interested in hemodialysis in the 1950s. Some patients recovered from acute kidney failure after painful short-term dialysis treatments. But chronic dialysis was an insurmountable problem, in part because every time a patient was hooked up to a dialysis machine, arteries and veins were damaged by the glass tubes that were used and doctors soon had no way to connect the machine. Scribner described waking up in the middle of the night with a solution to that inability to deliver chronic dialysis: sew U-shaped plastic tubes, or shunts, in an artery and in a vein. For each dialysis treatment, doctors could plug additional tubes into the device and attach them to an artificial kidney, creating a circuit through which blood could flow from the artery to be cleansed of toxic substances in the dialysis machine before returning to the body through the vein.

Four years after the device was invented, doctors implanted a Scribner shunt in the underside of Burl's left arm just above the wrist. He had to limit his liquid intake, even calculating how much water his food contained.

While they waited for a dialysis machine to be delivered to their home, Lou and Burl had to learn how to use it. They went to Sacred Heart twice a week for Burl's dialysis treatments and to train on the machine. Lou went twice more each week to learn how to perform other medical procedures, which included drawing blood and giving injections. It took three months—from August to October—to complete the training. Thereafter, she took a job in the hospital's human resources department. "We didn't know whether Burl would lose his job at the AP," she recalled. "And we needed the money."

7

The Model-T Days of Dialysis

Burl somehow balanced his treatments and his AP responsibilities during the autumn and early winter of 1964.

AP President Keith Fuller commented years later that after learning about his hemodialysis treatments, no one in management at the AP expected Burl to be able to continue to do his job. They thought AP work was far too strenuous for someone with Burl's condition, especially since the job required frequent travel. "I had no doubt he would succeed at some profession," Fuller told AP Special Correspondent Jules Loh in 1990. "But he was tied to a dialysis machine twice a week, and given the uncertainties of our work, the hours and the schedule and other demands, I didn't see how Burl could handle it."

But he did. "I took it day by day. I would say to myself, 'I can't die just now; I have to get the radio split out.'" During this time, Burl's stories—whether coverage of state football championship games as sportswriter or a report on escaped felons on the run as news editor—went out over the wires to be printed in small and large newspapers all over the country, especially in the region.

Burl became successful at juggling work with his biweekly hemodialysis treatments, but he thought he was still likely to die. He wanted to go home and say goodbye to his parents and brothers and longtime friends. He and Lou decided to travel home to Ashland for Christmas.

His treatments meant a cross-country driving trip wasn't an option, and the couple couldn't afford two pricey round-trip plane tickets. Burl would fly, and Lou would take a train.

Burl began to realize during his time in Spokane that as an AP newsman, he had a platform that could be used to inspire and encourage many other kidney disease sufferers worldwide. As such, he wrote about his Christmas trip on February 7, 1965, as he would any other A-wire article. It was the first of many such stories about his medical battle he penned in the coming months and years, stories that his fellow reporters and editors throughout the nation followed with keen interest. The editor's note that introduced his article read: "At 27, Associated Press writer Burl Osborne has lost the use of both kidneys and but for a miraculous machine would soon be dead. With courage and ingenuity, he pioneered a transcontinental trip via artificial kidney, giving hope to others for a more normal life."

Newsman Describes How It Feels to Bank on Machine to Stay Alive

SPOKANE, Wash. (AP)—My greatest fear as a beginning artificial kidney patient was not of death, but of bondage to the very machine that keeps me alive.

Now, because I wanted to take a cross-country vacation and because experts in the East and West are beginning to communicate, the fear is gone and the ties are relaxed.

Twice a week I submit to the maze of plastic and plumbing that cleans and purifies my blood — functions my own diseased kidneys no longer can perform.

With the treatments I am able to continue a relatively normal existence. Without them, in a matter of a few weeks, I would be dead. The disease is called chronic nephritis.

Under these circumstances, it seemed highly unlikely that I could make a 2,700-mile trip to Kentucky to visit my family.

Machines in predominant use in the East are built differently from those on the West Coast. My doctors and I were not sure I could switch from one to the other, even if one could be found near my home town of Ashland, Ky.

Tried "Pioneering"

We could find no evidence that such a transition ever had been made, but we decided to try.

We located a machine in Huntington, West Virginia, only 20 miles from my destination, and somewhat apprehensively, set out to prepare for a switch.

The eventual success of the experiment removed doubt and raised exciting prospects for freer travel about the country.

Doctors on the artificial kidney team here already knew that medically, both machines performed the same task — hemodialysis — so the problems, if any, would be mechanical ones.

The machines are built on an entirely different plan.

The Kiil sandwich kidney, which essentially is two rectangular cellophane envelopes sandwiched between three heavy plastic plates, is widely used here and in Seattle, where almost all West Coast kidney research and development is being done.

In the East, many centers are using a "twin-coil" kidney developed by Dr. William J. Kolff of the Cleveland Clinic. That machine looks like a stainless steel washtub with two coils of cellophane membrane stacked in the center of it.

Impurities Removed

In either system, the patient's blood — loaded with poisons and fluids his inactive kidneys failed to remove — flows inside the cellophane envelopes or coils. A chemical solution flows on the other side of the cellophane. Impurities are drawn from the blood, through pores in the cellophane, and carried away in the chemical bath. ...

By spacing the treatments four days apart, and undergoing treatment just before leaving and immediately after returning to Spokane, I was able to stretch the vacation to 12 days.

So, off I went with my wife, Louella, and a bag full of adapters, tubing, shunts, bandages, tapes and everything else that might have been needed.

Was Wary

When the time came to begin the first treatment, I had some misgivings about pumping the only blood I had through a machine I had never seen before.

The nervousness was compounded by an instinctive reluctance to have unfamiliar nurses make the connection to my cannulae [thin tubes inserted for delivery or removal of fluids].

My wife provided the solution. Since we both have been trained to set up, dismantle, clean and maintain the Kiil equipment, and since Louella is qualified to administer the treatment, she attached the adapted tubes to my cannulae.

By the end of this month, we will be using a Kiil kidney in our home, on a do-it-yourself basis. It is estimated that this will reduce the cost of treatment from $14,000 to about $3,000 or $4,000 a year. This way we hope to become independent, except for technical assistance and supplies of the Spokane and Inland Empire Artificial Kidney Center, where I now receive treatments.

In February 1965, Burl also wrote a letter to Gallagher thanking him for his assistance.

"Within a relatively short time, I feel confident completely portable equipment will be available or transplantation will be successfully demonstrated. Until then, I want more than anything else to meet well the responsibilities assigned me in Spokane—or perhaps elsewhere in the future—without this handicap becoming either a crutch or an insurmountable obstacle."

Burl waited all of February and March for the home dialysis machine, but delivery was delayed again and again. He continued to work.

Finally, on March 31, technicians installed the artificial kidney machine as Burl and Lou watched, wide eyed.

The first dialysis at the Osborne home took place on the evening of April 2. Doctors from the Spokane and Inland Empire Center alerted the media that something extremely rare was about to take place. Newspaper reporters joined the center's physicians and technicians in the spare bedroom housing the machine—now called the "treatment room." As they watched, Burl took a comfortable position on the bed, Lou fastened a disposable mask over her nose and mouth, and then she connected a pencil-size tube from the Scribner shunt in her husband's left arm to the artificial kidney. Moments later, Burl became the first person in Spokane—and one of only a few patients in the world—to be dialyzed at home.

And, yet, for all the wonders of the new machine, it soon became a deep source of frustration for both Burl and Lou. Not only was it exceedingly difficult to operate but also it had to be taken apart after each use, thoroughly sterilized, and then reassembled. Just cleaning the artificial kidney took an hour or more. It broke down often. Decades later Burl would refer to that time as the "Model-T days of dialysis."

Adding to their frustration, they also faced constant prognoses from doctors and other health care professionals who were convinced that home dialysis was destined to fail. "Everyone told us that home dialysis was never going to work," Lou recalled. "It was very technical, and it was a learning process every time I ran him on the machine. It was not easy. We were always having a crisis."

From the first day he used the erratic home machine, Burl knew it might not be sustainable. He began to wonder whether a kidney transplant might be a viable option, but such complicated operations were still in their infancy. In 1965, fewer than a hundred people worldwide had undergone a successful kidney transplant. Burl discussed transplantation with four doctors in Spokane; three out of the four told him, "You will never come back alive." He knew that the possibility for him was likely years away, if ever.

Despite the hardships of the process, twice a week Lou hooked Burl up to the machine for ten-hour to twelve-hour cycles, beginning in the evening and ending the following morning. While Burl slept for much of that time, Lou stayed awake through the night, for it was crucial that she monitor both the machine and the man. "I had to keep careful records every hour and make sure the machine didn't clot. I was injecting heparin every hour to keep it from clotting." She also had to keep a close watch on the makeup of Burl's blood, frequently analyzing the content for levels of sodium, potassium, chlorides, calcium, phosphorus, and sugar. These elements could all be adjusted by varying the amount used in the chemical solution that was part of the treatment.

Burl would sleep with one eye open, making sure that Lou was awake and on top of things. "The process was never fun," Burl wrote later, "and if, as happened in a few cases with other people, the cannula came apart while the patient slept, or a mistake was made in mixing the solutions, the result could be fatal."

Both husband and wife were very matter of fact about their new lifestyle. As Lou put it: "We had to run him on the machine, and that was that. No point in feeling sorry for ourselves."

Instead, Burl learned to manage the incredible pain involved in each stage of dialysis. He grew exceedingly restless on the machine, finding it especially difficult to keep his legs still. Being hooked up to the machine also made him itch, he had frequent nosebleeds, and his body regularly retained excessive fluids. Occasionally, one or both of the cannulae failed to function properly and had to be moved to another location on his arm or leg, which required minor surgery at the hospital.

Throughout these trials, Dr. Peter Ivanovich became Burl's tireless champion.

"Burl was never defined or limited by the challenges of his kidney disease. He was the ideal patient because he continued to go out and cover stories for the AP," Ivanovich said. "Dialysis was not meant to just keep people alive but also to keep them functional and continuing to do what they had chosen to do in their lives."

Ivanovich expanded years later on Burl's role as a pioneer in "what has today become the norm in the treatment of kidney disease for millions," recalling:

> Government health service officials were favorably impressed by on-site visits to the institutions' programs, but they were absolutely taken aback by Burl Osborne, especially by his willingness to self-administer home treatments that allowed him to pursue a full-time career for the AP. The favorable reports led to the establishment of a presidential blue-ribbon committee by President Johnson to study the large-scale feasibility of home hemodialysis treatment. Ultimately, in 1972, the U.S. Congress enacted legislation that directed Medicare to cover the myriad of expenses related to the treatment of kidney disease by dialysis or transplantation.
>
> I do not mean to imply, of course, that Burl was singularly responsible for this chain of events, but it is important to note that according to one of the Public Health Service officials who visited him on several occasions in Spokane, Burl's personal contributions and inspiration were most instrumental. Not only

did Burl influence those in government; he also demonstrated the feasibility of self-dialysis to physicians attending the Washington State Medical Society Congress in May 1965 by performing it [use of the artificial kidney] right there in the scientific exhibit area of the hall.

• • •

One of the first people internationally to entertain the possibility of a kidney transplant was American medical researcher Simon Flexner. As early as 1907, he predicted that healthy arteries, stomach, kidneys, and even hearts would one day be substituted for diseased ones. In 1933, a surgeon in the Soviet Union attempted the first human kidney transplant. A donor kidney was removed six hours prior to the operation and implanted into the patient's thigh. The organ was rejected, and the patient died after two days. A successful kidney transplant did not occur until June 17, 1950, when Dr. Richard Lawler successfully transplanted a kidney in forty-four-year-old Ruth Tucker in Illinois. Antirejection drugs had not yet been developed, so the donated kidney lasted only months—but in the meantime Tucker's remaining kidney recovered, and she lived for several years afterward.

The major barrier to successful organ transplantation rests in the recipient's immune system, which treats a transplanted kidney as a "non-self" and thus chronically rejects it. Medications to suppress the immune system were essential. Though routine use of such medications was introduced in 1964, the same year that Burl was hospitalized with renal failure, the risks involved in transplantation were still great.

• • •

In a December 1965 AP column, Burl continued to chronicle his personal journey for the country:

> All I want for Christmas is a kidney — that works.
>
> That's what I wanted last Christmas, and, chances are, that's what I'll be wanting next year.

I know my Christmas wish won't be granted this year, but it doesn't matter. Because I'm luckier than almost all the other thousands of persons whose kidneys have irreversibly failed.

I can wait until the solution is found.

And live.

It was in July of 1964 that my kidneys ceased functioning; no longer filtered from my bloodstream the deadly poisons that accumulate in the life processes.

Since then, life has been sustained by twice-weekly treatments on an artificial kidney machine — first in the Spokane and Inland Empire Artificial Kidney Center here, then at home, in my own bedroom.

The club to which I belong is tragically exclusive ...

Only about a dozen, including me, are treating themselves at home.

Life on an artificial kidney is not ideal. But it is life. And it is near-normal enough so that I want to go on living it.

There are good days, in which I have the world by the tail. There are bad days, when I don't want to get out of bed.

But even the worst days are brightened by the hope — and the conviction — that a solution is on the way. All I have to do is hold on, live one day at a time. That's what I intend to do.

The solution to my problem — and the problem of others like me — will be transplantation. Except in extreme cases, it is not yet feasible. But soon it will be.

Until then, the artificial kidney is my solution. It has become as much a part of my life as eating and breathing. I am aware of it the instant I awake, and it is always the last thing on my mind when I drift off to sleep.

He concluded: "My life could be better. But I walk, I talk, I work, I play. It's almost another Christmas. And I live."

8

The Decision

As the first anniversary of his home-administered hemodialysis treatments approached, Burl filed another personal update on April 10, 1966: what it was like to live with two diseased kidneys that were killing him.

The version of the story that ran in the *Walla Walla Union-Bulletin* included an introduction: "Burl Osborne has a home machine, and all it does is keep him alive. It's an artificial kidney, and it'll have to do until the doctors perfect kidney transplant. In the meantime, this AP writer works, plays, even travels, with courage and good cheer."

In his article, Burl wrote, "I am able to work full time, without upsetting office routine with sick leaves, and my social life has not suffered unduly ... My wife and I have time for a night on the town now and then, or a movie or a trip to the mountains. The actual treatments require about 10 hours apiece, plus about two hours cleaning and preparation time. That's a total of 24 hours a week — and I spend about 16 of those hours sleeping. So the demands on my time are not too high. It's really a simple process. Much like a medical laundromat."

The story reflected Burl's s optimism tempered with realism, although it omitted the private strains that came from a young marriage and extreme health problems. Husband and wife had both grown resentful—Burl because he had grown dependent on Lou and Lou because she hadn't planned to become a nurse to her husband.

Burl also chose not to include that for some time now his dialysis treatments were marred by a frightening new problem. On occasion—about once every three to four weeks—he would begin to involuntarily shake and then suffer a full-scale convulsion during his treatments. He would thrash about uncontrollably on the bed, sometimes foaming at the mouth, while Lou struggled to move him onto his side to keep him from choking. At the same time, she labored to keep one hand on his cannula so that it wasn't torn out as his arm flailed about. Burl blacked out during the convulsions—which typically lasted four to five minutes—and had no memory of them afterward.

Lou and Burl told Dr. Peter Ivanovich about the disturbing episodes, but neither he nor any other doctor at the Spokane and Inland Empire Artificial Kidney Center could determine what caused the convulsions or how to prevent them. Burl couldn't simply stop dialysis; it was keeping him alive. So he lived with the convulsions, unpredictable and upsetting as they were.

Eventually, however, he also began to experience severe pains while on dialysis. "He just started feeling bad all over," Lou remembered. "He was given Demerol, which he said took away the pain but made him feel like he was floating on a cloud."

Depression set in because of the extensive problems with the machine and the convulsions, which were becoming more frequent and more frightening. About this time, Burl told a writer for Sacred Heart's newsletter that he planned to write a book about the psychological aspect of his treatment.

Burl continued to work long hours even after spending the previous night on dialysis. Or, alternatively, he had enough energy to follow a twelve-hour shift in the bureau's offices with twelve hours on the machine. But not always. One morning, after he had suffered a convulsion during treatment, Lou insisted she take him to work. "I wouldn't let him drive. I drove, and I rode up on the elevator with him to his office. He had to sit down in the elevator going up." On the days when the elevator was not working, Burl would take one flight of stairs at a time, stopping on each floor to rest before tackling the next set of stairs.

Then came a watershed event. One evening the home dialysis machine broke down. This time Lou and Burl couldn't figure out how to fix it. They immediately called Ivanovich, who told Burl to come immediately into the dialysis center for his treatment. As Ivanovich vividly described Burl that night: "He came into the kidney center markedly weakened, as happens with high serum potassium. I recognized this, and we got him to his dialysis station."

As Burl was lying on a table, waiting to be hooked up to the artificial kidney, he went into cardiac arrest. Ivanovich took over, pressing on Burl's chest while Lou connected him to the dialysis machine. Then Ivanovich injected epinephrine directly into Burl's chest.

"His heart had stopped beating," Ivanovich said. "If Burl hadn't come into the center that night, he would have died."

•   •   •

The staff didn't let Burl go home after the incident. Instead, they moved him into Sacred Heart's intensive care unit while doctors discussed what to do next. Ivanovich was worried. This time they were lucky that Burl's heart stoppage did not cause brain damage or lead to his death. If there was a next time, however, they might not be as fortunate.

"That was one of the complications that made Burl and me consider other options for treatment," Ivanovich said.

They soon narrowed it down to one: a kidney transplant.

Not everyone agreed. "My mentor had personally warned Burl *not* to get a transplant," Ivanovich said. "He told Burl that it would end his life."

Burl trusted Ivanovich, who told him that if a transplanted kidney didn't work, he could always go back to the far-from-ideal hemodialysis. One did not preclude the other. At the time, about 70 percent of patients who received a kidney from a blood relative lived for about a year, and half that many lived up to four years longer. Transplanting a kidney from a cadaver or a nonrelative reduced the chance of a patient's body accepting the organ. Although the likelihood of success was greater with live donations from family members, they were still rare at the time.

For two months following his cardiac arrest, Burl carried on the transplant debate in his head. He wondered not only whether he would survive such an operation but also whether it would be ethically right to accept a kidney from a member of his family. Would that family member be subject to greater risk with only one kidney?

Burl asked doctors to explain in great detail what the risks would be for the donor, and they assured him that a person can easily survive with only one kidney.

Did he want to be a test patient for such a risky operation? Did he face even greater risk *not* undergoing a transplant?

"Together we decided that we didn't really have a choice," Lou said. "Because of all the problems with home dialysis, it seemed obvious to us that a transplant was the only answer. Burl wasn't afraid. He just accepted that this is what he had to do."

Burl later wrote of his decision: "After checking major transplant centers throughout the United States, my family and I settled on the University of Colorado. First, because doctors there were willing to do the operation and, second, because of its reputation as one of the world's foremost transplant centers."

Burl chose Colorado for one other essential reason. Ivanovich was a colleague of Dr. Thomas Starzl, one of the leading transplant specialists in the world, who would later be referred to as "the father of modern transplantation." He was on the surgical faculty of the University of Colorado's hospital.

Coincidentally, he was the nephew of Frank Starzel, the general manager of the AP when Burl was hired, who, he wrote in his book *The Puzzle People*, had legally changed his last name to Starzel "because his journalist colleagues could not learn to spell and pronounce it correctly." Starzl remembered that Burl "never failed to dwell on his affection for my uncle Frank." Burl especially admired that Starzel "knew every employee in the organization and interviewed all new recruits before hiring them." He prioritized "genuine kindness" over "expediency."

Ivanovich spoke with Starzl about Burl's condition and the imminent danger he faced. Starzl agreed to take on Burl as a patient. Arrangements for Burl's kidney transplant were immediately set in motion.

• • •

Before a donor could be selected, his or her blood and tissue matching had to be tested. This was something of a logistical nightmare in this case, though, because the patient was in Spokane, the potential donors were in Kentucky, and the premier blood and tissue testing center was at the University of California, Los Angeles (UCLA), under the direction of Dr. Paul I. Terasaki, a well-known expert in blood and tissue matching.

Added to that complexity was the obstacle that members of the AFL-CIO International Association of Machinists union were on strike, effectively shutting down 60 percent of the country's commercial airline industry. Burl found a solution. He had a news source and friend in Spokane at the

Washington Air National Guard who volunteered to handle all the arrangements for transporting the blood and tissue samples to UCLA's laboratory in a timely manner.

Thus, the Osborne family members' blood and tissue samples—taken in Ashland—were picked up by a Washington Air National Guard jet at the airport in Charleston, West Virginia—the nearest airport that could supply the special jet engine fuel for the flight. Time being of the essence, Burl's brother David raced to Charleston with the samples to meet the plane.

Another jet, with Burl's samples from Spokane, was dispatched to arrive in Los Angeles in concert with the jet from Charleston.

Three Osborne family members told Burl they wanted to be donors: his mother, Juanita, and his two brothers, David and Rick. Oliver's blood type was not a match.

The test results revealed that David was the best match. Burl's mother was a close runner-up. Delighted, and not a bit frightened, Juanita said matter of factly that she gave Burl life once and she wanted to give him life a second time. She insisted on being the donor because David was still young and newly married. She felt that it was too risky to put another of her sons through the surgery, and she didn't want to lose them both.

Burl took the highly anticipated call about midnight on July 20, instructing him to be at the University of Colorado Medical Center's Colorado General Hospital in Denver by Friday, July 22. The transplant was scheduled for Wednesday morning, July 27. Burl and Lou flew, while Ivanovich, who would join Starzl in the operating room, drove Burl's red Corvette the nearly 1,100 miles from Spokane to Denver.

As Starzl wrote in his book *The Puzzle People*, Burl would be only the third person in the world to be treated with triple-drug antirejection therapy that included antilymphocyte globulin, a serum drawn from the hindquarters of a horse. The injections were horribly painful. Later on, Burl likened the pain to what he imagined it actually felt like to be kicked in the rear by a horse.

David drove his wife, mother, father, and brother Rick to Denver so Juanita could begin prepping for the surgery five days prior to the appointed date.

Meanwhile, following Burl's decision to have a transplant, executives at the AP's headquarters in New York asked Spencer to do the necessary work of preparing a "biographical sketch" of Burl that could be used as an obituary should he die during or soon after the operation. The first line of Spencer's sketch read, "Burl Osborne was only 27 years old when death moved in as a close neighbor."

9

Is It Working?

The day Burl arrived in Denver for pre-op procedures, a letter from Gallagher arrived for him at the center: "I just learned today from the news report—and it is a good place to learn something—of your impending kidney transplant operation. I know I speak for all of your friends in the AP, who have long admired your courage and ability, when I wish you complete success in the operation and a speedy recovery. We are all looking forward to having you back in good health."

Fuller sent an immediate follow-up letter to Burl assuring him that Gallagher had "asked me to inform you that despite your limited eligibility, you will be on full pay during your convalescence."

Starzl told Burl that he would need to stay in the hospital for at least a week after the operation and that he should plan to remain in Denver to be monitored as an outpatient for an additional three weeks. Burl and Lou rented an apartment within walking distance of the hospital for themselves and Juanita as she recovered from her surgery.

Burl later recalled that the last thing he remembered on the Wednesday morning of the operation was seeing his mother smiling a cheerful hello as staff wheeled them into their separate operating rooms. He didn't think about dying as he entered the room on a gurney. Nor was he frightened, which he suspected stemmed more from the preoperative drugs than bravery. He felt he had everything to gain and very little to lose by undergoing the transplant. He had waited a long time for this moment, and he was more than ready.

If anyone was nervous about the operation, it was Starzl. As he wrote in *The Puzzle People*, the connection between Burl and his uncle Frank meant "my anxiety was higher than usual."

During the five-hour operation, Starzl removed Burl's spleen, his appendix, and both his useless kidneys. In another operating room, Dr. Thomas L. Marchioro removed Juanita's left kidney. Starzl then transplanted Juanita's healthy kidney into the lower right abdomen of Burl's body. The incision left a zipper scar down the front of Burl's midsection.

When he awoke from the operation, Burl asked one question: "Is it working?"

"It's functioning perfectly," Ivanovich told him. In fact, the kidney had begun functioning while he still was on the operating table.

As Starzl wrote, "Except for complaints of a sore buttocks from the hated . . . injections, his recovery was uncomplicated." Burl's "full disclosure" rebuttal, as it were, went like this: "The next thing I remember [after waking in recovery] was excruciating pain that continued without letup for a full twenty-four hours. Painkillers might put added stress on the kidney. So it was grin and bear it. Pain was a small enough price to pay."

Burl was only the 130th person in the world to undergo a kidney transplant from a living donor. The nurses had their patient up on his feet the very next day. He took a few steps with their support. Each day thereafter he grew a little stronger. His postoperative therapy involved taking heavy doses of the steroid prednisone plus the immunosuppressant azathioprine to help his body fend off rejection of the kidney. Two days after the operation, his body did show mild signs of rejecting the transplanted organ, but that didn't progress. Soon his entire body began functioning normally.

• • •

A month after the transplant, Burl wrote to the AP's Gallagher. "I just want to say thank you for the support you and the AP have given me during the past two years—and especially during the past few weeks—when my kidney ailment has been a particular problem. That support has been something I have been able to lean on when the going has been particularly rough. Now that a happy ending is in sight, I find I cannot begin to measure the worth of that help. Again, although the words seem inadequate, thank you."

Starzl soon discharged Burl, comforted knowing that Ivanovich would continue to look after him. Once back home and resettled in Spokane, Burl returned to work full time on October 1, 1966.

• • •

During those early years of dialysis, Burl's personal accounts had gone out on the A-wire and ran in AP member newspapers worldwide, read by many people afflicted with kidney disease. Now he could give them something more important—hope.

Under his byline, he wrote:

'It's Functioning Perfectly': Kidney Transplant Has Given Him a New Life
November 3, 1966

SPOKANE, Wash. (AP)—For the first time in my adult life, I can savor the full difference between living and just staying alive.

Medically, I should have died two years ago when both my kidneys failed — and left my body without their vital blood-cleansing ability. I have lived since then only through twice-weekly visits to an artificial kidney machine.

But now a new and radical operation has given me a new kidney — a transplanted kidney that is working at the 24-hour-a-day job of keeping my body fluids stable, letting me eat and drink with freedom again, and releasing me from the tyranny of living by benefit of machine.

Like a Pardon

I'll never forget when doctors told me after the operation, "It's functioning perfectly." Nothing will surpass the joy I felt when I heard those words. It was like a pardon from a life sentence.

It was a new experience — just feeling well. After the effects of the surgery passed, I could tell I was becoming stronger every day, stronger than I had been in years. I don't have to pretend anymore, because I do feel well. I want to get out of bed in the morning, and once I do, I feel like going, doing, living like other people. The off-limits signs are gone from the swimming pool, the golf course, the bowling alley.

Perhaps most people won't understand my joy when the nurse brought me a big chocolate milkshake after the operation. I was spellbound by the first big pitcher of water she put at my bedside, with instructions to drink all

I wanted. I had been limited to three small glasses of liquid a day, and I had to figure into that total how much water was in my food.

My salt-free diet ended with my first breakfast of bacon and eggs. I had avoided salt for so long I was almost afraid to eat the bacon. And when I did, it tasted too salty.

Walked Quickly

I was on my feet the next day, with nurses supporting me, but managed to hobble only a few steps. After that, I could feel improvement each day. And what I couldn't feel I could see on a big chart in front of my bed. Within a few days almost everything was normal.

My body tried mildly to fight off the new kidney a few days after the surgery. It happens in nearly every case. Drugs to control the rejection were administered.

Burl concluded his story with some additional good news: "My mother, Mrs. Oliver Osborne, 45, is home again and feeling fine."

• • •

The Osborne family's concerned friends in neighboring West Virginia were pleased to learn of Juanita's good health and her son Burl's progress.

"It's with a lot of happiness that we can report that Burl Osborne, former AP star here ... is in good health again after a kidney transplant at Denver," Currence wrote to readers of the *Bluefield Daily Telegraph*. "Buckskin plays golf, swims and does a full day's work (and much more, probably) for the worldwide news service. He returns to Denver ... so the medicos can have a look at him, but they have drastically cut down on his medication and he is now living what just about amounts to a normal life."

10

Imagine What He Could Do with Two Kidneys!

Burl would soon be returning to Denver for more than medical reasons. At summer's end, Gallagher promoted him to news editor and assistant bureau chief in Colorado's capital. Effective September 15, 1967, Burl would be in charge of the AP news and photo reports for both Colorado and Wyoming.

With its half a million residents, Denver was booming in the mid-1960s.

Instead of having just one office, Burl operated out of two: the AP's offices at *The Denver Post* and those in the *Rocky Mountain News* building. It was "terribly inefficient," but that was the setup Burl inherited, and he didn't try to change it.

> We had offices in both newspapers, several blocks apart. At four o'clock in the afternoon, you packed up a satchel with the reports, and you went from *The Denver Post* to the *Rocky Mountain News*. And, around 6:00 a.m., or something like that, you repacked at the *News*, and you lugged the reports back over to *The Post*.
>
> The thing I remember most is that *The Denver Post*, which was historically the leading newspaper in Colorado, had a view that it couldn't happen until they reported it, and they weren't going to report it simply because the AP reported it. And so stories would linger around. . . . On the other hand, the *Rocky Mountain News* was sort of gritty, and they were way behind and widely considered to be the second choice, but they didn't care where they got it if they got it first. And so, after a while, one could quietly play that and wind up on page one of the *Rocky Mountain News* many times with stories that *The Post* hadn't had.

For the first time in his career, Burl would spend less time traveling, reporting, and writing news stories. Instead, he would focus his attention on the newspaper and broadcast members of the AP. Burl said, "[Denver] was the first time that I actually went out to find out what the problems were and get them fixed or, if we had a new service, to try to get someone to buy it. So I was to make sure the members were properly served and as happy as they could be, which wasn't always the case."

For example, in Colorado Springs, one particular newspaper—which had been started by a union—openly disliked its competitor, the *Gazette Telegraph*. That presented Burl with the constant challenge of managing the two of them and, as he put it, "not letting them bring the AP into their fight."

Burl loved membership work. That delighted Denver's Bureau Chief, Noland Norgaard, a Norwegian who went by the nickname "Boots," who *did not*. Burl recalled,

> Boots had a very imposing mustache and was somewhat formal in his approach. And I was then, and I guess still am, somewhat less so. It was good for me because he didn't interfere with what I wanted to do, which was handle the complaints, run the news desk, make sure the trains run on time, and get out and do membership work. And if you can find some spare time, then do some reporting, but that really wasn't what the job was. Boots was very good about giving me a free hand to do those things, especially if it didn't interfere with his love for skiing. And so I was able to do a lot of different things, including *some* reporting.

Burl lived in the same apartment building with his UPI counterpart and competition. He recalled:

> Periodically I would ask the doorman whether he had seen Paul. If he said, "Not yet today," I would say, "Would you tell him that I left on a dead run?" Paul did it to me as well. So we had fun with each other.

Though his top priority was customer service, Burl's output over the A-wire was just as prodigious as it had been in Charleston. Oftentimes, he worked side by side with Denver AP Photographer Bob Scott, who called him a "whirling dervish." At the age of ninety-one in 2019, Scott still recalled Burl fondly. "Oh, that mind of his was just unbelievable. I just wish I had had some of his knowledge. I always wished that."

The furious pace Burl kept up in Denver likewise caused Gene Foster, radio editor for the AP in Denver, to shake his head and exclaim, "Imagine what he could do with *two* kidneys!"

• • •

With newfound energy since the transplant, Burl soon took up snow skiing. Although he put in exhaustive hours at his day job, when the weekend came, he and friends headed for the slopes west of Denver.

His transplant surgeon, Starzl, wrote in his book about a chance meeting with Burl. "The next time I saw him [post-transplant surgery], he was on his way to Aspen for a ski vacation. Although moon-faced from steroids, he was bursting with energy and confidence." Upon hearing Burl describe his plans to hit the slopes, Starzl cautioned, "'Please don't go.' I could imagine that his bones, thinned and weakened by the steroids, would crack with the first hard fall. He went anyway, and did so every year until I left Colorado at the end of 1980."

Realizing that his patient had no intention of taking his advice, Starzl soon began joining Burl on the mountains. Sometimes, after a day in the operating room, he would call Burl on the spur of the moment to arrange a quick ski trip.

Burl spoke fondly of Starzl throughout the years. "Tom Starzl and I became very good friends when we were both in Denver, and we still are. He is a brilliant researcher, and he's always been way ahead of his peers in knowing what had to be, what needs to be, done. I got back to Denver in time to be assigned to cover Tom's work in transplantation, which would cause him periodically to threaten to withdraw my treatment because he wasn't always especially happy with what I was writing."

Among the many of Starzl's cases Burl covered was the touching story of four girls who underwent historic liver transplants in the summer and fall of 1967. As Burl wrote for the AP on November 22, 1967: "Four little girls — too young to know they're making medical history — offered hope for thousands Tuesday when doctors outlined their progress as the most successful liver transplant patients in medical history. As recently as four months ago, there was no known record of anyone surviving longer than 34 days following any type of liver transplant. Now there are these four. The first, Julie 'Ju-Ju' Rodriguez, daughter of Mr. and Mrs. John Rodriguez of Pueblo, Colo., had her transplant 122 days ago on July 23 [just nineteen months old]."

Burl went on to describe the other three girls and the results of the operations to date. "There have been some serious but so far not insurmountable complications with these cases, but generally doctors ... are optimistic. They are hopeful progress with livers will parallel advances in kidney transplantation, a field where some patients are doing well five years after the surgery."

In the spring he filed an update: Julie was going home.

Liver Transplant Girl Goes Home

PUEBLO, Colo. (AP)—Squealing, "Daddy!" even before he walked through the door, 2-year-old Julie Cherie Rodriguez welcomed her father home from work Thursday.

And that completed a homecoming for a pretty, dark-haired and wide-eyed little girl who has lived longer with a transplanted liver than anyone else known to medical science.

"I didn't think it would ever happen," said John C. Rodriguez after he learned his daughter had been sent home from the hospital more than 10 months after the operation.

"I wanted to shout it from the rooftops: My baby's going home," said Julie's mother, Louise. "God let Julie come home and I can have my two kids together. That's what I'm thankful for. We're a family again ... Julie is a different person out of the hospital. She even hugged and kissed 5-month-old John. She knows he's her brother."

In the middle of June, Burl received a letter from the AP's Gallagher: "In making some changes, a chief of bureau opening will come up in Montana. If you would like to succeed Wick Temple . . . as chief of bureau in Montana and accept the job enthusiastically, it is yours. . . . I want you to know you have done an excellent job as news editor there [in Denver], and there will be further advancement for you in news alone if you choose this for your career."

Burl replied on June 17, first in a phone call, then in a follow-up letter. In both he emphasized that he was deeply interested in running a bureau and all that entailed—travel, management, member relations, and such. At the time, however, he could not accept the job in Helena, Montana, for personal reasons. He and Lou had separated.

They had thought the kidney transplant would bring them closer together, but it did not. They were both still very young, and their future after the transplant was uncertain. Five years was about all the doctors would give Burl as a time line for life after the transplant. Burl wanted children. Lou, exhausted, did not want to be a young widow with children.

With the marriage ending and their situation unresolved, Burl did not want to take a new assignment. But he assured Gallagher that his personal circumstances "would not affect his ability to do his job" and that he was "qualified to do a competent job as a chief of bureau."

"I did not intend to leave any impression that I feel I am indispensable in Denver. I know better. But I have been here just a short time, and we have barely scratched the surface," Burl wrote. He closed the letter by vowing to "continue to do the best job I know how in Denver until I can move into something with more responsibility."

• • •

On August 27, 1968, Burl composed a story he had hoped never to write. "Julie Cherie Rodriguez, who lived with a transplanted liver longer than anyone known to science, died of cancer Monday evening at the University of Colorado Medical Center."

"It was a blessing ... She had suffered so much. I'm glad God came and picked her up," said her father. "We're not bitter or sorry that we went through it.

We're grateful we had this chance to keep Julie a little longer and, with what doctors have learned, help humanity a little."

• • •

While in Denver, Burl continued to follow new developments in human organ transplants.

In a September 17 article, Burl wrote: "Transplanting human organs is not a perfected art, but it appears to have become an accepted clinical treatment — not an experimental long shot — when vital organs fail." Citing that at the University of Colorado, "214 kidney transplants have been performed since 1962, with 127 survivors," Burl conveyed the surgeons' assertion that the lessons learned in kidney transplants "provided the foundation for later attempts at transplanting the heart, liver, lungs, pancreas, spleen and thymus." The article concluded: "Because doctors around the world are becoming less reluctant to try transplantation, the future for victims of irreversible heart, liver, kidney and lung disease appears brighter. They have a chance to live where none existed before."

• • •

Managing the newswire was a unique challenge in Denver because of the vast territory for which the bureau was responsible. Denver was a place where a lot of wires crossed for the AP—literally. The available technology limited transmission speeds to sixty-six words per minute. Burl recalled:

> Just filing football, for example, on a college Saturday, you had several conferences that you had to cover. . . . We had a gallon of stuff and a quart of wire time. As you did triage near the end of the day or of the night—where you may have gotten a story, some agate,[6] and a follow-up at six o'clock by eleven o'clock—you were lucky if you got the score.

His boss was pleased with how Burl balanced the job responsibilities. Norgaard wrote to Gallagher on January 22, 1969, praising Burl's "driving energy, resourcefulness, and hard work." He wrote:

Your assignment of Burl to this job has proven to be one of the
best things that ever happened to the Denver bureau. Our news
output has improved immensely, both as to quality and quantity,
under his immediate supervision.

Norgaard followed up that letter a little over a year later, writing to Fuller.

"I offer two names for your list of AP employees who may be
considered good prospects for administrative jobs. First, let
me repeat earlier recommendations that Burl Osborne be kept in
mind for a bureau chief opening. He is ready for it. As I have
mentioned before, both to you and to Mr. Gallagher, he would be
an ideal nominee to succeed me here in Denver."

11

It's a *Nude* Story

While the senior executives at the AP's headquarters discussed Burl's immediate future with the organization, Burl continued to pluck the choicest assignments. One was an invitation to fly in a B-57, an opportunity he was now healthy enough to take.

As explained in the editor's note for the following story, "Three or four times a month orders are issued for a surprise air attack on North America to test the Air Defense Command. The bombers are real, but they carry no bombs or missiles. It's a friendly enemy that 'attacks.'" Burl and Scott were guests on one such "night mission." AP Canadian and U.S. member newspapers picked up their account.

North America Under Air Attack; But It's Only a Make-Believe Game
By Burl Osborne
Associated Press Writer
June 21, 1970

NORTH BAY, Ont. (AP)—Jim Goodnight fiddled with [his] white and fluorescent orange flight helmet until it was more comfortable. He gently braked the taxiing bomber, its twin jet engines at a screaming idle, until it halted.

Ahead, a kaleidoscope of blue and red and yellow runway lights blinked in the prickly hard, spitting snowfall, swirling across the runway in the glare of the plane's landing lights.

Goodnight peered out of the plexiglass canopy, now locked in place and shutting out some of the engine noise. Airmen, moving stiffly like oversized puppets in massive, Arctic weather parkas and huge gloves, moved up to the plane for the "last chance" visual inspection before takeoff. The crew leader, his face all but hidden by the furry lining of his parka hood, turned thumbs up.

"Here we go," Goodnight said softly, with a trace of his native Mississippi accent.

The B57, its long wings rocking gently up and down, eased to the head of the runway. Its engines screamed at high pitch. Power indicators in the cockpit spun from idle to 100 per cent.

From the tower: "Cleared for takeoff, Apex 82."

The fat rubber wheels thumped, faster and faster, as the plane gained speed across the seams in the concrete runway. Then it lifted softly into the night. The bomber, with black and brown and olive camouflage, was hardly visible once it cleared the ground.

The pilot, unlike his plane, was a combat veteran. Air Force Maj. James Goodnight was a veteran of 204 missions over Vietnam, 44 of them night patrols over North Vietnam.

This flight had many trappings of combat. But there were differences: this B57 carried no bombs or missiles. There would be no ground fire. No fighters would shoot back. Jim Goodnight would destroy nothing, kill no one. Except on a computer read-out sheet.

Ahead of Goodnight, and behind him, two dozen or more other crews were performing the same ritual.

Their assignment: slip through North America air defenses for make-believe attacks on eastern Canada and the northeastern United States.

Moonlight gleamed dully on the camouflaged wings. When Goodnight banked, he sometimes could see the snow-draped Canadian countryside through wispy holes in the overcast.

He adjusted his oxygen mask, pulled a card from the leg pocket of his flight suit and rechecked his mission notes, taken in an earlier briefing at Hill Air Force base in Utah: to James Bay at 25,000 feet. Turn south. Descend to 10,000. Then 8,000. Low-level run. Firing point 40 miles north of North Bay. Near Rouyn. Target: Niagara Falls power plant and the Buffalo, N.Y., chemical plant complex.

Goodnight put away the card and set a course to James Bay.

The half-million residents of Buffalo didn't know their city was a marked target that crisp, cold night. Many were settling down to watch "Catered Affair," with Ernest Borgnine and Bette Davis, on the late movie. Others prepared to turn in. One, Mary Anne Shea, a pretty graduate student at Niagara University, parked her car, ran inside and decided on a snack after a late evening class in educational psychology. She saw no cause for alarm.

Nor was there alarm in the town of North Bay, snuggled on the shore of Lake Nipissing, about 200 miles north of Toronto. But nearby, in the Blue Room, most protected sanctuary in a fortress hewn deep underground from granite-like rock two billion years old, Capt. Chick Campbell spotted a new blip on his radar screen and tensed.

It was moving quickly from the north. There was no flight plan for aircraft in that sector. That's near James Bay, Campbell figured silently as his radar console, one of about 20 in the room, fed information on altitude, speed, location and direction into the sprawling banks of high-speed digital computers humming two floors below. In a fraction of a second, the computer confirmed his suspicion. The plane on his radar was an unknown. The computer assigned it a track number: M264.

Other radar consoles, some manned by Americans and some by officers of Canadian Armed Forces, like Campbell, were turning out similar reports. There were more than two dozen tracks, all from the polar north.

One floor below was the command post for the two-million-square mile 22nd region of the North American Air Defense Command, the joint U.S.-Canadian agency charged with defense of North American air space. The information was displayed there on electronic wall screens.

The decision was made quickly. Scramble the interceptors.

Val d'Or is a small town with a musical-sounding name that rolls off the tongue. It is about 100 miles north, and slightly east, of North Bay. It was there the waiting ended for Capt. Ross Betts, a tall, handsome Canadian jet fighter pilot.

Betts, 24, who likes to ski nearly as much as he likes to fly, usually was stationed at Bagotville, Que., with "Les Alouettes," the 425th All Weather

Fighter Squadron. But he and other supersonic CF101 pilots were on alert at Val D'Or.

The scramble order sent Betts and his navigator, Capt. Lloyd Booth, trooping for their plane, the Canadian version of the 1,200-mile-an-hour CF101. They strapped themselves into the ejection seats and quickly taxied for takeoff. The jolt of the afterburners pinned them back. The CF101 lifted, Betts pointed its nose to the sky and they climbed to 35,000 feet, then leveled off at better than 600 miles an hour, near the speed of sound.

The radio crackled: "Kilo November 17, your target is NORAD track Mike-264."

And, as it happens dozens of times a year, the stage was set for a "friendly enemy" attack on North America:

- Bombers converging on industrial and military centers.
- Interceptors speeding to meet, identify and, if necessary, destroy them.
- Missile batteries at the ready.

And people in dozens of cities, like Mary Anne Shea in Buffalo, by now snacking on steak left over from a dinner party the night before, who weren't aware of anything out of the ordinary.

"We're over James Bay," said Goodnight. His B57 had been airborne about an hour, climbing through the soupy overcast and now skimming along the cloud tops.

"We're a little past the turn point," he said, "but there's nothing to worry about." The turn point, over the bay, was where the B57 became a blip on Campbell's radar, instead of the artificial, computer-made track the radar first showed.

"Beautiful. We're right on the nose. Probably a little early. Maybe three minutes," Goodnight said.

"You can see the stars at least," he said as the soft moonlight flooded the cockpit. The soft red light of the instrument panel reflected on the transparent canopy.

"We're going down now." The altimeter spun from 25,000 feet to 20,000 feet in a minute. The moonlight became blackness as the B57 dropped back into the overcast. Air speed was 350 miles an hour. Heading almost due south, toward North Bay. Toward the small town of Rouyn. Toward the firing point.

On course now. There was time for conversation.

"Is this like Vietnam?"

"Well, yes and no. Pilots don't fly over snow in Vietnam; they fly over jungle. No one has been shot down in an exercise over Canada."

"But like Vietnam, the contest is a serious one."

"Vietnam is really something," said Goodnight, who at 34 is looking to retirement from the military in seven years. "It's really beautiful country ... if we don't put so many bomb craters over there you can't see the green any more."

From the air, he said, "Pleiku is like Kansas. But Da Nang is like eastern Tennessee and Kentucky."

At 13,000 feet, the conversation ended. Another pilot, another "bad guy," "faker," or "black hat," radioed to the mission controller that his wings were icing.

Goodnight said nothing, but beamed a cockpit spotlight first on the starboard, then the port engine. "We're picking up some too. See, on the cone and on the leading edge of the wing."

"Apex Control. Request permission to change altitude because of icing."

No response.

"I have to go up."

Two minutes later, where the temperature was 40 below zero, the plane lifted out of the mist. The ice slipped away, bit by bit.

The plane whooshed along, pushed by engines that each generate 7,000 pounds of thrust.

It was quiet for a few minutes.

"That's not right," said Goodnight over the intercom linking the front and rear cockpit.

"Apex Control. Do you have a position on me?"

"Negative 82. We lost you some time ago in the jamming and haven't seen you since." The showers of aluminum chaff, dropped by the intruders to confuse — jam — defensive radar, had lost Goodnight as well.

It was almost two hours into the mission. Apex 82 should have been 50 miles north of North Bay, less than two minutes from the spot where its make-believe missiles would be fired.

The area should have been swarming with interceptors. But the ABS54, the gadget which detects radar on an approaching plane, was not lit.

"We're off course," said Goodnight matter-of-factly. "We're in a hell of a crosswind. That's got to be what it is. We're off maybe 20 or 25 miles. We're east of Val d'Or instead of west."

Goodnight altered course to the west and south. The DME — distance measuring equipment — finally locked in on the North Bay radio signal. Sure enough, he was not 50 miles from North Bay; he was more like 120 miles out.

The B57 eased back into the clouds, dropping to 8,000 feet. He was 110 miles from North Bay and 70 miles north of Rouyn, less than 15 minutes from "firing" at Buffalo and Niagara Falls.

At the corner of Rosary Avenue and Lackawanna in Buffalo, Mary Anne Shea was at home and ready for bed. She decided against the late movie and instead decided to read some more of Sinclair Lewis' "Main Street."

Capt. Betts and his navigator were barreling along to the southeast. They still got directions by radio, looking for M264—the "bad guy," Goodnight. Their course was set over Lake Kipawa, about 40 miles north of North Bay.

In the rear cockpit of Goodnight's B57, the radar detector remained unlit. "That's funny," said Goodnight. "We should be having company any time now."

It was black outside. The stars and moon were hidden by the murky overcast. The cockpit glowed red from the instrument lights. It was quiet. The firing point was 30 miles away — five minutes.

Fuel gauges showed just how far off course the wind had taken him. Still, there was enough to complete the mission and get back to North Bay.

The only sound was the deadened engine noise. The firing point was 15 miles away.

Ten miles away.

Eight miles away.

Six miles — one minute.

There was no sign of interception.

"There he is!" shouted Goodnight. A small light flashed suddenly in front, from left to right.

"He got us. I know he got us."

That's all there was — a flash of light — to getting "shot down" in a make-believe battle.

Goodnight didn't get to his firing point. But the margin was not great. It often isn't. Forty seconds more and in this serious game of make-believe he could have pushed the button. But these "bad guys" get that extra 40 seconds only 5 per cent of the time, and this test was no exception.

Betts and the other interceptor pilots returned to their bases to confirm their "kills."

Goodnight returned to North Bay, then to his house unit to plan another "attack," on Florida.

Mary Anne Shea put down her book and went to sleep.

She saw no cause for alarm.

Another select assignment was a promotion that Burl and Scott covered together for the 1970 big-screen movie *What Do You Say to a Naked Lady?* Although the event was more the domain of entertainment news than hard news, Scott remembered Burl avowing: "This is a story we must cover. It's a *news* story." To which he retorted, "Yes, Burl, but it's a *nude* story."

The press conference was held in a hotel room, at the center of which was a svelte brunette sitting on a table, wearing nothing but a floppy hat and a feather boa. Several newsmen were gathered around her trying to figure out just what to say to a naked lady. Burl masked his own thoughts: wearing a placid look on his face and holding a tape recorder in one hand, he asked her matter of factly: *"Are you cold?"*

12

Things Are Going to Be Different

That September, Gallagher reached out to Burl.

I have a new job to offer you. . . If you are prepared to accept it enthusiastically, I would appoint you Chief of Bureau in Kentucky . . .

The Kentucky bureau is an important one to us with a very strong membership situation and a very demanding group of newspapers not only in Louisville but in other sections of the state.

I am sure you will find it a challenge.

Burl was headed home.

• • •

Burl first showed up at the Louisville bureau in mid-October 1970 wearing bright red shorts and a casual shirt opened at the neck. It was a Saturday. Not many staffers were around; those there were more than a little intrigued.

"Burl stood only about five feet five," recalled then-staffer Terry Hunt about that day, "but he moved with complete confidence. The AP office was located just off the newsroom of *The Courier-Journal* newspaper in Louisville, a pretty staid, coat-and-tie kind of place. We had never seen anyone in shorts in the office. Ignoring our shock, Burl introduced himself as the new AP bureau chief. I remember thinking, 'Things are going to be different.'"

Having read up on the AP bureau in the largest city in his home state, Burl knew pretty much what to expect. "Louisville was less complicated than Denver. The sports were more contained, the state was easier to cover, and there were—at the time—no serious multistate obligations. It was easier to focus. I would say it was a traditional AP bureau, with a mix of people ranging from very new to very old."

Then–staff writer Bill Winter described the bureau's setup, which heightened everyone's awareness of one another.

> The bureau was in a room at one end of the *Courier-Journal* and *Louisville Times* newsroom, its glass walls allowing those of us on the AP side to peer out at the much larger newsroom of the world-class sister newspapers on the other side. One side of the bureau was lined with noisy, clattering, slow-speed AP teletype machines that churned out paper copies of stories at sixty-six words per minute. The CRTs [cathode ray tube word processors] that were replacing typewriters in AP newsrooms at that time were on the other side of the room, mere feet from the glass enclosure that was the bureau chief's office.

As part of Burl's transfer to Louisville as bureau chief, Burl flew to New York to meet with Gallagher. AP bureaus in states like Kentucky were ruled by their budgets, which were set in New York. No money was allocated for overtime work.

Burl recalled their conversation: "He said, 'You know, I want to tell you one thing. You've got to watch your budget. However, if there's a big story and you go after it, and you go over your budget, that'll be okay. If there's a big story and you don't go after it, and you stay within your budget, I will fire your ass.'"

Gallagher had a second admonishment: "Now remember, you're the bureau chief. You don't go cover every story yourself. You have—that's why you have a staff. You do not; you stay in the office, and you make sure everything runs properly."

Gallagher's words were still fresh in his mind when, shortly after noon on December 30, 1970, Burl learned of an enormous coal mine explosion and collapse outside the town of Hyden—where it was said of miners "they's worth more dead than when they's a-livin'!" It was a year to the day after passage of the Federal Coal Mine Health and Safety Act of 1969. And it was an event so tragic that two songs were later written about what became known as the Hurricane Creek mine disaster: Tom T. Hall's "Trip to Hyden" and J. D. Jarvis' "The Hyden Miner's Tragedy."

As many as forty miners were feared dead. The mine was a risky eight-hour drive over snowy mountain roads. Burl knew he couldn't waste those hours traveling by car. Fortunately, the editors at *The Courier-Journal* had chartered a plane to Hyden and had one seat still available. "You can have the seat, but we're going right now," they told Burl. He decided not to do as Gallagher ordered—that is, to stay in the office and send a staff reporter. Instead, Burl went to the scene of the tragedy himself.

"I left the bureau and took the seat [on the plane] and went to the story," he recalled. "And I decided it was easier to beg forgiveness than permission."

Burl and the few reporters from *The Courier-Journal* were among the first on the scene. And, for most of the day, they were the *only* reporters on the scene because the foot of snow that fell around the time of the accident made the roads to the mine nearly impassable.

Late that night Burl phoned the Louisville bureau. Hunt distinctly recalled their conversation. "A weary Burl called in around 11:00 p.m. to say goodnight, but I had to tell him that New York wanted him to write a feature story for the overnight cycle. I thought he'd sit down, compose something, and call me back a little later. Instead, he sighed, said okay, rifled through his notes, and then began dictating a story off the top of his head. It was perfect. And he blew me away!"

Only One Man Lived

HYDEN, Ky. (AP)—One by one, the worst fears were confirmed in the tiny valley.

The coal dust–blackened miners' boots, extending from the blanket-covered stretchers, were still.

Thirty-nine men had been working in the Finley Coal Co. mine, burrowing from two openings underneath a southeastern Kentucky mountainside.

Now, 38 miners were dead, and only one man was out to tell the tale.

A.T. Collins was near the mouth of the mine Wednesday when an explosion sent rock dust billowing through the honeycombs of the mine and spewing out its mouth. Collins survived with slight injuries. His coworkers farther back were felled.

Most of the wives and children left the mine area before the men were found dead.

They trudged through the cold night along the muddy road for more than a mile to the main highway. Then they headed for their homes in this small mining town about five miles west of the mine.

As the hours of waiting and uncertainty wore on, women who might be widows became increasingly somber and reflective.

"Seems like I don't really believe he's dead or anything," 18-year-old Brenda White said as pools of tears welled in her eyes. "It just doesn't seem real to me. That's why I'm so calm," she whispered.

Her husband, Elmer White, the father of a 5-month-old daughter, is missing. He had worked as a miner for only three weeks.

At the mine site, only man-made light crept through the darkness and reflected on the snowflakes and the pools of mud and water.

There was no moon. There were no stars.

Some miners and others clustered around four fires to ward off the biting cold.

A half mile inside the mountain, searchers worked quietly.

The ambulance driver eased toward the site shortly after the disaster was reported to him.

Rescuers initially probed about 1,900 feet into the mine but were driven off by deadly carbon monoxide gas.

About 6 p.m., another rescue operation was started.

The crowd had swelled to more than 200 by the time the first bodies were brought to the surface. They were taken to a makeshift morgue set up in the gymnasium of the Hyden grade school. Some were identified by name tags they wore or by information in their billfolds.

BURL

H. N. Kirkpatrick, state commissioner of mines and minerals, said that after all the bodies were removed, the mine would be sealed to "rest for a few days" before the federal-state underground investigation began.

Finley said he could offer no explanation for the blast.

The worst disaster in Kentucky coal mining history occurred on Aug. 4, 1917, when 62 were killed at the No. 7 mine of the Western Kentucky Coal Co. near Clay.

The previous second high toll was on Christmas Day 1945, when 31 died at the Straight Creek mine in neighboring Bell County, 20 miles from Hyden.

Leslie County Judge George Wooton, who passed through the crowd of friends and relatives of the miners, encouraged them to keep up their hopes.

"This is the most terrible thing which has happened to us in my time," he said. "We have so many problems here it seems unfair for this to happen to us."

Leslie County is one of the most remote and underdeveloped counties in the state. Its single industry is the mining of coal.

"It's a damned hard life," observed Leon Roark, whose brother-in-law was among the missing.

Roark, who gave up the mines after suffering a crushed disc in his spine, said, "If I have any say so, no son of mine is ever going to go down under."

"Hyden cemented his reputation as a news god for his staff," Hunt said.

"He simply wasn't going to allow himself to be defeated," Winter said. "His enthusiasm was inspiring to his staff."

• • •

Once settled into a rhythm at the bureau in Louisville, Burl even found a way to keep skiing. The Louisville Ski Club arranged a winter vacation in Chamonix, at the base of Mont Blanc, the highest summit in the French Alps. Before the transplant, such a trip was unthinkable. Burl kept the lift ticket, dated January 4–10, 1971, his whole life.

In Kentucky, Burl also found more time to spend with his parents and brothers. Anytime he scheduled appointments with AP member newspapers or broadcast stations near Ashland, he would visit. He could also now more easily spend holidays with them.

Currence noted one Christmas visit in 1970, writing in the *Bluefield Daily Telegraph*'s "People and Things" feature on January 24, 1971: "Buckskin is headquartered in Louisville and on a visit here not long ago was in the best of health."

• • •

As bureau chief, Burl also had a new responsibility: mentoring and championing the younger reporters.

"Burl was instrumental in kick-starting my career," said Hunt. "After more than a year in Louisville, I was anxious to move up. That would mean that Burl would have to ask New York for a replacement, then find a good candidate and train him or her. But he didn't hesitate to push for my promotion or try to slow it down. He said he felt it was his job to help me rise."

Hunt recalled this firsthand example of Burl's thoughtful mentorship and clever workaround in the face of budgetary restraints:

> Burl approached me one day and asked if I wanted to write a feature story about a juvenile detention center in Ashland, Kentucky, where inmates were allowed to leave confinement and go to college during the day. He said he couldn't pay me overtime for working on days off and over the weekend, but he would cover a hotel, mileage, and meals. I jumped at the chance, since all I did in Louisville was work on the desk, handling sports stories and scores and rewriting local stories from other newspapers. I was the most junior staffer in the bureau, just back from two years in the army in Germany. This was my first AP news feature. It turned out to be two to three thousand words. I gave it to Burl. He gave it a hard edit, made a lot of changes, and turned it into a terrific story. I was thrilled. That's one thing I really appreciated about Burl, that he was such a good teacher.

Hunt was eventually promoted to AP's Rhode Island bureau before moving to Washington, where he became chief White House correspondent for the wire service.

"Burl was really hard charging, and he was perfectly capable of barking at you," Winter said, "but he also understood that not everyone was talented. If someone made a mistake, he wouldn't stomp across the room and call them an idiot. He would address it in a way that was compassionate. He had a pretty good empathy for the human condition."

One experience as bureau chief that Burl never had prior to arriving in Louisville was having to fire an employee. As he recalled years later:

> The toughest thing, the absolute toughest thing I'd had to do [then] was to terminate somebody who wasn't making probation. And I haven't forgotten the lesson. This was a young woman who was a very nice person, and she just couldn't do radio. She wasn't able to do the work. I finally decided, with the probationary period running out, she's not cut out for this at all. So I bought a box of Kleenex, and I called her into the office, and I said, "So-and-so, you know, this isn't working out." And she looked at me and said, "I've known that for two months and was wondering if you would ever figure it out" [*laughs*]. The lesson is don't assume that you're the only one who knows that this person isn't working out. They may know it before you do. And most of the time, they do, I think.

Burl actually oversaw three AP offices in Kentucky: the Louisville bureau itself, plus two "correspondencies," defined as an office with just one or two correspondents. One was in the state's second-largest city, Lexington, seventy miles east-southeast; the other was in the state capital, Frankfort, about fifty miles due east. In addition to visiting staff in those satellite offices, Burl often met in person with the broadcast membership in Kentucky. That included both AP member and nonmember radio and TV stations. He was issued a company Chevy to carry him around the state.

As always, part of the job was keeping an eye on UPI, the rival newswire service. UPI was constantly trying to make inroads and was heavily discounting its prices. The competition was heated. Was UPI trying to steal papers away from the AP? Were there UPI client newspapers Burl could win over to the AP?

"Louisville was competitive," Burl recalled. "So I spent a lot of time traveling the state with matches in one hand to set a fire under their customers and a water bucket in the other to try to put out the fire they had set."

Lift ticket, Chamonix, 1971

13

Camelot

Burl would visit the *Lexington Herald-Leader* often, and over time, he became friendly with the president's secretary. During one visit she suggested that Burl join her, along with some other friends, one evening for drinks at a popular bar called Camelot. Burl was game, and they set a date.

When Burl showed up at Camelot, the secretary introduced Burl to her friend, who had brought along a friend of hers. The friend of the friend was Betty Sue Wilder, a brunette with pale skin, large brown eyes, and a radiant smile. Just twenty-one years old, she had both the natural beauty and the poise of someone older and stood about an inch taller than Burl. He was instantly smitten.

They chatted with each other while also socializing with the others seated around a large table. As the party thinned, they continued talking after most everyone else had left. Then they were the only ones left at the table. It grew late. When the band called for the last dance of the night, they found themselves one of only a few couples on the dance floor. The two parted ways that night but not for long.

The following morning Betty was at her desk at General Telephone in Lexington when she received a phone call from Burl. He asked her to meet him for lunch. She agreed to meet him but explained that her lunch break was a short one. Burl chose a nearby Long John Silver's fast-food restaurant as the venue. Betty remembers the first comment Burl said to her after they were seated: "I just had to see if you looked as good in the daylight as you did in the dark."

"I think we knew from our first meeting that we wanted to be together," Betty recalled.

Although Betty was twelve years younger than Burl, the couple found that they shared many life experiences, chief among them growing up in similar hardscrabble circumstances in Kentucky. "I didn't have to go into detail to explain to Burl the kind of house in which I grew up," says Betty. "He completely understood. We spoke a similar eastern Kentucky language. Early on in our relationship we would sometimes try to 'out-poor' each other, to see whose story about growing up in poverty was more compelling."

Betty continued to work and live in Lexington, where she had friends and a busy social life. Shortly after she and Burl met, she was promoted to the head of the department at General Telephone. In addition to working full time, Betty took night classes at the University of Kentucky, working toward her bachelor's degree. Despite their busy schedules and the seventy miles that separated them, Betty and Burl found time to see each other.

That distance would soon stretch even farther, however, because in March 1972, after less than eighteen months in Louisville, Burl would be leaving Kentucky. The AP had a problem in its bureau in Columbus, Ohio, and Gallagher decided that Burl was the person to fix it.

• • •

Ralph Langer, then managing editor of *The Journal Herald* in Dayton, had lobbied AP management for a change in Columbus. "Burl's predecessor as bureau chief [Al Dopking] was someone who was one of the last World War II reporters, a nice guy, but his idea of his job was to wander around the state and play a round of golf. But Ohio is a damned important state. I complained to the AP in New York that we needed government covered more efficiently. So they promoted Burl and sent him to Columbus."

On the second day he assumed his new post, Burl drove one hour to Dayton to personally introduce himself to Langer. The two men discovered that, along with their shared love of journalism, they had been born just thirty-five days apart. They became fast friends.

Burl soon learned from several sources that Al Dopking had been a terror in the office. "Dopking would storm through the newsroom, and he'd be yelling and screaming at people, and you never knew what was going to set him off," said AP Broadcast Executive Mark Thayer, who worked out of the Columbus bureau selling AP services to radio and TV stations in both Ohio and Michigan.

Then Burl came in to settle things down because not only was the staff not happy with Dopking, but the member newspapers didn't care for him either. Burl wasn't a screamer or yeller. You could tell when he wasn't happy because he'd get a little red in the face, but you didn't see that very often. If you got beat by UPI, Burl wouldn't get angry, but he'd want to know exactly why and how it happened, and he'd say, "Let's make sure that never happens again." He definitely wanted to be first. He'd go through *The Columbus Dispatch* and circle AP and UPI stories, and he didn't want to see many UPI stories in the paper.

Ohio had several large newspapers and television stations spread across the state—from Cleveland and Toledo on Lake Erie to central Columbus to southwestern cities Dayton and Cincinnati. The position required pursuing and maintaining relationships with the nearly one hundred editors in all those places. Burl said:

I guess the challenge in such a big state as Ohio was really twofold. Number one, you have a state with a large number of large newspapers: Cleveland, Akron, Dayton, Cincinnati, Columbus, and so on. And then a large number of other newspapers, all of which thought they were just as important as these larger cities. So that was part of it. And they were spread out, and so just getting around was an issue... If we had been able to figure out a way to spend 90 percent of the time in the office and 90 percent of the time on the road, everything would have been fine, but one couldn't do that... [In Ohio] they had large numbers of members, and their needs were complicated and varied, and so it required a lot of time on the road. Lots of great people. I liked Ohio.

AP's Columbus bureau was located inside the building that housed both the Wolfe family–owned afternoon newspaper, *The Columbus Dispatch*, and the Scripps Howard morning paper, the *Columbus Citizen-Journal*.[7] The bureau was an exciting place to work, and the staff's energy and enthusiasm grew exponentially with Burl in the driver's seat. Among the changes he envisioned for the news report and discussed with staffers were:

- A few weekly features on such topics as state and local government initiatives and consumer interests.
- An additional weekly in-depth column in the sports section on the accomplishments of a given team, strategy, or player.
- A weekly background story from the Ohio statehouse that focused on pending legislation, committee or legislative actions, or the role individual legislators played.
- A weekly grocery column that compared prices on ten to twelve grocery items at several chain grocery stores in the state.

Joe McKnight, Burl's assistant bureau chief in Columbus, appreciated Burl's management style.

"He often made suggestions about the news report, but I never knew him to say, 'Do it my way,'" McKnight said. "He was a consummate listener and invited ideas from the bureau staff on how to improve the news report. He briefly opened up conversations among the staff and editors of AP member newspapers, too, then listened closely as they responded. Then he got them to elaborate. He led by suggestion and request, never by mandate." Member newspapers were eager to share their input and grateful for the new material.

Burl oversaw implementation of a new initiative that was one of the AP's first important steps toward digitizing its news operation. Distributing computer terminals to all the state bureaus was prohibitively expensive, so several AP bureaus were designated as twenty-four-hour "hubs" that would consolidate smaller bureaus' electronic input, editing, and distribution of news copy. Columbus became the hub for Ohio, West Virginia, and Indiana. McKnight recalled:

> The idea was a good one. It was ahead of the technology, I
> think. We had just begun to bring [computer] terminals into
> the bureaus. They were clumsy and awkward to use, but
> nevertheless, they represented an advance. Part of the idea was

that you could save money if you consolidated certain editing functions in these hubs and then ran the wires for the states out of there... Fortunately, technology caught up so that it worked better after a while.

On June 2, 1972, Gallagher wrote to Burl, "with total confidence that you will make the Columbus hub the same success that you have made of your other assignments." He was raising Burl's salary from $17,500 to $19,000 a year to acknowledge just how well the transition had gone.

AP Board Member Thomas Vail, who was publisher and editor of *The Plain Dealer* in Cleveland, had commissioned David Rimmel, assistant to the executive editor of *The Plain Dealer*, to survey the state's news media. He sent his findings to Vail in a June 9, 1972, letter:

> Until just recently the state wire of the AP was poorly edited, lacked substance, and was woefully deficient in enterprise stories. Arrival of Burl Osborne . . . has changed all this. He has chopped into the trivia, cut out the incessant rewriting, and is having his staff concentrate on editing and writing and improving the news report. . . AP staff in Columbus is at full strength, [with the] added editors and reporters experienced AP workers.

• • •

Just as Burl's career was on the upswing in Columbus, so was his personal life. Throughout the year between spring 1972 and spring 1973, he and Betty continued to see each other as often as possible. They usually met in Cincinnati, the halfway point between Columbus and Lexington. Sometimes, they had lunch or dinner together; at other times, they took in a Cincinnati Reds baseball game. Often, they dined at the homes of friends or colleagues. "It didn't matter where we were; we were just always so happy to be together," said Betty.

Betty was fully aware of Burl's medical past. Early in their relationship he had confided to her in detail just how traumatic life had been before his kidney transplant. He also warned her that although his kidney was operating well, there were no guarantees. History had shaped his mindset, which was to live each day as though it were his last.

In late summer 1973, Burl came to Lexington to see Betty. He gave her an engagement ring and asked her to move to Columbus with him. The couple wanted to try living together before they set a date.

Betty found a job as a coordinator of the management training program for the Buckeye Union Insurance Company and enrolled in evening classes at Franklin University.

"I told my father when I left to go to Columbus, 'Burl may not live a long life, but I want to be with him now, even if I don't have a long life with him,'" Betty recalled. "We spent the holidays that year with his family in Ashland, which cemented our commitment to each other. I loved his family. They liked me too." After the holidays, they set the wedding date: February 14, 1974.

"Farewell Kentucky, hello Ohio" (Credit: Osborne family collection)

14

Don't Worry—Go Buy the House

Burl was the best-dressed person in the Columbus bureau. David Tomlin, associate general counsel for the AP in New York, who worked in Columbus with Burl, recalled:

> Burl was very stylish. He dressed very carefully. The prior generation of AP managers were kind of rumpled. The men who were still in the bureau from earlier generations wore white shirts, black ties, and black pants. Often the shirts were short sleeve. Maybe they wore a pocket protector. But that wasn't Burl. He always looked kind of snazzy. He wore zip-up ankle boots that had a heel. He paid a lot of attention to his hair. It was long and very stylish. He must have had it professionally done. He looked sharp in a way that was a very new thing for AP management.

Both men and women in Burl's work and social circles took note of his fashion sense and charisma. Tomlin continued:

> When he arrived in Columbus, we were told that he had this reputation of being someone who women were attracted to. On one hand, I could see that, but on the other hand, he had a sort of gnomish look. And I said to my wife once, "He's very short and not a great-looking guy, but he's got this reputation." And she said, "The thing about Burl is that when he's talking to you, you feel he's really focused on you. You're being paid attention to." My wife came away feeling he was paying attention *only* to her. It was remarkable.

Andy Lippman, who worked out of the Cincinnati bureau reporting to Burl in Columbus, said that Burl could command a room without opening his mouth. "He just had this enormous persona. There are people who have it and people who don't. But he really had it. Sometimes it's not a good thing because they are all ego, but that wasn't Burl at all. He just had great presence."

• • •

Burl's staff of reporters and writers and salespeople particularly appreciated that their boss didn't hover over them. He communicated what he wanted done, and then he would go away and let them do it. In part, that was because his philosophy was to be hands off; in reality, he also wasn't able to be in several places at once. Eventually, Burl was spending 75 percent of his time on the road visiting member newspapers. By the end of his first year in Columbus, he had logged approximately fifty thousand miles on AP business.

"The competition with UPI was very tough," said Thayer. "Three major dailies in Columbus, Cleveland, and Cincinnati, plus television in Cincinnati and Cleveland, were owned by the same people. About half the broadcast stations were UPI subscribers, and the other half were AP."

Lippman recalled: "If there was a problem at a newspaper and the paper complained, Burl was on it right away. He was very quick to find out what the problem was and solve it. He was always so quick; he just didn't put anything off, and that probably was one of the reasons for his success."

Rich Oppel, then AP bureau chief in Michigan, recalled an uncomfortable meeting to discuss a problem in Toledo.

There is a strong bond that unifies AP men and women, and especially the bureau chiefs who run staffs of ten to fifty or more people, who are responsible for state reports and major breaking news in their areas and are the first line of contact between AP and its members. What prompted our meeting was a joint visit to the editors of the *Toledo Blade*. Burl was chief of bureau for Ohio. The *Blade* was a colorful, old-fashioned newspaper with editors who were demanding in colorful, old-fashioned ways. Burl was the primary AP representative for the *Blade*, since it was an Ohio paper. But since Toledo borders Michigan at the western end of Lake Erie, the newspaper also took the AP Michigan state wire, for which I was responsible.

Our meetings with the *Blade* managing editor consisted of sitting with him over a cardboard box filled with printouts of the AP wire, on which he had jotted notations. Burl was a stickler for grammar and spelling, and he found an uncomfortable number of violations in the Michigan report. My first tendency was defensiveness. However, I followed Burl's example of great patience and serious attentiveness, and in truth these were the proper responses of an AP executive. That said, we couldn't wait to get to the old Holiday Inn Tower in Toledo for a couple of stiff drinks.

With the hands-on attention, the AP's problems in Ohio soon began to disappear.

Loren G. Schultz, managing editor of *The Daily News and Sun* of Springfield, wrote to Gallagher: "In my opinion, and I have been with the Springfield, Ohio, newspapers for 30 years, The Associated Press in Ohio has been 'backsliding.' ... Burl Osborne has been on the scene in Ohio less than one year, and there has been a complete turnaround. We are going up—not out.... Don't move Osborne out of here until we get this thing really booming. The way we are going now, that shouldn't take more than two or three years. I was asked by many Ohio AP members to send this [letter] along."

• • •

Two and a half years after they met, Burl and Betty married in a quiet ceremony in the small chapel at the First United Methodist Church in the town of Milford, just outside of Cincinnati. They invited family members and a few treasured friends.

Burl had gone skiing in Vail a few days prior and had an accident—the results of which he was unable to hide on Valentine's Day as he walked down the aisle, his arm in a sling. "While Burl was skiing in Vail," Betty recalled, "I spent time in Ashland with Burl's mother, an accomplished seamstress, and together we made a simple wedding dress."

Steve Pyle was the AP photographer in Columbus. He took photos, and his wife, Sharon, was Betty's bridesmaid. Betty stayed with Sharon's mother the night before the wedding while Burl had a bachelor's dinner at the Golden Lamb. Burl's AP colleague Dorman Cordell flew in from Denver to be best man.

Pyle's mother hosted the reception at her home in Milford. Dinner for the wedding party and a few others followed that evening at Mike Fink, a floating restaurant, docked just across the Ohio River from Cincinnati in Covington, Kentucky. In 1958 one of Burl's first feature stories at *The Ashland Daily Independent* had been about the *Delta Queen*, and Burl had had an affinity for steam-powered paddle wheelers ever since.

Thayer asked Betty whether she was going to be a good AP wife. To him that meant keeping the drink glasses filled and the ashtrays emptied in the hospitality suites they rented during member conventions. Betty replied that she would be a good wife to Burl.

Burl and Betty flew that evening to New Orleans for their honeymoon. They stayed at the Fairmont hotel. By this time Burl's friend and colleague Bill Winter was the AP correspondent in Jackson, Mississippi. He and his bride, Glenda, drove over to New Orleans to see the newlyweds. When Burl and Betty arrived at the hotel, a congratulatory note from the Winters had been left for them at the front desk, which read—"Ain't legality dynamite!"

Burl's friend and colleague Ed Tunstall had also recently been assigned to his dream spot, New Orleans, where he'd grown up and gone to college. Ed planned much of the itinerary for Burl and Betty's honeymoon. Breakfast at Brennan's and dinner at Galatoire's and Antoine's. They visited Jackson Square, shopped for art in the French Quarter, and savored chicory coffee and beignets at Café Du Monde. They were guests of the Tunstalls at the Krewe of Carrollton's masked ball. The king of the ball, who was masked, honored Betty with a dance and a small gift, which was customary. Only later did she discover it was Ed's father-in-law.

One subject Betty and Burl didn't discuss before they married was children. "I was so young. I didn't give any thought to having children or whether that would be possible given Burl's health," Betty said. He had taken heavy doses of steroids and other medications for many years. Whether those drugs had left him infertile was not something the infatuated couple ever really considered.

Upon returning from their honeymoon, one of the first congratulatory calls they received was from their friend Dr. Peter Ivanovich. At the end of their conversation Betty asked: "What about babies? Can we have babies?"

Ivanovich didn't hesitate at all. "I don't see why not."

• • •

In the early spring of 1974, the newlyweds began looking for a house in Columbus but were hesitant given Burl's career trajectory to date. Burl called Fuller and said: "Look, I'm not asking you to tell me anything you don't want to tell me, but I was in Kentucky only a year and a half, you know. If you think you're going to move me somewhere would you tell me, so I don't buy this house?"

Fuller's response? "Don't worry—go buy the house."

So in June, they did.

Not three months later, they'd have to put the house on the market.

15

A Washington Outsider

In September, Fuller called Burl and told him to fly to Washington, D.C., and, specifically, to go to the Washington Hilton to talk privately—secretly, that is—with Marvin Arrowsmith, the Washington bureau chief. Leadership in New York was planning to assign Burl to Washington as assistant bureau chief. When Arrowsmith retired, Burl would succeed him.

Roughly 60 percent of all news on the AP wire came from Washington, and Burl had wanted to work there his entire career.

Burl recalled thinking: "Geez, that's terrific! Sign me up."

Two months later, almost to the day, Burl received a confidential word from Gallagher that in light of Burl's transfer to Washington, he had approved a merit increase raising his salary from $27,500 to $30,000.

> Dear Burl:
>
> In anticipation of the good job I know you will do, and also you are going to find Washington difficult financially, you will find the attached PC [personnel change form]. There will also be generous moving expenses in view of your recent acquisition of property.
>
> Washington is not a cheap place to live, and you should expect this, and housing is difficult at the moment. You will probably have to settle for a rental apartment at least for the time being.
>
> You can expect the Washington staff to try you out and make things more difficult than the usual staff since they always do this with a newcomer, doubly so when he is an executive. But I am sure you will be able to handle it.

• • •

Burl and Betty treated themselves to a long-overdue and much-deserved vacation before they made their way to Washington in mid-January 1975. Burl confessed in a letter to his friend Richard Jones of the Ohio Arts Council in Columbus that they were "a little uneasy about [the move] but it was one of those offers I just couldn't refuse."

Giving his *Bluefield Daily Telegraph* readers an update on "Buckskin" in the December 15, 1974, edition, Currence wrote: "Burl Osborne, 37, ex-AP man here, has been promoted from Ohio AP bureau chief to assistant Chief of its big Washington, DC, bureau."

Burl had been in the Washington bureau for only nineteen days when, on January 25, 1975, a twin-engine plane, navigating through rain and fog, struck a broadcasting tower, exploded, and crashed on the campus of American University.

All five people in the plane died, including a close friend: Edgar T. Wolfe Jr., the forty-nine-year-old publisher and board chairman of *The Columbus Dispatch*.[8] Wolfe and two prominent Ohio businessmen had been heading to Washington to meet Ohio Senator Robert Taft Jr., "as his guests to the annual dinner of the Alfalfa Club."

Burl, sad and somber as memories of Wolfe and Columbus played in his mind, found himself assigned the grievous task of collaborating with the Columbus bureau on coverage for the AP wire.

The AP article quoted President Gerald Ford's telegram to Wolfe's brother, John Walton Wolfe: "Edgar Wolfe Jr. was an outstanding publisher and a patriot in the finest tradition of your great family. He will be long remembered as a man of achievement and dedication in the fields of commerce, communications and civic affairs."

• • •

In his letter to Fuller in New York reporting on the funeral for Wolfe, Burl mentioned that Robert B. Smith, managing editor of *The Columbus Dispatch*, had shared with him "that he and the Wolfe family noted and appreciated the way we handled the story of the airplane accident." In contrast, UPI had erroneously reported that a prominent man had been on the airplane and blamed Smith for the mistake. "He is seeing red and appears unlikely to forget it anytime soon," Burl wrote.

Smith wrote to Burl and his successor as AP Columbus bureau chief, Jim Lagier:

> Through mutual efforts between your bureaus and my office The Associated Press had by far the most complete, accurate, and earliest story.
>
> It was reassuring to work with competent and able newsmen like yourselves and members of your staffs.
>
> Thank you for your understanding, speed, and accuracy in covering this tragic story. It only proves once again that when you think of competence in news coverage, you think of The Associated Press.

· · ·

Two months into the job, and despite the initial rush of the plane crash coverage, Burl began to experience the reality of being second in command and a Washington outsider. As Michael Putzel, a reporter who joined the AP Washington bureau in 1972, explained:

> It was very unusual to bring someone in from the outside, as Burl was to the Washington bureau. There was a lot of inertia in the bureau. It was a bureau of older men, experienced Washington reporters, who had seen a lot. Many of them had covered World War II. Part of being a good reporter is knowing the history of the bureau. And Burl, because he was new, did not know the bureau's history. So he'd order up a story, and if you couldn't show that it had already been done, then someone was going to do that story. That was Burl's refusing to accept things the way they had always been. He didn't take the standard response as an answer.

Burl knew the reporters and writers would need a honeymoon period in which to adjust to his management style and priorities for the bureau—and he to them. He recalled:

> They were really a quite extraordinary bunch of people. Fran
> Lewine was part of the White House group, as was Frank
> Cormier. They each covered six presidents during their tenure
> in Washington. I've never been quite sure why I was there, and
> I suspect they wondered the same thing. Because I hadn't come
> up through the bureau . . . that had been its history. I think you
> sort of had to prove that you belonged. These are friends of mine,
> but they test you. They want to know whether you mean what you
> say or not.

Burl found Washington frustrating from early on. Congratulatory letters from across the country kept arriving. On occasion, Burl used his replies to let off some steam of irritation—and incredulity too: "Thanks for . . . the vote of confidence. It comes in handy in a town where just the simplest task is like swimming upstream in molasses."

Because the nation's capital really had only two major newspapers—*The Washington Post* and *The Washington Star*—the membership work Burl so enjoyed was fairly limited. Instead, the bureau chief's main responsibility was the news report that hummed through the teletype machine all day long. The second-biggest job involved making decisions about personnel. Arrowsmith, biding his time somewhat as he awaited retirement, delegated those responsibilities to Burl.

Reluctance on the part of the bureau's veterans to accept Burl because "he didn't fit the mold very well" reflected the way the city of Washington was too. Speaking about the oldest and one of the most prestigious journalistic organizations in the district, for instance, Putzel noted: "You had to have been in Washington for ten years to be considered for [membership in] the Gridiron Club. Burl never qualified because he hadn't been there that long."

• • •

In response to a year-old competitor, the Capitol Hill News Service, Burl and Christopher "Kit" Kincade, Louisville bureau chief, proposed a new initiative.

In a four-page single-spaced letter to AP Executive Editor Lou Boccardi, Burl stressed how "readers want to know what their government is doing to them or for them" but the current ways the AP was handling the report from Washington were not providing "stories that . . . relate to the special interests of our states and to individual congressional delegations. It is this void we should fill."

Burl then outlined a system of redeploying the AP's manpower. Some members of state staffs would be physically located in Washington. "The Ohio man would be an Ohio staffer who happened to be assigned to cover Ohio-interest stories in Washington. . . . If a story is of interest to more than one state, that's fine too." The new system offered two other advantages: improved morale among the top people assigned to Washington and more motivated staff who perceived that the assignment was within their reach.

By month's end, Burl and Kincade had each heard from New York headquarters. Conrad Fink, vice president and assistant general manager, objected because of the dollars. Although he agreed with the value to member newspapers of Burl's and Kincaid's "highly desirable goal" to enhance state coverage from Washington, the plan would add "substantial sums" to AP members' weekly assessments in the current "cost-conscious era."

• • •

Until Washington, Burl had worked autonomously in each of the bureaus where he served. For the first time ever, he had someone looking closely over his shoulder.

That someone wasn't Arrowsmith, however. It was Boccardi, based in New York City, who had a habit of micromanaging the news report out of Washington—Burl's main responsibility.

Though they admired one another, their relationship ran hot and cold. Burl, who "had little patience for nitpickers who didn't check their facts before accusing," had to spend time defending his actions. The bureaucracy weighed on him. He recalled:

Part of my role was to answer the memos—in the Washington bureau or from New York. I decided that the only way you could defend yourself was to create more paper than you got. I answered the questions. And it was easier to answer all of them than to try to figure out "OK, which ones really matter?" And it's important to know why the other person is asking.

Washington and New York had a creative tension between them, and it was there before I got to Washington. The source of that tension is news: differing news judgments, differing priorities, differing perspectives on the news, differing ideas about what we should be doing, control issues, differing notions about what's important.

Arrowsmith was a former White House correspondent and a wonderful man to work with and for, Burl said. "He was an elegant, distinguished, white-haired presence. The nicest person you could ever, ever want to know."

Arrowsmith was planning to retire. Burl's predecessor, Walter Mears, had been set to take his place until Mears left the AP in a surprise move to *The Detroit News'* Washington bureau.

"He was lured away," Burl said. "And that then set off a round of musical chairs and themes and speculation and rumor."

Burl had been brought in to get settled and eventually take over the bureau.

Unexpectedly, Arrowsmith then postponed his retirement.

Around the same time, Mears decided he didn't like his new job. And Burl found himself in the unenviable position of recruiting Mears back, ensuring Burl would not get the bureau chief position when Arrowsmith ultimately stepped down.

"I'm there in Washington a little while, and I met with Walter—by then Walter and I knew each other. I start hearing that he's not really liking it, Detroit. I report back to [Keith] Fuller. I said, 'I don't think Walter's really happy there.' 'Hmm. Well, you keep working—let's get him back.' So I said, 'Okay, we'll try to get him back.' And eventually he came back."

Well versed in office dynamics, Burl saw the pros and cons of Mears' return as the prospective heir apparent:

That was a wise decision for him, in my judgment, although at the time I wasn't quite sure where it left me because there really was no question about who—of the two of us—had there ever been a question, there really wasn't one. He really should have been the bureau chief.

I got to edit Walter's copy. Walter's unique ability was that he could smell the lead in a story. It was second nature to him. Most of us have to think about it and work on it. And he could do it on the fly; he was very fast. He had a personality that allowed him to be really close to people of almost any political persuasion, and he never got himself tagged as too much this way or too much that way, too far right or too far left.

Burl used his speeches to reporters to remind each audience that he understood them implicitly, having paid his dues in the fields they still ploughed. "I do ask you to remember one thing: the next time you complain about the effete eastern liberal snob reporters in Washington, just keep in mind that I'm there, too, and I'm one of you."

• • •

Burl was "a good reader of horseflesh," as his mother, Juanita, would say, which led him to hire first-rate men and women for the bureau and to judiciously fire those who could no longer pull their weight. Putzel provided this real-world example from his time as White House correspondent under Burl's leadership:

He was the person to decide who was going to get promoted within the bureau but also who was going to get promoted to a higher job in another bureau. That was critical to Burl's success. He promoted people even when it left him without a great reporter working for him. There has always been a feather in the cap of the bureau chief who spotted talent and promoted him out of the bureau. Burl was excellent at that.

Putzel's wife, Ann Blackman, also worked in the Washington bureau when Burl arrived. Her father was Sam Blackman, who had been managing editor of the AP when Burl joined the organization in 1960. Burl highly respected the elder Blackman and had a soft spot for his daughter as well.

She remembered Burl as a demanding, ambitious boss who always wanted to win—not least against UPI. In that period when newsroom staff everywhere ran faster than the other person to reach for the phone, Burl—channeling his Marshall University mentor, Mr. Journalism—demanded that the reporters take the time to get the story right. UPI, on the other hand, went for getting the flashy lead . . . even if it *wasn't* quite right. AP staffers called that "hyping a story."

Burl had a softer, more endearing side, too, which Blackman recalled fondly. He could also be very witty.

> There was a story that I've always gotten credit for, but it was Burl who did it. I covered the National Zoo in Washington, and I think I got more sex onto the AP wire than there ever was before because of the sex lives of the pandas I was writing about. The zoo was trying to breed the pandas, Sing Sing and Ling Ling, and they had been unsuccessful. So Burl walks over to my desk one day and says, "What's going on with the pandas?" I said, "They're not mating." So Burl says to me, "Sing Sing and Ling Ling haven't done a thing thing."

That's the lead we went with. Burl wrote it. He was very clever. Very quick.

16

Fireworks

When Burl and Betty moved to Washington, they first lived at a temporary apartment in Foggy Bottom while waiting for a house under construction to be completed some thirty miles west of Washington, in the Fairfax County town of Vienna, Virginia, which is home to Wolf Trap National Park for the Performing Arts. "By July 4 we were in our new home, which was within walking distance of Wolf Trap," said Betty. "That evening we walked over to watch the fireworks. The mosquitos were so bad Burl and I left early. We opened a bottle of Château Margaux and made our own fireworks."

Although they loved their house in Vienna, Burl hated the forty-five-minute commute into the capital. Eventually, they sold the house and moved to the Plaza condominiums directly across the street from the infamous Watergate complex. The Howard Johnson hotel—where the Watergate burglars had kept a lookout in room 723—was another neighbor. "Burl was much happier being at the center of activities in Washington without the commute," said Betty.

When out-of-town friends visited, Betty recalled, "we would take our after-dinner cocktail and walk over to the Kennedy Center and take in the sights on the rooftop, passing the Watergate each time."

Betty took a job in the accounting department of the Golden Arch Realty Corporation, which owned several McDonald's restaurants in the D.C., Virginia, and Maryland area. "It seems to me that I always had a job to help supplement our income," Betty recalled.

She also enrolled in classes at George Mason University, but discovered she was pregnant shortly after classes began. "I suffered from terrible morning sickness," Betty said. "Not just in the morning but all day long. I couldn't work and go to classes. I was too sick."

Washington was Betty and Burl's first experience on the East Coast. Early in 1976, Burl saw an ad in *The Washington Post* for protocol classes. The Osbornes were on a social registry and got invited to glamorous events, including several embassy parties. Burl, always looking to the future, knew an invitation could one day arrive from the White House. Betty recalled:

> The classes were taught at the home of Mrs. Gladstone Williams (Helen), whose husband had been a newspaper man. Her School of Protocol drew foreign diplomats, newly appointed and elected officials, and top military brass. The classes would begin with a sip of sherry. Then Helen would give a lecture. One lecture demonstrated how to eat an artichoke, which neither Burl nor I had ever done before. During another class, we would practice making cocktail party conversation. We were taught to never ask someone, "What do you do?" That's a faux pas. She also taught us how to "turn the table" at a dinner party, to speak first to guests on your left and then on your right, or vice versa.

Burl referred to Mrs. Gladstone Williams' etiquette class as the "class class."

• • •

On March 18, 1976, a week early and nine months after Burl and Betty's Fourth of July fireworks, Burl Jonathan Osborne was born at Fairfax County Hospital.

Jonathan was the first baby in their condo building. "The developer, who also developed the Watergate, sent us a huge bouquet of flowers to congratulate Jonathan's arrival," Betty said.

Thirty-eight-year-old Burl was beyond delighted to be a father. In the coming weeks, however, he worried that his son might somehow have inherited his kidney disease. "Burl was looking over the railing of the crib when Jonathan was sleeping," Betty recalled. "He said to me, 'I just hope that he doesn't have to suffer as I did as a child.'"

Jonathan developed a urinary tract infection. His parents both worried that it could be related to his kidneys. Tests and an x-ray revealed that his kidneys were just fine.

Dayton, Ohio, friend Ralph Langer, then editor of Washington State's *The Everett Herald*, was one of the first to congratulate Burl. "Dear New Dad," he began the letter, "I understand from talking with Steve Pyle today that you have a new son. He thought everyone was in good shape and I hope that's correct."

Burl replied about six weeks later (he and Betty were busily juggling work life *and* parenting, after all). "Now that I have been certified as a barely adequate diaper changer, I thought I'd try to tell someone about my achievement," he wrote. "I cannot say that no one ever told me that the arrival of a child changes the sleeping habits of everyone around it, but I didn't quite understand how much. Anyway, Jonathan is now getting close to eight weeks, and he and Betty are doing very well. Betty is getting back in shape and making noises about really learning to play tennis. If that happens, I will be in a lot of trouble."

• • •

That summer, the nation's capital was still sizzling with the sex scandal on Capitol Hill *The Washington Post* had broken in May. Beauty pageant winner Elizabeth Ray alleged that Democratic Congressman Wayne Hays from Ohio kept her on the federal payroll as his "mistress" for two years. She famously admitted: "I can't type. I can't file. I can't even answer the phone."

On June 9, Burl sent a letter to Jim Harris congratulating him on becoming publisher of Ohio's *Steubenville Herald-Star*, which included this jibe. "We've been trying to get to the bottom of the Hays-Ray business, which has been prime news in Steubenville. I must confess the closest thing to a sexy woman I've seen while working on it is a waitress at the hamburger joint down the street."

In his speech for the South Dakota chapter of the AP managing editors annual meeting in mid-September that year, per their request Burl tackled the issue of printing news versus gossip, citing the Hays-Ray story. "It requires that we not lose a sense of perspective and a sense of what is, or isn't, significant. If her charges are supported and proven, it is possible there could be a fraud charge against at least one important figure in the national government. That, in my opinion, is legitimate news."

• • •

The Osborne family had established a comfortable routine as city dwellers. As Betty recalled: "When time and weather permitted, I pushed Jonathan in his stroller the ten-minute walk to meet Burl at the AP offices and walk home with him after work. Sometimes we met halfway where there was a small wine shop. Burl liked to stop and shop for a bottle of wine for dinner. Sometimes Jonathan and I walked to the Watergate Safeway to shop, where we'd run into Arthur Burns, then head of the Federal Reserve, who lived at the Watergate. He would often be outside smoking his pipe. We talked while he admired my baby and the family dog, Brandy."

Betty returned to work about three months after Jonathan was born. She worked as the office manager for *Washington Calendar* magazine. Jonathan's babysitter lived nearby her office. "I loved that job," Betty said. "I worked with some very creative folks."

• • •

Betty could tell Burl was growing more and more unhappy in Washington, even with the AP earning a Pulitzer for its coverage of the 1976 presidential campaign.

In his December 2, 1976, letter to a friend, Charlie Boren, of Idaho's *The Lewiston Morning Tribune*, Burl alluded to his frustrations.

> Although I have been in Washington now almost two years, I still find that it is just as screwed up as I imagined it might be. We are trying to refocus what we are doing here so that it bears some meaning for readers more than three miles from the Potomac. I wouldn't have missed the chance to work here for the world, but getting the simplest kind of task done here is a major undertaking. It never seemed so complicated in Spokane.
>
> In case the gossip didn't catch up, I remarried a couple of years ago and finally figured out how to make an heir. Jonathan is eight months old and propositions girl babies. So I guess my recovery took. I'm considered one of the old fogies now, rather than one of the new kids on the block, and I don't care much for the role. But I'm growing into it.

• • •

On March 9, 1977, three buildings in Washington, D.C., were seized by twelve armed members of the Hanafi Movement—an African American Muslim group founded in rivalry with the Nation of Islam. The gunmen, led by Hamaas Abdul Khaalis (born Ernest Timothy McGhee), took 149 hostages during the seizure.

Armed with shotguns and swords, the group took control of the headquarters of the Jewish service organization B'nai B'rith before storming the Islamic Center of Washington, a rival mosque. Two blocks from the White House, militants then shot their way into a government building, killing radio journalist Maurice Williams and Mack Cantrell, who was a security guard.

Khaalis told reporters that he organized the attack in an attempt to bring attention to the murder of his family several years prior. In 1973, his wife, two children, and grandchild were all killed in their home after Khaalis publicly criticized Nation of Islam leader Elijah Muhammad.

When Sgt. Albert M. Skoloda of the metropolitan police encountered Khaalis at the B'nai B'rith headquarters, Khaalis said he would kill the captives and roll their heads down the stairs if his demands weren't met.

"He said Washington had never seen as much blood as would flow," Skoloda said. "He said no one cared about the bloodshed when his babies were killed at 16th Street."

The gunmen demanded that the men who had been convicted of murdering their seven relatives be handed over to them, as well as those responsible for killing Malcolm X.

An AP log[9] published later that month titled "Some Unusual Angles of the Hostage Story" noted that Burl "coordinated coverage of the story from the start for more than 24 hours without a break."

AP Reporter Robert A. Dobkin published an article on the second day of the siege, writing, "Khaalis, angry, shouting at times, abruptly switching thoughts, spoke by telephone with reporters through the day and night Wednesday from his 'command post' in the cafeteria at B'nai B'rith's national headquarters. Nearly 60 hostages are being held there."

Dobkin interviewed Khaalis on the final day of the siege, asking, "Are you making any progress in your negotiations?" and "Have you set any deadlines?"

Negotiations for the peaceful release of hostages were conducted by the Washington police, the ambassadors of three Islamic countries, and State

Department officials. Burl "snatched a few hours' sleep while efforts to release the hostages were stalemated," noted the AP log, "then returned for another 18-hour stint through the negotiations that preceded the release."

After the siege, the twelve men were charged with armed kidnapping. *Time* magazine wrote, "The heart of the capital was under siege. Everywhere, it seemed, was the wail of sirens, snarled traffic, milling crowds, police marksmen poised on rooftops, swarms of reporters interviewing one another in the glare of floodlights."

• • •

Burl's bosses in New York were duly impressed. Boccardi wrote Arrowsmith commending the Washington bureau's performance as a whole and Burl in particular. Managing Editor Robert Johnson wrote to President and General Manager Keith Fuller: "I thought you should know further that when this story broke, Osborne virtually took over the bureau. He was given full command of the story and its handling. We were fortunate to have a spot news–oriented executive of Osborne's caliber in Washington when this story broke."

In the spring, Arrowsmith finally retired. The AP announced that Walter Mears would succeed him. Burl expected to be relocated to another bureau chief position.

The decision makers at the AP's headquarters in New York had a different plan:

No, Burl wouldn't take over the D.C. bureau as originally planned.

No, they wouldn't send him to another bureau.

Instead, they would bring him to New York and promote him to the position of managing editor of the entire organization.

His antennae up whenever Burl was concerned, Currence made note of this development in the *Bluefield Daily Telegraph* on May 12, 1977, under the headline "AP Executives Are Promoted."

Former colleagues were ecstatic upon hearing of Burl's advancement to New York to run the wire. With typical self-effacing humor, Burl joked about his promotion: "All this move means is that I am getting another job in the complaint department" and "Let me assure you that they haven't taken the Kentucky out of the boy."

Among the dozens of letters Burl received and responded to, he cherished two in particular. Langer, his friend from Ohio, wrote: "I imagine the littlest Osborne is growing fast and eating sirloin by now. Now he'll grow up with a New York accent."

Burl replied, "Jonathan is, as you guessed, growing and eating. He also managed to break a bottle of wine the other day. Probably because I wouldn't uncork it for him. I hadn't thought about a New York accent, and it's frightening. His grandparents wouldn't be able to talk to him."

And Spencer, the Seattle bureau chief during Burl's time in Spokane who'd stuck by him during his kidney failure and transplant, wrote: "Nancy and I are just bursting with pride at the fact our little protégé has been given a big, big job with the A.P. It couldn't happen to a more special person, and having watched your career ever since 1964, I marvel at the way you played your cards to overcome some real obstacles."

Burl wrote back, "I confess I have been carrying your letter around, savoring it, for a few days before answering. Thank you doesn't seem like very much to say. I don't know how things will go in New York. But I will give it my best shot. You both know, and I know, that there would have been zero chance of this happening without your help and understanding. I will be ever grateful. Love, Burl."

• • •

Always aware of human frailty and the randomness of fortune, Burl took stock of all he had accomplished during his seventeen years with the AP. On the home front, he was happily married, the proud father of a bright little boy, and enjoying a healthy body that freed him to live life to the fullest.

"I remember waiting, day by day, hour by hour [after the transplant] for the rejection I felt was inevitable. Those were the first days of my life when laboratory results one day came back equal to or improved from the day before," Burl said. It had taken years for him to face lab tests with confidence. Now he had blood tests twice a year, and the numbers had been stable for seven or eight years.

Standing confidently on that foundation, Burl rented a van to move their "beginning art collection" and loaded the Chevy Nova with Jonathan and their dog. Burl driving the van and Betty the car, they set off as a caravan of two, New York City bound, as the summer of 1977 began.

17

The A-Wire

Burl arrived at the AP headquarters at 50 Rockefeller Plaza in mid-July 1977 as the number two news executive in the entire organization, right below the executive editor. "I was excited to go to New York. It was—is—a great job in the AP. In many respects, it's maybe the best job in news because it's *the* hands-on job," Burl reminisced. "It really is hands on. All day, every day; all night, every night."

If Washington was the origin of much of the AP's news, the New York headquarters—specifically, Burl's fourth-floor office overlooking the skating rink at 50 Rockefeller Plaza—was the epicenter.

If, for example, a commercial airliner crashed in Atlanta, a reporter from that city's AP bureau would communicate the on-site interviews and details to the Atlanta editor, who would craft them into the story that was sent to the General Desk in New York. Almost certainly, additional input from several other sources would be needed to flesh out the story. In this instance, the Federal Aviation Administration would have something to say about it, so the Washington bureau would get involved. Burl would then compile the various pieces of the puzzle into one major story that was sent out on the A-wire.

• • •

July 13, 1977. Two lightning strikes that evening, just minutes apart, shut down Con Edison's power system for most of the city within an hour. Electricity wouldn't be restored until late the next day.

The blackout took place during a severe financial crisis. By 1975, New York City had run out of funds to cover normal operating expenses and faced bankruptcy. Recounting the city's dark mood many years later, *Time* magazine wrote that, for many residents, the blackout was merely "a metaphor for the gloom that had already settled on the city."

When the lights went out in 1977, the subway screeched to a halt, elevators stalled, and a populace already primed for discord began to erupt. According to *The New York Times*, in the "sweltering" twenty-five hours before power was restored, more than 1,000 fires were reported, 1,600 stores were damaged by looting and rioting, and 3,700 people were detained by police in what became the largest mass arrest in the city's history. The *New York Post* wrote, "Even the looters were being mugged."

This was not the city's first blackout. Twelve years earlier, in 1965, New York had gone dark, but the city's mood had shifted sharply since then. "They set hundreds of fires," *Time* noted, "illuminating in a perverse way twelve years of change in the character of the city, and perhaps of the country."

Yet, in the midst of chaos, small moments of comradery arose. "People left their homes to help direct traffic in the suddenly darkened streets," reported the *Times*. "Often armed with flashlights, they took up their impromptu stations at intersections and guided drivers and pedestrians."

Burl recalled his firsthand experience of the blackout at a regional meeting of AP editors later that year.

> Con Ed at first said the blackout was caused by an awful act of God. [But] Mayor Abe Beame and some of the New York papers suggested it was caused by a god-awful act of Con Ed. I had been in New York two days and just barely had learned how to get to the train station to get from home in Connecticut to New York. I had been there such a short time, the guy who sold me the Brooklyn Bridge hadn't even had time to deliver it. In the office, I had barely learned to find the can, but not the candles. My home telephone had been installed the day of the blackout, so somebody was able to tell me it was happening, and that required me to try to get into the office. So I drove into New York for the first time. . . . It was a surprise to go all the way in without ever having to stop for a traffic light, without ever running into a traffic jam, without so much as seeing a taxi, without hearing a horn honk, without having anybody run me off the road.

For ninety minutes the AAA wire was out, and staff dictated copy to the AP bureaus in Philly, Newark, Chicago, and Albany, whose staffers relayed national and international stories through regional computers to state wires.

Adding to the New Yorkers panicking that night were the yet-to-be-solved murders committed by a serial killer in their midst. The following month, an AP article allayed some of the uneasiness.

> The .44-caliber killer is the target of the greatest manhunt in New York City history. But it is doubtful if any of the 300 police officers hunting him would recognize the so-called "Son of Sam" if they sat next to him on the subway.
>
> Four different sketches of the gunman have been prepared at one time or another during his yearlong reign of terror — testimony to the divergent descriptions obtained from a handful of witnesses.
>
> The newest sketch was based on details obtained from the killer's latest of eight attacks — last Sunday morning's fatal shooting of 20-year-old Stacy Moskowitz, fifth female victim of "Son of Sam." One young man also died.

Assuring news followed a few days later, picked up by dailies nationwide. The front-page headlines such as "Son Of Sam Suspect Captured!" and "'Sam' Suspect Mystery Even To His Neighbors" and "Car Ticket Leads To 'Son Of Sam'" declared that suspect David Berkowitz had been taken into custody August 10.

> A $35 ticket for parking too near a fire hydrant led police to a reclusive postal worker they said was "Son of Sam," the night stalker who killed six young persons and wounded seven with his .44-caliber revolver.
>
> The arrest came as David Berkowitz, 24, left his apartment house Wednesday night in suburban Yonkers and encountered police, who had staked out the building.

Police said that as Berkowitz stepped into his car, they asked him who he was, and Berkowitz replied: "I'm Son of Sam. Okay, you've got me."

• • •

Things quieted down somewhat in New York thereafter. But not for the General Desk at AP headquarters, where the thirty-plus editors and the new boss were still getting acquainted. "It was like a super desk operation, except it's the national report and, indirectly, the international report," Burl said. "It was basically dealing with the—what was then the—A-wire report and making sure that that was where it needed to be and that the trains were running on time and occasionally inserting yourself into it and rewriting somebody's lead, just so they wouldn't forget you were there."

Throughout Burl's initial months in New York, senior management frequently sent him memos evaluating his job performance. One such review came from Tom Pendergast, vice president and assistant general manager, commenting on Burl's interoffice memo to the General Desk regarding a rewrite of a particular "Minneapolis offering." "Your memo should have been sent to every chief of bureau for morale reasons alone. It's the first time I can recall, at least since coming to New York, that anyone in authority on the news side has had the courage (or intelligence) to suggest the obvious: 'When rewriting is needed, and in this case it was not, let us have the originating bureau do it if there are no compelling reasons to do it here.' Congratulations! Thinking like a bureau chief, as you did here, will make you a great ME."

Burl, Betty, and Jonathan had moved into a contemporary home in the Cos Cob neighborhood of Greenwich, Connecticut, overlooking a portion of the Mianus River Gorge.

After settling in, Betty began a job search and came across a radio station manager looking for an assistant. "The idea of working at a radio station intrigued me," she recalled. The WGCH AM radio station manager and his wife became good friends of Betty's, as did many of her coworkers.

Burl had an A-wire printer installed in the basement. Each morning just before he left for work, he would tear off the pages that had come in from midnight on so he could review them on his commute into Manhattan. "I would read everything on the train and say whatever I had to say about it and mark it up," Burl said. "So by the time I got to the office, I was up to speed on where we were, to the extent you could be in those days. It's a desk supervisory role, where you're really trying to manage the flow and make sure that the flow's right and the timing is right, and so on."

Mike Silverman, a national editor on the General Desk, remembered those days with Burl well: "He would come into the office already fully aware of what had moved in the preceding twelve hours, and he would have marked up things he liked or didn't like. But mainly he read the wire copy in the morning on the way to work so that when he got there, he could hit the ground running."

Twice daily, both morning and afternoon, staff conducted a "plate check" of a number of newspapers across the country to see which ones used AP stories and which used UPI. Silverman recalled the procedure well.

> We asked them to tell us which service they used that day and where they displayed the story. Those [data points] were compiled religiously. We might do an expanded plate check if there was a really big story. This gave us a really good sense day in and day out of how we were doing.
>
> *The New York Times* took both AP and UPI, and they used a fair amount of wire copy from around the country. They would use AP or UPI on some stories, and there was always considerable interest from Burl in whether they had used AP or not. If it was a UPI story that *The Times* had used, Burl would want to know why. *Precisely* why. Sometimes you could tell from the story: maybe they had a better lead, or maybe we hadn't done the story at all. Burl would occasionally call up a paper and ask them why they had used UPI on the story. There usually was a good reason.

Lou Boccardi had been the AP's managing editor for six years before his promotion to executive editor. (An AP "lifer," he served in that role for nine years before becoming its president and CEO for nineteen years.) He pronounced that the AP was overwhelmingly better than its major head-to-head competitor, UPI:

UPI was graced by some good writers, and I'd be a fool to tell you they never outhustled us on a story. But a newsroom mantra when there was a surprising news development was commonly, "Yeah, but what does AP say?" That's a reputation one earns; it doesn't come out of a marketing brainstorm. A major advantage for AP was its hard-won reputation for accuracy.

Silverman described the electric atmosphere of the General Desk area this way: "Beating UPI even by a minute or two—or by seconds—was crucial to the competitive game. If you were a minute ahead, that mattered a lot."

By the late 1970s, it was becoming apparent that UPI was unlikely to survive. What was once a "healthy" competition between the AP and UPI at its peak in the 1960s was becoming disastrous for UPI.[10] Profits were rare, and newspaper loyalty was uncertain.

In his book 2005 book *Reporting from Washington*, Donald Ritchie wrote:

> Competition with the AP eventually pushed UPI into financial collapse. With expenses rising and income falling, UPI could not match the AP in worldwide outlets, technology, or reputation.... Newspapers dropped UPI while keeping the AP.... Unable to pay competitive salaries, UPI suffered increased staff turnover that further diluted its reporting.

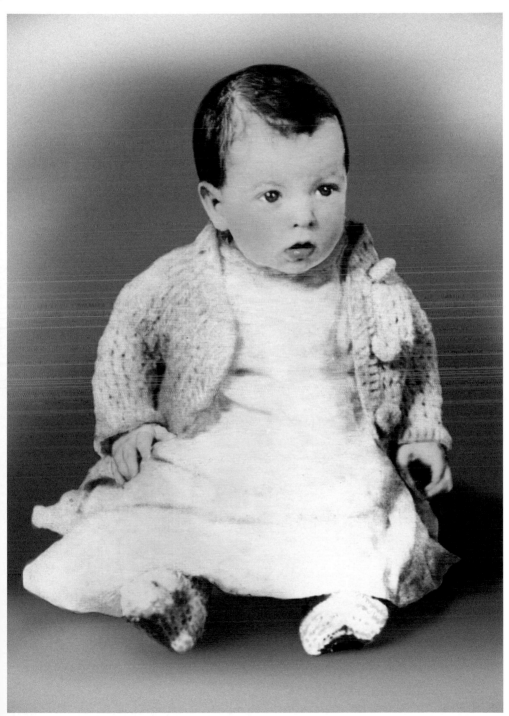
Baby Burl (Credit: Osborne family collection)

Juanita, Oliver, and Burl Osborne (Credit: Osborne family collection)

Burl's high school photo (Credit: Osborne family collection)

WHTN TV reporter, Huntington, West Virginia (Credit: Osborne family collection)

Sixteen-year-old Burl reading *Hot Rod Magazine* (Credit: Osborne family collection)

Burl behind the wheel of his 1960s Corvette (Credit: Osborne family collection)

A very sick Burl at work in the Spokane AP bureau with canulae in his left arm used for dialysis treatment (Credit: Osborne family collection)

Denver, post-transplant; Burl reading the AP wire, 1968 (Credit: Floyd H. McCall, *Denver Post*)

Burl climbing into a B57 for the "Friendly Enemy" story (Credit: Bob Scott, AP)

Burl: *What do you say to a naked lady?*
(Credit: Bob Scott, AP)

"Farewell, Denver" (L–R) Burl, Rulon Pusey, and Keith Fuller (Credit: Gene Foster, Jr.)

(L–R) Dorman Cordell, Burl, and Olympic skier Jean Claude Killy, Vail, Colorado, 1974 (Credit: Osborne family collection)

Burl, Betty, and Jonathan, Vail, Colorado, 1979 (Osborne family collection)

Washington, D.C., AP bureau colleagues celebrate Burl's promotion to managing editor (seated at left is Marv Arrowsmith, D.C. bureau chief) (Credit: Osborne family collection)

AP colleagues bid Burl "happy trails"; (L–R) Jim Mangan, Bob Johnson, Burl, and Keith Fuller (Credit: Osborne family collection)

(L–R) Keith Fuller, Walter Mears, and Jim Mangan (Credit: Osborne family collection)

The infamous cowboy boots (Credit: Osborne family collection)

"Goodbye NYC" party at the home of Bobbie Seril; (L–R) Burl, Betty, Jonathan, Bobbie, and Steve Downs, WGCH radio station manager (Credit: Osborne family collection)

The Dallas Morning News'
executives welcome Burl to
Texas; (L–R) Robert Decherd, Jim
Moroney, and Joe Dealey, 1980
(Credit: *The Dallas Morning News*)

The Dallas Morning News' "Rock of Truth" (Credit: David Woo, *The Dallas Morning News*)

18

Kentuckians in the City

In early February 1978, a three-day blizzard brought record snowfall and hurricane-force winds to New York City. Cars were buried, streets were flooded, and the public schools were forced to close. The AP reported on February 8 that President Carter declared a state of emergency for Massachusetts, Rhode Island, and Connecticut. Betty recalled the drama of the family's first winter in the Northeast:

> Early on the morning of Monday, February 6, Burl tried to pull out of the driveway for the twenty-minute drive to the train station in Greenwich, but his car got stuck in the driveway. The noise from Burl gunning the car and trying to get through the snow awoke our neighbor, who fortunately owned a jeep. Understanding the urgency for Burl to get to 50 Rock that morning, he offered him a ride to the station. If he hadn't, I believe that Burl would have walked the many miles in the storm to get to the train station. That's how important he saw his role at AP.
>
> Burl eventually did get to the city, where the only accommodations he could find were at the Pierre hotel—a ten-minute walk up 5th Avenue from AP's offices in the best of times. Burl made it home four days later.
>
> While Burl had luxury accommodations at the Pierre, I couldn't arrange for the driveway to be plowed until Wednesday. The snow was so high it blocked our front door.

Jonathan developed a high fever, which had me worried. As soon as the driveway and car came out from under the mountain of snow, I was able to take him to the doctor.

• • •

A key component of Burl's position as managing editor in New York was expanding his already rich and geographically expansive network of meaningful friendships with publishers and editors in chief of numerous newspapers around the country. National newspapers were the AP's primary revenue base, and the AP staff's main concern was with their happiness, their welfare, and their satisfaction with the news report. Burl's assistant, Bobbie Seril, observed him firsthand on a daily basis capably "schmoozing the members, being very responsive to their needs and desires."

Seril said Burl brought a new culture of responsiveness to the office. She recalled him saying, "Let's not allow the phone to ring more than twice. When we do, it just permits the person on the other end—whether a member [newspaper] or the general manager—to wonder whether we're paying attention."

One time when Burl was on the phone with Katharine Graham, publisher of *The Washington Post*—an AP member paper—whose family owned the paper, a call came in from Betty. Seril remembered Betty apologizing for interrupting Burl's workday, but it was important. So Seril motioned to Burl that Betty needed to speak with him. Burl put Graham on hold and spoke briefly with his wife. After he had ended both calls, Burl said to his secretary: "Did you know that that was Katharine Graham I was talking to? You're going to have to prioritize." Without missing a beat, Seril responded, "I know, and I did." Burl thought a moment and exclaimed, "Touché!"

• • •

Burl loved seeing those who worked for him advance and proudly said, "The price of having excellent help is encouraging them and losing them quickly."

Seril remembered Burl's words when she told him the AP's director of personnel wanted to promote her to the membership department. "Burl said to me, 'You can leave, but you've got to find your replacement.' I did. But the person after me also didn't work for Burl very long. Eventually, a group of us who had worked for him for just a short time before moving on became known as 'Burl's Girls.' Working for Burl became a career starter, a stepping-stone to something better at the AP."

· · ·

Burl found the responsibility of leadership fulfilling, and he kept his focus on the future of the news business. He discussed the prospect of transmitting news via satellite at a speech to AP members in Minnesota.

A reporter covering the speech wrote, "The idea sounded a little futuristic. A satellite high in the sky, moving with the Earth. A large dish alongside or on top of each newspaper office. But those were the prime ingredients in a plan unveiled last weekend by Burl Osborne."

Burl explained that the AP and UPI, though typically rivals, would split the cost of setting up the satellite transmittal system, which was in the neighborhood of $11 million.

Burl concluded his remarks by admitting that such monumental change was "not going to happen right around the corner, but it won't be long before newspapers move a bit further into the space age." He said that it looked technologically promising but was hardly the panacea many thought it would be.

· · ·

Burl enjoyed a comfortable level of camaraderie with his fellow AP executives in New York, but he stayed away from long lunches at the Athletic Club's dining room and long stretches in the steam room. "And I figured out pretty quickly that you've still got to get the AMs report out, and martini lunches didn't comport with that, so I didn't go," Burl recalled.

Outside of work, Burl and Betty were asked to join a small group of New Yorkers with ties to Kentucky. Not surprisingly, they called themselves the Kentuckians.

Creed C. Black, chairman and publisher of the *Lexington Herald-Leader*, wrote to James Bowling, senior vice president, and assistant to chairman of the board, Philip Morris, on October 10: "At a state AP meeting here over the weekend, I learned that AP's new managing editor . . . is a native Kentuckian. He is, of course, as brilliant and personable as the rest of us and would make a worthy addition to the Kentuckians. He also has a lovely wife—a Kentuckian too—who would make an even worthier addition. I mentioned the organization to Burl, and he seemed interested, so you might want to follow up."

The Kentuckians' twice-yearly spirited gatherings at New York's University Club were fun, where—to quote Black—"Bluegrass comes to Fifth Avenue . . . and everybody goes home in a mellow mood." That could be because on each table at the dinner sat a bottle of Maker's Mark. And everyone had to stand and sing "My Old Kentucky Home" at the end of the evening.

• • •

Betty saw an opportunity in her new job with WGCH AM radio, which subscribed to UPI's wire and audio services. She spoke with the news director, Dirk Van, about the station's needs, and thereafter, the AP's broadcast executive for the New England states and AP's Hartford bureau chief paid Van a visit. They learned that WGCH's three-year contracts for UPI would soon expire; Van was willing to review the AP's services.

In April 1978, the AP's broadcast executive sent Betty a note that read, "Cheers for your great work in the sale of AP service to WGCH. . . . Victory could not have been achieved without the help and guidance you lent us all the way."

In a private letter to Burl, Fuller wrote: "I am authorizing a rather expensive dinner at a restaurant of your choice for you and Betty since you were successful in convincing her new employer to drop UPI and take AP."

On September 22, following a trip to Paris, Burl sent a private letter to James Tomlinson, the AP's treasurer, in which he wrote: "You may recall that Keith invited Betty to take me to a 'rather expensive dinner' following the application for membership from WGCH. He suggested we might do this during our vacation, so we did. The enclosed bill is in French francs, and our share of it is one-half. I think you will agree it met his offer." With views of the Seine and Notre Dame as a backdrop, the Osbornes had feasted on pressed duck (each with its own numbered certificate) at the famed and Michelin-rated La Tour d'Argent. *C'était délicieux.*

• • •

In April 1978, two local sheriff's officers entered AP offices in Helena, Montana, and told Bureau Chief Hugh Van Swearingen they had a search warrant for a recording of a telephone conversation between an AP reporter and a man accused of slaying a Montana highway patrolman. The officers allowed Swearingen to make a call before they started their search. "For the next three hours, while AP lawyers worked rapidly in New York and Helena, I stalled for time," Swearingen said.

In New York, Burl kept Swearingen on one line while coordinating with AP lawyers on another.

The attempt to search the AP premises was ultimately halted by court order. An attorney for the AP "argued that the search warrant violated both the federal and the state constitutions and Montana's reporter shield law because the AP was not accused nor suspected of a crime."

The April 11, 1978, AP story was headlined "Sheriff's quest for tapes stopped Monday: Judge invalidates news office search."

Interviewed later, Burl said: "When the press has material [that] law enforcement officials believe they need, there are constitutionally permissible ways to obtain it. The proper procedure is to obtain a valid subpoena. It is not proper to invade a newsroom and threaten to break open desks. That is what the sheriff did, and it is this we resisted."

• • •

Boccardi valued Burl as a colleague. "He had a broad array of talents. He was a sound newsman, a good organizer and motivator, hard working and ambitious, very popular with the members." But he admitted that he was the only thing keeping Burl from reaching the top of AP management. "We were roughly the same age, and I had the next job on the AP ladder."

Burl felt a growing desire for responsibility. He later recalled:

> I think it was probably about the time I came to New York that I figured out, "I think I'd like to do something that I'm accountable for." There was no epiphany. But over time, it became clear that here's what you can expect, here's the way you can live, here's what you're going to be doing. And as much as I loved being managing editor, doing that for another twenty years wasn't really what thrilled me.

Executives in the industry around the country were beginning to take notice of Burl's successes and soon began to try to poach him.

Throughout the month of August 1978, for instance, Burl exchanged a number of letters with executives at *The Charlotte Observer* in North Carolina. Editor Dave Lawrence and President and Publisher Rolfe Neill offered him the managing editor position. Both men expressed great disappointment when Burl declined their first offer. Seizing on the droplet of hope that the possibility of leaving the AP "must be percolating or you wouldn't have been talking to us," Neill wrote Burl that *The Observer* "as one of the country's twenty best" was aiming "to be in the Top 10, not least because the paper [is] willing to innovate."

After more soul searching, Burl's answer didn't change, but he wrote to Neill:

> I signed on in this job with some very clear objectives for improving what the AP does with its news report. I believe it is fair to say that we have made some progress. It also is true that we have not moved far enough so that I can say, to myself, that I have succeeded.
>
> You noted, quite correctly, that the possibility of leaving was in my mind.
>
> What it came down to was this: whatever discomfort there is with my present circumstance yielded to the need, for my own peace of mind, to do some more where I am. I have been here barely a year, and that just was not enough time to get enough done.

19

The Information Business

After turning down the job offer from *The Charlotte Observer*, Burl communicated more often to his bosses exactly what he wanted to accomplish at the AP. On August 24, he sent a four-page letter to Fuller in which he outlined "what I think we can do to raise measurably the proportion of AP play in competitive papers." Among the tasks he listed were:

- We're going to tighten the report and improve copy flow.
- We are aiming for 25 percent more stories without raising the total word count.
- We will have stronger General Desk supervision.

Having learned from his earlier rejected proposal, Burl added, "Many changes I propose involve reallocating resources without adding costs. Some would need approval for investing some money in our future. Some can be done quickly; others may be months or years away," he explained.

Then, under the main section headings NOW, NEXT, NEXT, and AFTER THAT, Burl delineated his ideas and metrics and deliverables under such categories as Assignments, Service, Writing, Reporting, Bureau Participation, What's Wrong?/Right? Member Survey, Electronic Storage/Library, Membership Glue, Growing Readers, R&D, and Growing Staff.

He concluded with the disclaimer: "Staffers who must make the system work have been brought informally into the discussions. The conclusions are mine and do not necessarily reflect the views of others, into whose territories I may have strayed. Perhaps this summary, in roughly the order we might want to undertake any change, can serve to start a discussion."

In mid-November, Burl was back managing a big global story.

Jim Jones, pastor of the Peoples Temple, and more than nine hundred of his followers died at the cult's Jonestown settlement 150 miles northwest of Georgetown, the capital city of Guyana.

The special challenge the AP faced, according to its A-wire article "Additional Jonestown Survivors Return," was that "the Guyana government denied a report published by the AP that Home Minister Vibert Mingo ordered the police commissioner to call off an investigation into Jonestown prior to the tragedy." The allegations were "contained in a series of articles written by AP Special Correspondent Peter Arnett on the basis of documents obtained in Jonestown."

Interviewed in New York, Burl defended the AP and its writer's integrity. "The papers and Peter Arnett's dispatches speak for themselves. Arnett requested comment from government officials, waited a week for it, and left Guyana only after he was informed no comment or interviews would be forthcoming."

• • •

In 1979, Burl, Betty, and Jonathan moved away from their house in Connecticut. "We loved the house and hated to leave it," said Betty. "But I told Burl— especially after what we endured during the Blizzard of 1978, I wanted to live where we could walk to the train station, the grocery, and a doctor's office if need be." In January 1979, they bought a townhouse that was still under construction in Dobbs Ferry, in Westchester County along the Hudson River where George Washington had established one of his many headquarters during the American Revolution.

The Osbornes moved to their new townhouse in April. Just fifteen miles north of Manhattan, it was an easy trip for the working couple as well as for friends and colleagues they invited for dinners in their home. Burl loved his walk from Grand Central to Rockefeller Plaza as well as to Fifth Avenue—and the window shopping both coming and going.

Betty soon started work again on her undergraduate degree at Mercy College. She continued working part time at the radio station for a while but then enrolled full time to finish her degree. Sister Ethel, a retired teacher, ran a preschool next to the campus. Betty could leave toddler Jonathan in her care while she attended classes. "I decided not to work and concentrate on being a full-time mom and student," Betty said. "I loved my time with Jonathan." A great business law professor at Mercy inspired her to seriously consider going to law school in the future.

. . .

Yet another major news story broke on March 28, 1979. The nuclear power plant on Three Mile Island in Londonderry Township, Pennsylvania, located on the Susquehanna River just south of Harrisburg, had a partial meltdown. A competitor ran a story suggesting there was a risk of imminent meltdown, although the AP didn't find the source credible. Burl did not hesitate or waffle in his decision. Said AP Special Correspondent Jules Loh: "He sent people to the area immediately, even though everyone knew it would be dangerous. Everybody was working. And everybody knew what their job was. He made sure of it." Fortunately, no one was hurt. Years later during an interview, Loh said of Three Mile Island: "It [was] vintage Osborne. Unflinching. Unafraid to make tough decisions. Smart, fair, and competitive. Above all, competitive."

In 1978, in the wake of the Iranian Revolution, Burl read about the worldwide OPEC oil crisis and found himself in the rare position of not understanding the news:

> In the late seventies we went through a spike in energy prices, and there were stories about obscene profits by the oil companies. And the oil companies felt that they were unfairly treated [by the press], and they were complaining. On the other hand, people who thought [the oil companies] were gouging were also complaining. And I kept reading our business report, and I couldn't figure out what was what. I decided, "I'm going to sign up for a graduate course in reading financial statements so that I can understand this and carry on a decent conversation."

Coverage of stock and bond markets in U.S. newspapers at the time was commonly criticized as "dry," "listless," and generally out of touch with the concerns of the average reader. By the late 1960s, readers were clamoring for "consumer news" and more qualitative analysis of the statistics that typically dominated business coverage. But most newsrooms maintained that consumer trends were not newsworthy, and that attitude didn't begin to change until papers started losing readership to more personalized radio and TV programs in the 1970s. High inflation rates and rising unemployment created a growing popular interest in business coverage.[11]

Burl made it a goal to improve the depth and sophistication of the business news report, with the goal of "writing in terms that newspaper readers can understand and that economists can abide."

To bolster his knowledge about economics and finance, Burl enrolled for the fall 1979 semester in Long Island University's MBA program marketed to working executives. Classes were held at the Dobbs Ferry campus, close to the family's home. "I did a basic accounting course, and then I did some statement analysis, and one thing led to another, and I thought, 'Well, this is pretty interesting stuff. I think I'll just keep going.' And I decided that I would see if I could complete work on an MBA while I was still working." Burl studied for his classes on the train ride home from work and attended classes on certain weekday nights and weekends.

When the AP refused to reimburse him for his studies, Burl took out a student loan. "When I asked to be placed in the tuition reimbursement program, it didn't fit, so the answer was no. I said, 'OK, I'll file that away,' and I did it on my own."

• • •

In July, during the Republican National Convention, a rumor spread across TV networks and radio stations that the Republican nominee for president, California Governor Ronald Reagan, was going to choose former President Gerald Ford as his running mate. Acting quickly to beat UPI with the scoop, Burl had a reporter write up the story. A bulletin went out on the wire, but it wasn't accurate. Reagan chose George H. W. Bush—not Ford—to join him on the ticket. It was a rare mistake for the AP and Burl.

In a story evaluating the coverage, Betty Anne Williams of the AP wrote that "news executives generally agreed that Ford himself was largely responsible for what one of them called 'the roller coaster effect' of the reporting" through several misleading TV appearances that night.

• • •

"In the late 1970s and early 1980s," Burl later recalled, "we were in one of our periodic self-flagellation cycles where we were all worrying about whether newspapers were going to be around another ten years." In an attempt to future proof, the AP moved into what Burl called the "unsettled new field of information retrieval."

The AP Political Databank was a computerized library, updated daily and available through almost any computer terminal, on the 1980 campaign. The AP provided the product, and *The New York Times* Information Service provided the computer, distribution, and marketing systems. Burl negotiated the revenue-sharing agreement with *The Times*.

He also negotiated with NBC News to jointly conduct national public opinion polling with the AP. This cost the AP a fraction of the cost of independent polling and gave it national television exposure.

Burl wrote his thesis on it to complete his marketing course requirements at Long Island University, then submitted a copy of the twenty-three-page document to the AP's president and general manager.

"We can overcome the hurdle of newness," Burl wrote. While competitors existed, that newness meant "we can stake out our own territory without having to try to take it away from someone else."

Through this service, news would "be especially written, edited, and formatted for delivery on a television screen, rather than on paper. It will allow for graphics, headlines, and color—all beyond the capability of teleprinter delivery."

The paper opened with what was essentially a Strengths, Weaknesses, Opportunities, and Threats (SWOT) analysis. "If we believe that we are merely in the news business, and not in the information business, then we are headed for big trouble," Burl wrote.

20

The Interview

In the early spring of 1980, Robert Decherd, the executive vice president of *The Dallas Morning News*, was nearing the end of a six-month cross-country search for an executive editor. His paper was the clear underdog in a newspaper war that was capturing national attention, up against the much wealthier *Times Herald* owned by the powerful Los Angeles–based Times Mirror Company. Both were vying to be king of the media for the entire southwest region of the United States. Decherd's family had owned *The News* for four generations. He was preparing to take the company public, so he wanted to professionalize the management of the paper.

One day Decherd took a call from AP's Dallas bureau chief, Dorman Cordell, who had been best man at Burl and Betty's wedding and had remained a close friend. As Decherd recalled the conversation: "Cordell said, 'You can't attribute this to me, but you need to meet Burl Osborne. I know him very well. He reports to [Executive Editor] Lou Boccardi, and they're a year apart in age.'" Decherd understood that to mean Boccardi wasn't about to retire in the near future, and, from the standpoint of career advancement at the AP, Burl was boxed in.

Decherd quickly followed up on Cordell's recommendation. He phoned Burl, who "was a little reticent," Decherd recalled. "He said, 'I'm happy at the AP.' He was circumspect. He said, 'I like where I am.' And he did. He was in a position that had been a huge lifetime dream for him, being managing editor of The Associated Press."

But Decherd would not be deterred. He contacted Fuller who had formerly been a reporter at *The Dallas Morning News*. Fuller suggested that Decherd come to New York and meet with several AP senior managers over lunch. Burl was among the group invited. Boccardi was also included. Fuller explained that Decherd was collecting the names of qualified candidates for the editorship at his paper. Burl prepared a list of people—"quality editors who represented the best in our business"—drawn from his personal network nationwide.

It was a pleasant, low-key lunch in the AP's large dining room at 50 Rockefeller Plaza. The following day, by prearrangement, Decherd and Burl had a private lunch across town. "We went over to the Carlyle and had a very elegant lunch," Burl said. "We talked very broadly about what he was hoping to do and what I was hoping to do at the AP. By then, I was into the MBA program and made some comment that my interests were going far beyond news management into a more general management area."

By the end of the lunch, Burl realized that Decherd was still interested in *him* for the job. "I came home that day and said to Betty, 'I could swear, if I didn't know better, I would say it was just like being on a job interview.' Well, turned out that's what it was."

Decherd invited Burl to Dallas, writing:

> As I have said, it is our plan to invite three, perhaps four, candidates to Dallas during the latter half of August. We hope to make a final decision in early September.
>
> Prior to your visit, you might forward a résumé and any background material you would like for Jim [Moroney] and me to review as we come to a final decision. Of course, we can provide you any information you feel is important to your decision when you are here in Dallas. Let me know what materials you would like to see and we will arrange to have these available while you are in the city . . .
>
> It goes without saying that I admire your abilities and believe there is much commonality in our thinking about the prospects for *The News* to become a paper of real distinction. I am looking forward to our visit.

Burl sent a comprehensive cover letter enumerating what he had achieved throughout his work history.

"My AP experience has included virtually every field job that we have," Burl wrote. "I missed only a foreign service assignment, although some of my friends tell me that my early West Virginia days amounted to the same thing." Burl noted his administrative background ranged from running the AP's smallest office to its largest bureau, Washington, where he had supervised more than one hundred staffers, to overseeing the full AP news report in his current role.

• • •

Mid-August arrived. Burl sat down for his official interview in Decherd's office. He recalled:

> I think the cleverest thing Robert did was to say, "I'm going to give you something to look at," and he gave me a blank organization chart for *The Dallas Morning News*, and instead of names in the blocks on the chart there were numbers. He said, "Look at this awhile, and then we'll talk." Well, I figured out fairly quickly that the numbers were ages. And if you looked at that and at the management of the newspaper, it didn't take a rocket scientist to figure out that in a reasonably short period of time, there were going to be a lot of people leaving and somebody had to replace them. That was sort of his way of formalizing the discussion.

Another facet of the interview process was a psychological assessment conducted for *The News* by the outside consulting firm of Lifson and Trego. The test rated Burl on a scale of 1 to 9 on eleven aspects of his personality, ranging from his ability to deal with people to his durability under pressure. He scored highest on his intellectual power, a 9; the quickness of his work pace, an 8; and how socially outgoing he was, an 8. He did less well on the ease with which he himself could be managed, a 4/5; his attitude toward rules, a 4/5; the style with which he dealt with people, a 5; and his pressure durability, a 4.

The first paragraph of the test's "assessment summary" read: "Mr. Osborne's assessment results indicate that this is a highly intelligent individual who is both action-oriented and planning-oriented. Although his reserve may lead to his appearing somewhat cold in initial contacts, he is actually a forceful and socially comfortable individual who should deal effectively with people in most situations."

Further in the summary these traits were highlighted: "He may at times be touchy, something of a prima donna. . . . He is advancement oriented and will probably not be content to remain in the proposed position indefinitely."

Finally, under "placement considerations," the report stated: "The candidate's characteristics must be evaluated in light of position demands. If Mr. Osborne can be given a position demanding an independent, hardworking analytical problem solver who can direct others forcefully, he can be a highly effective performer."

Burl came away from the interview process both exhausted and invigorated. The idea of joining the Texas newspaper began to have greater and greater appeal.

> My impression was that this may be the last truly great opportunity to do something really special in this business. That, as Robert described the marketplace—the tradition of the newspaper and, most importantly, his aspirations to make it truly wonderful—coupled with what we knew to be the economic viability of that market, it seemed to me this is a very high-risk proposition but with a wonderful potential payout. . . . To hear a discussion about how to build a great one was a very inspiring kind of discussion.
>
> I had a very secure path where I was, but I saw this as an opportunity. This was kind of the Wild West. There are very few opportunities to have a real impact on an organization, but this looked like if I got it right, we could really do something great.

But as interested as he was in the job in Dallas, Burl doubted it would be offered to him. "I had thought the chances of anything developing from this were small because of my long career in the AP and the relatively brief experience I'd had in newspapers would probably cause [Decherd] not to be interested."

"Au contraire!" said Decherd. "He was running a large news organization at the AP and the talent equation is the same. It didn't bother me at all that he hadn't run a newspaper."

Even if Burl were offered the job—a big if, he thought—he wasn't sure he was willing "to walk away from twenty years in the AP, a sure thing, a bird in the hand, and go roll the dice in Dallas."

Decherd agreed with Burl that it would be a significant gamble. "He was taking a very big career risk. He had a very high-profile, influential role at the AP in New York, and he was going to give up all of that to become editor of a newspaper that had unrealized potential."

Burl returned to New York with much on his mind.

• • •

Burl continued with AP business as usual. But as he reflected more and more on Decherd's goals for *The Dallas Morning News* and on his own professional goals, he saw just how congruous—and desirable—they were. He said:

> There's probably some limit on the length of time anyone should do any job of any importance to the person. After a while, you begin to say, "I've seen this before." And that's really good if it helped you not to step in the same ditch you stepped in the last time. But it's really bad if it causes you to have a programmed, sort of rote response to circumstances that may in fact have changed. I think we all need change periodically.
>
> I loved the AP. I'm surprised it wasn't scratched in my forehead somewhere.

Burl wanted to run a company, and it was apparent that the AP wasn't going to be that company. He realized he could be in his current role—a great job—for the rest of his career, or he could roll the dice.

Burl apprised Fuller of the conversations and interviews he had had with Decherd and other executives at *The Dallas Morning News*. The AP's president had taken an interest in Burl's career from its early days, and Burl felt he owed him.

Fuller said, "You can stay here, and you will be the executive editor of the AP." He was candid with Burl about what would happen, what could happen, and what would not happen. "If I were you, I would go find out how good you are."

Buoyed by that discussion, Burl decided he wanted to roll the dice. He had Betty's support, and Decherd would pay him double what he was making in New York. "What it came down to, in my mind," Burl later said, "was a chance to do or be part of something truly terrific."

21

A Roll of the Dice

Decherd also asked Burl to undergo a thorough physical that was mandatory for all top executives planning to join *The News*. He'd made arrangements for Burl to see doctors the newspaper hired to administer the exam and corresponding tests before he left Dallas.

When Burl confided during one conversation, "I've got this health situation," Decherd listened carefully yet heard nothing that set off an alarm bell. "He presented his history very directly. He said, 'I'm interested in this role, and I need to tell you about my health. I'm fine. I think I'm going to live a long time. But there are reasonable people who would say that's not a certainty.'"

The doctors advising *Dallas Morning News* President and CEO, James M. (Jimmy) Moroney Jr., considered themselves reasonable people, and they were not certain about Burl's longevity at all. Reviewing and re-reviewing the lab results from Burl's tests, they said: "Do you know everything about Mr. Osborne's health? It's remarkable, but there's considerable risk here that it could deteriorate suddenly and rapidly." Armed with disturbing x-rays, one of which showed scar tissue on one of his lungs, they recommended that Moroney not hire Burl.

"He was absolutely crushed when the doctors said no," recalled Betty.

At Burl's suggestion, Decherd contacted Ivanovich, who was now chief of the hemodialysis unit at Northwestern University. He remembered taking Decherd's call. "He said, 'Can you assure me that Burl will live five years?' And I said, 'Burl will certainly live five years. Don't worry. He's got a good functioning kidney.'"

Ivanovich arranged for Burl to fly to Chicago, where he would undergo a battery of new tests at the school's renowned teaching hospital. Meanwhile, he contacted the University of Colorado's Health Sciences Center, where Burl's kidney transplant surgery had been performed in 1966. Their records showed that the scar tissue on his lung was preexisting, and when Ivanovich compared the old and new x-rays, it appeared that the scar tissue had remained unchanged. The old scar tissue was nothing to worry about, he argued.

Starzl's advice to *The News* "was to judge his candidacy in the same way as for any other healthy and talented executive being considered. There were no guarantees for anyone."

The News' doctors still weren't convinced.

Decherd recalled that Moroney and Joseph M. (Joe) Dealey, publisher of *The News*, "said to me, 'You're recommending we hire him, and our prominent internal medicine people are saying there's a big risk here?' That's when I said, 'Burl Osborne could accomplish more in five years than anyone else I've met could accomplish in twenty years.' I told them that Burl was the only person I'd met with who had the potential to become the publisher of *The News*. After I said this, they said, 'Okay. That's it, then.' And they never brought it up again."

• • •

The official announcement went out to AP member newspapers on Friday, September 26, 1980.

DALLAS (AP)—Burl Osborne, the managing editor of The Associated Press, has resigned to become the executive editor of the Dallas Morning News.

Keith Fuller, president and general manager of the AP, announced Thursday in New York the appointment of Wick Temple as ME.

James M. Moroney Jr., president of the Morning News, said Osborne's appointment will be effective Oct. 15.

As executive editor, Osborne will direct all news gathering and editing functions of the Morning News, including the newspaper's bureau operations, special news sections and Sunday publications.

"We are convinced that Burl Osborne's skill as a news executive will set new standards for journalism in Dallas and throughout the Southwest," Moroney said. "Our goal is to build the Morning News as a newspaper of distinction, and Burl Osborne can establish the directions necessary to achieve that goal in years to come."

• • •

Burl's former assistant, Bobbie Seril, threw a heartening going-away party at her home. Some colleagues questioned the wisdom of Burl's move—apart from the demands of the job, which would be substantial, wouldn't Dallas feel too conservative, too right wing for Burl, especially after his years in Washington, D.C., and New York?

Burl recalled, "At my farewell party, Jim Mangan, who ran the membership department, told me I was absolutely out of my eff-ing mind because, he said, 'You'll never get along with those people down there.' That was *not* the most encouraging send-off I could have had."

"We were all sad to see him leave," Seril said. "His colleagues really loved and respected him." They showed it by giving him a pair of cowboy boots as a farewell gift. And Seril had her favorite New York jeweler craft a pair of silver-and-gold cufflinks in the shape of the AP logo.

Once more, letters of congratulation poured in. To the AP's Atlanta bureau chief, Ron Autry, Burl wrote of his career change, "I believe it will be challenging and stimulating, and I look forward to getting in harness. The last 20 years have been mostly good ones, and I leave with more than a little sadness."

To his friend Bob Hartley, executive editor of Toledo, Ohio's, the *Blade*—who wrote, "Welcome to the unreal world and good luck"—Burl quipped: "Thanks. I think. . . Don't be surprised if you get a call asking for advice."

• • •

"You have instincts about people," said Decherd. "My instincts were very positive from the moment I met him. Everything about Burl felt good and then quickly began to feel right."

Burl was confident that he, too, had made the right choice. When he flew from Chicago to Dallas in late September 1980—a clean bill of health and a signed contract in hand—he vowed to make good on all within himself that had spurred Decherd to name him executive editor of *The Dallas Morning News*.

"I thought he had exceptional leadership abilities because he lived every minute," Decherd said. "He was in a hurry."

PART II

The Dallas Morning News

22

Big D

There was no good reason for a town to grow where Dallas did—no confluence of rivers, no topographical features to make it a good stopping point for settlers. The town got its quiet start as a trading post in a lean-to on the bluff overlooking the ford in the narrow Trinity River.

After a few years, the town consisted of two log cabins with families of ten or twelve. Nevertheless, the hyperbole that brought Dallas into the national consciousness in the 1960s and into worldwide notice via televised sports in the 1980s was there from the very start. It was a place made not by nature but by men, specifically those with a talent for self-promotion and aggrandizement. One settler wrote in his diary: "We soon reached the place we had heard of so often; but the town, where was it?"

In the late 1800s, a happy combination of political tricks in the Texas legislature and a purchase of $100,000 worth of railroad bonds brought the transcontinental Texas & Pacific Railway to Dallas. Without this coup, Dallas would have remained a hamlet or disappeared altogether. Instead, within a few months, the town was bustling with more than 7,000 residents.

Alfred Horatio Belo founded *The Dallas Morning News* in 1885 in a one-room shack in Galveston. George Bannerman Dealey, an immigrant from England who had devoted himself to the paper from its first edition, bought the paper from Belo's heirs in 1926.

Dealey bought and promptly shut down the sole competing morning paper in town, leaving *The News* with a morning monopoly, and moved it to Commerce Street in Dallas.

In the first two decades of the twentieth century, Dallas grew into an important center of commerce. After expanding *The News'* building nine times—yet still needing more room—*The News* moved on March 20, 1949, to what one staffer declared "the most modern newspaper plant in America." This new headquarters was a large four-story building on the corner of Houston and Young Streets in the southwest quadrant of downtown Dallas. Some reporters nicknamed the building "the Rock" after the quotation by Dealey chiseled in large letters into its limestone front:

> Build the news upon the rock of truth and righteousness. Conduct it always upon the lines of fairness and integrity. Acknowledge the right of the people to get from the newspaper both sides of every important question.

Although oil was not discovered in Dallas, banks grew up in the city to house the oil money made in other regions of the state and the southwest. The city's population grew, oil boomed, and real estate became king.

Rival newspaper the *Dallas Times Herald* also had its roots in the late 1800s, originating from the merger of two older newspapers. The Times Mirror Company bought the *Times Herald* in 1969, and competition between the two papers had escalated from that time onward. The *Times Herald* even introduced a morning edition in 1977, ending the monopoly Dealey had started. *The News* trailed its rival in circulation in Dallas County, and it sold less advertising. Many Dallas readers considered *The News*—often referred to as the "Gray Lady of Young Street"—stodgy and boring, alternatively labeling it *"The Dallas Morning Snooze."*

• • •

Decherd gave Burl a mandate the day he offered him the job of executive editor for *The Dallas Morning News*: win the war against the *Dallas Times Herald*.

"At that point, *The News* was a middle-of-the-road regional newspaper with some real talent and some genuine mediocrity," then–Business Editor Bob Mong said. "The *Times Herald* was much more aggressive and putting out a better paper. It was a zero-sum game. One of the papers was going to survive but not both."

Burl analyzed the criticism. "Whether fairly or not, the newspaper had a reputation for complacency, for not being aggressive about pursuing news, for just sort of rocking along. Our competitors—who were then owned by Times Mirror—made much of that and promoted themselves as the aggressive, young, assertive, creative, innovative people while we were considered the stick-in-the-muds. Like most hyperbole, there was less truth to that than was stated, but there was some, and we had to deal with that."

Times Herald Editor Roy Bode recalled, "When Burl first arrived, the general feeling among reporters and editors was pretty dismissive. I think people thought, '*The News* just hired someone as bland as they are, from the gray, bland AP. The feeling at the *Herald* was that the AP was just all facts. Their feeling was that the AP is competent and very pedestrian, while we at the *Herald* are so much more than that."

Tim Kelly, then the *Times Herald*'s deputy managing editor, put it this way: "I'll never forget when Burl got to Dallas. The day he was named and it came across the wire, I was in the newsroom with some people, and they were all kind of like, 'What's this AP guy doing?' Our editors were from *The Washington Post* and *The Philadelphia Inquirer*. People in the newsroom were saying, 'What does this AP guy know about running a newsroom or being an editor?'"

Kelly was a native of Ashland, Kentucky, and worked at the *Lexington Herald-Leader* many years after Burl had moved on, but he'd followed Burl's career closely. Desperately wanting to escape Ashland as Burl had, Kelly made note of Burl's advancement up the ranks of the AP. He warned his *Times Herald* colleagues about dismissing Burl. "I spoke up and said, 'Listen. Don't underestimate this guy. He's like the world's longest-living kidney transplant recipient, and I know him.' I explained that you just couldn't sell him short; he was a fighter, a battler. He had worked his way up from the humblest of beginnings to a successful career at the AP, and he had done all of this despite his health problems."

• • •

On Friday, September 26, 1980—the same day that newspapers coast to coast announced his selection as executive editor of *The Dallas Morning News*—Burl stood beside Decherd behind the glass partition that separated the executive office suite from the newspaper's bright, expansive newsroom. This was to be Burl's informal introduction to in-house reporters and editors in advance of his official first day two weeks later. Inviting an outsider—the first in fifty years—to come run the paper was, for some, difficult to accept.

As the two men stepped past the glass partition, a reporter shouted across the room, "Fuck you!" Burl pretended not to hear it. Decherd chose to overlook the offense and launched right into his introductory remarks.

"And that was Burl's introduction to the newsroom," recalled then night City Editor Stuart Wilk, who was seated a few desks away from the man who released the F-bomb. "I think the pressmen three floors away heard it. 'Well, we have nowhere to go from here but up,' I said to myself."

City Desk Reporter Steve Blow had a similar reaction when he heard the expletive. "I had expected the worst. After all, a big shot from the AP had been hired."

Unlike its member newspapers, the AP didn't have a published product—just a constant stream of breaking news stories that went out over the A-wire. Burl had never dealt with production, a printing press, or circulation or delivery issues. But the difference was more philosophical than that: as an AP correspondent, Burl had worked alongside reporters and editors in an untold number of newsrooms but had never belonged in any of them.

Burl's musing about how the newsroom perceived him that day encapsulated it best. "We had the combination of somebody nobody ever heard of showing up and also somebody who basically has never worked in a large newspaper, ever, and who didn't know anything about production and didn't know anything about anything, much, except some thought he knew a little bit about news."

Decherd told the staff that he respected Burl's talents both in the newsroom and in the business office. And he spoke of what he termed Burl's "special insight" into how to go about the business of journalism and the art of journalism. He reminded them that as the executive editor Burl would "direct all news-gathering and editing functions of the paper, including bureau operation, special news sections, and Sunday publications." Then Decherd turned the floor over to Burl, who seized the moment for his own clear, straightforward communication.

He told the staff he'd been reading their paper. "There is an awful lot that is good in it." He was "persuaded that there is a commitment that runs to the bottom of everyone's toes to make this a great, distinguished, excellent newspaper. And that's why I want to be a part of it. I ask you to let me be a part of it. I ask you to help me. I will do everything I can to help you."

He said this would likely be the last time they saw him with a coat on. He would be in the newsroom often, not hidden away anywhere. "I will be there to help, and I will be asking you an awful lot of stupid questions. But I will keep asking until the questions aren't stupid anymore. The door's always open, and the light's on in the hall."

Then he addressed Decherd's directive about the newspaper war:

> I would like to put as much daylight between *The News* and the *Times Herald* as it is possible to do. I think the competition is great. It's one of the attractive reasons for coming here. But it has to be true, real competition. As far as I'm concerned, that means I am going to do everything I can to beat them every way I can in every department I can, every day I can. And I have the sense that all of you feel the same way. If they are able to compete in that environment, I wish them well.

After the meeting ended, Steve Blow's boss, City Editor Don Smith, called him over. "On my way into the newsroom earlier, Don had said to me, in his morose way, 'This is the worst day of your life.' And I said, 'Why?' and he just repeated, 'This is the worst day of your life, and you'll find out soon enough.' Well, now Don says to me, 'You get to interview the new editor and write a feature for Sunday's paper.' I agreed with him. *The worst day of my life.*"

> They summoned me into Burl's office when he was ready for me. I go back there, and I say, "I'm the guy who's drawn the black bean. I've got the job of writing about you for Sunday's paper." He kind of laughed and expressed his condolences. He was very nice. He knew I had a tough job. He talked about a dog caught in a coal mine back in Kentucky, and he said it was one of the first stories he had ever covered.

What I was sweating was something you couldn't escape noticing, which was that Burl was very short. If you were doing a profile of anybody else, you would say this is a very short guy. I was thinking, "How am I going to handle this?" You couldn't not mention it when writing a profile about Burl. It would be leaving out something important if I didn't mention it, and I was wrestling with the ethics of this. Can I be true to myself and my journalistic ethics and not mention it?

And then Burl gave me a gift. I asked him whether he expected to have a high profile in the city, beyond the newsroom, and he joked, "I'm too short to be high profile." So when it came to writing the piece, I had to explain this quote. But even then, I remember wrestling with myself and with my editors as to how to explain his height. The editors just kept saying to me, "You'd better get this right." They were making no bones about the fact that if Burl didn't like the article, it was all on me.

In the profile he composed, Blow diplomatically settled on describing Burl as a "small, squarely built man."

Blow admitted that reading the article now "mostly reminds me of how quickly Burl Osborne put me at ease. He was funny and forthright and self-deprecating. I remember he said, for instance, 'I don't know very much, but I know it at great length.' Writing the story was a pleasure."

23

A Trip Back to Washington

October 15, 1980. Burl reported to work early. He recalled:

> The first day, I walked in, and I hadn't even toured the building; I didn't know where anything was. And Robert says, "OK, well, here's your office, , , Come with me; there are some people I want you to meet." So he drags me off, and we go up some elevator, and I walk in—I didn't realize they had an auditorium—and there were about four or five hundred people sitting out there who all had questions to ask us.

Taken a bit by surprise, Burl nevertheless stood comfortably at the podium for his first official "getting-to-know-you" session. He spoke a little about himself and his goals before opening the floor for the Q&A. One of the first questions was posed by the department head for the lifestyles section. As Burl recalled the moment:

> She kind of smirked and said, "Well, what's your policy about free trips and free travel?"
>
> And I said, "Well, I just got here, but the answer is no. Why would we do that?"
>
> She grinned, and I said, "What?"
>
> She said, "Well, you do know that the wife of your predecessor [*laughs*] is a travel writer who takes all these free trips?"
>
> I said, "Well, if she wants to keep doing that, we'll give her a budget, and she can live within her budget, and we'll go where we need to go, but the answer is still no."

Burl made it very clear in the auditorium that the days of travel writers and editors accepting free gifts, sports writers accepting free tickets, and society writers accepting everything from flowers to clothing and jewelry were over. He explained that he was determined to avoid even the appearance of a conflict of interest by his reporters and editors. He told the assembled group that *The New York Times* and the *Los Angeles Times* and a handful of other major newspapers across the country had recently instituted the same rule.

"This was hard for a lot of people to swallow," recalled a reporter who was in the auditorium that day. "It was early proof that things were going to change at *The News*. Some of the benefits that we were all used to were going to go away in the interest of the paper's integrity. Even though people didn't like it, it was a good thing he was doing. It was a very good thing for the reputation of the paper."

• • •

From the time he was in high school, Burl had loved fast cars. That wasn't about to change now that he had more than doubled his salary. Roby Terrill, who worked at Dallas' Park Place Motorcars—one of the nation's largest Mercedes dealerships—recalled that he sold Burl the first car he bought in Dallas, a Mercedes SL roadster convertible. "He wanted red because red stood out. He not only had the ego that wanted that car, but he also had the smarts to go with it. Burl always negotiated with me on the price. He was a very smart businessman. He didn't throw his money away."

Betty had thirteen hours left to go on her degree in business administration and minor in accounting. "I immediately enrolled at the University of Texas in Dallas to complete my last thirteen hours," Betty said. She graduated summa cum laude and with honors in her major soon after.

Jonathan enjoyed school and played sports through YMCA-sponsored little leagues. "Being an only child," Betty said, he "got his share of attention." Burl and Betty volunteered to run the clock and keep score for many of his youth basketball games. "Burl loved it," Betty said.

• • •

Shortly before Burl joined *The News*, a research firm had analyzed the Dallas market and found that the *Times Herald* was winning in every major category, including the two that were most important to Dallas readers: sports and business. With its advantage of being a morning paper, *The News* should have been far ahead in both those areas.

Bob Mong had been promoted from assistant city editor to editor of the business section about a year before Burl arrived at *The News*. At the time, only six or seven newspapers in the country had an entire standalone business section. Even *The New York Times'* "Business Day" was only a few years old. As was the case at many other newspapers, the business stories published in *The News* appeared haphazardly in the back of the sports section.

"We were the first turnaround section of the paper because we'd already started working on the section before Burl arrived," Mong said. "The *Times Herald* had announced it was expanding its business section, and Robert Decherd [*Morning News* executive vice president] had put me in charge of the section."

The *Times Herald's* success was due in large part to its executive editor. Tom Johnson was a former Lyndon B. Johnson aide who had managed the former president's Austin-based broadcast properties and joined the paper in 1973. Charismatic and articulate, Johnson did much to change the *Herald's* image by hobnobbing with Dallas city fathers and overseeing some investigative projects. Within two years, his flair had won the paper a mention in *Time* magazine as "one of the five best newspapers in the South."

In 1975, Tom Johnson became the publisher, and the *Times Herald* recruited Kenneth Johnson from *The Washington Post* to become its executive editor. Ken Johnson was a West Virginian with an earthy wit and pronounced drawl; he was the epitome of a veteran newsman, save for his meticulous manner of dress; and—according to *Newsweek* magazine—he was "appalled by the state of journalism in Texas."

Ken Johnson set about raiding newspapers—in his case, Detroit, Philadelphia, and Washington—to supplement, complement, or replace the staff he inherited.

Burl mulled over the reality that despite the *Times Herald* outdistancing *The News* in the race, his paper nevertheless "had a pretty good reputation even though we didn't have much of a product."

Empowered by Decherd, just weeks after arriving at *The News*, Burl launched a search to raid a big-city newsroom for an editor who could transform its dull, sleepy sports coverage that paled in comparison to the *Times Herald*'s much better-written and more exciting section.

The research firm's study had revealed that it was impossible either to put too much money into sports coverage or to have too many articles about the Dallas Cowboys. It also found that 55 percent of local readers—male and female—considered themselves serious sports fans, compared with 46 percent nationwide, and more than two-thirds of them regularly read the sports pages. In the language of the report, Dallas was a "sports-happy" market.

Burl zeroed in on Dave Smith, the highly respected manager of the sports section at *The Washington Star*. Smith was used to competing against the larger, more influential *Washington Post*. He had been sports editor at *The Boston Globe* from 1970 to 1978, and *Time* magazine had named that paper's sports section the best in the country in 1977.

Burl and Robert both flew to Washington to meet Smith in person.

Smith was very receptive to going to Dallas, in part because *The Washington Star* had begun "pulling back" resources (the paper folded six months later) but also because he could feel Burl's enthusiasm. That, plus the city's five professional sports teams and two hundred golf courses. "It wasn't a hard sell."

He recalled: "They both said, and it was incredible advice, 'Dave, before you come in and start making all sorts of changes, realize that Dallas is not Boston and Dallas is not Washington. It's Dallas.'"

On that same trip to D.C., Burl also arranged to meet with staff in *The Dallas Morning News* bureau to get a feel for how their operations were going.

En route to their offices, he ran into former AP colleague Carl Leubsdorf in the Mayflower Hotel. Leubsdorf had been the AP's chief political officer when Burl was assistant bureau chief, and he was currently Washington bureau chief for *The Baltimore Sun*. The two hadn't seen each other in nearly five years and decided to catch up over coffee.

Burl jumped at the chance to pick Leubsdorf's brain. Reporters in Dallas referred to the paper's Washington bureau as "*The Morning News* Embassy." He told Leubsdorf he wanted *The News* to be seen as a player in Washington.

Leubsdorf told Burl it was important to have a good deputy to run the day-to-day operations. "Then you also have to focus your attention on areas that are of special interest in Texas, such as the economy, energy, and defense." Burl took in everything he said.

Leubsdorf recalled:

> Then I got to thinking, I wonder whether I would be interested in doing what I'd just described. At that time, *The Morning News* didn't have a good reputation. The *Times Herald* was the hot item down there. The *Times Herald*'s Washington bureau was much better than *The Morning News'* bureau.
>
> I wrote Burl a note summarizing what I'd said over coffee. I got back a standard, official-type note that said, "Thank you for your note, etc." But then I noticed that there was a little note tucked in with it that said, "Might you be interested in this? I'd hate to think we'd go through all of this and find out later that you might have been available." I wrote back a cryptic note that said, "Thanks for your thoughts. This might be the time."

For a month, Leubsdorf heard nothing else from Dallas. But Burl was thinking hard about *The News'* Washington bureau and had decided to utilize the structure that they had discussed: having both a writing bureau chief and a managing bureau chief. Leubsdorf would be the writer who would "head an expanded Washington bureau that would make sure that the areas most important to us were covered—energy, defense, economics."

Leubsdorf recalled how he made his decision. "I knew people at the *Times Herald*, and most of the people there seemed to think that positive changes were coming to *The News*. It was gearing up to fight back against the *Herald*. Burl had certainly given me a lot to think about. He said they were trying to build the best paper in the region. We had a long talk, and I agreed I would go to Dallas."

Both he and Burl wanted his presence to be felt right away. As Leubsdorf recollected: "I called the press secretary for the newly elected vice president George H. W. Bush. I said, 'I'd like an interview with the vice president,' and they agreed to it. So I interviewed him." The piece appeared the day before

Leubsdorf's first day at *The News*. "I think this was Burl's way of saying, 'Hey, guys, it's going to be different now.'"

Shortly thereafter, word went out that the *Times Herald* planned to hire a political columnist to counter Leubsdorf, whose academic credentials (a master's, with honors, from Columbia's Graduate School of Journalism) and professional experience were estimable. "I was frankly concerned that they might hire my old *Baltimore Sun* colleague Fred Barnes who both had strong opinions and was an aggressive reporter who could break stories," wrote Leubsdorf in *Adventures of a Boy on the Bus*.

> As it turned out, they hired Jody Powell, a non-journalist who had been President Carter's press secretary. I breathed a deep sigh of relief; Powell, writing an interesting though predictable column, was no threat to our goal of news dominance, and he eventually left to establish one of Washington's most successful public relations firms.
>
> Fortunately for us, the *Times Herald* often preferred to run wire stories on the major Washington stories, freeing up the bureau to write sidebars. That strategy was exactly the opposite of ours, which was to put our stamp on every major story.

24

Action!

The research firm's survey also guided Burl on business coverage. Dallas was business focused as a city, and the market was ready. "Burl was on the cutting edge of seeing how much opportunity existed in business coverage," Business Editor Bob Mong said.

But he felt something was missing from the business section prototype *The News* was testing. In November, he put the brakes on the project, knowing full well that bruised feelings might result because a lot of people had put a lot of effort into it. "The reason that we pulled it back," he said, "was that it didn't seem to me to say, 'Action.' It wasn't newsy. It had the look of a feature section that would appear in a Sunday paper, which I did *not* want." Burl tinkered with the arrangement:

> We created this digest down the left side, and we made the pages a little more vertical and changed the mix of the content a little bit and got ready to go. We made it more active and more vibrant, and we launched. In a very short time, of course, it occurred to us that if it makes sense on Tuesday, it probably makes sense on the other days too. In a reasonable period of time we were able to publish a separate business section every day of the week, which had not been done in Dallas before.

"This move by Burl helped establish *The News* in the same echelons as *The Boston Globe*, the *Miami Herald*, *The Washington Post*, and other papers that were expanding and improving business coverage," Mong said. "*The News* moved quickly to a seven-day-a-week business section, one of the first in the country to do so."

Burl authorized Mong to hire journalists for the expanded section. As Burl recalled, what Mong found during his efforts to recruit reporters was that "increasing numbers of young people were deciding there is a strong future in business news reporting, and they were preparing themselves to take a piece of it." From that much larger pool of reporting talent around the country, Mong chose men and women capable of "more instructive and explanatory writing" who could fashion "stories that will explain where we are and how we got that way." He sought out writers who could take economics—until recently considered "the dismal science"—from the abstract to the concrete, showing the ways in which it affected how individuals live. The department tripled in a matter of months, from five to fifteen reporters.

Burl also decided it would be smart to have presidents and comptrollers of companies and banks meet informally with editors of the business section when no story was involved. The meetings—always off the record—were casual and conducive to members of both sides becoming better acquainted.

Burl commissioned a survey seeking feedback on the new layout and coverage. The response from readers and advertisers was immediate: they liked it. One CEO wrote, "It is Dallas and Texas business news that we can't find anywhere. And it's indispensable. I'm glad we're finally finding it in *The Morning News*."

In a speech he delivered to executives in the greater Dallas community, Burl outlined the new standards for *The News* business section.

> We should insist that reporters have education and/or experience in business before trying to write about it. Editors should be able to read and understand financial statements, should know something about economic theory, about finance, about the various measures of a company's health. We ought to know what we are doing.

To that end, Burl met with officials of Southern Methodist University's (SMU) Edwin L. Cox School of Business to describe the program he envisioned. He asked them to design a special curriculum for reporters and to recruit members from among their faculty to teach the classes. *The Dallas Morning News* would pay all expenses. Ultimately, six, three-hour sessions, spread over six weeks, were conducted at the Communications Center during working hours. All *Morning News* staff were encouraged to participate.

Burl explained his rationale: "It was not practical for us to try to make every business reporter an economist, although a couple of ours arc. It was reasonable, we felt, to try to see that business staffers understand the language and principles of business and the economy that are essential to writing knowledgeably about either."

The goal was to further empower Mong (nicknamed by staff the "obscure genius") and his team to interview business leaders and digest financial analyses with confidence.

For veteran reporters it was great refresher training; for neophytes it was akin to taking a graduate-level course. The six core classes addressed such fundamentals as how to read an annual report and how to understand a spreadsheet, as well as such key elements of financial decision-making as the impact of taxes and debt versus equity financing. The case study method—using examples from local companies—was used extensively and provoked lively discussion. The program even included instructions on how to determine whether financial data were being inflated or suppressed.

As Burl told Mong and his team: "It should not surprise reporters, but sometimes does, to learn that it is perfectly acceptable for companies to make bad results look better merely by choosing a different set of accounting rules. It should not surprise us, but sometimes does, that a subject as complex as the economy won't submit to the neat, event-oriented formulas we'd like to use to describe it."

Mong said that the program with the SMU business professors was ingenious. "It really accelerated our understanding of business." Mong's staff reporters and writers would go on to specialize in energy, electronics, and entrepreneurship—all topics of great interest to Dallas residents.

The business section eventually grew to fifty-seven staff. Cheryl Hall, who later succeeded Mong as business editor, said, "In this town it made sense for Burl to focus on business. Everything, including sports, is a business here in Dallas."

Of the improved coverage of both business and sports, Burl recalled:

It is one of the ways that we ensure that reading *The Morning News* is not merely a nice thing to do or enjoyable, but it is necessary if, in fact, you wish as an individual to be informed about those two areas.

In a speech he delivered to the Dallas Rotary Club, Burl described the relationship between corporate America and the press in recent history:

Reporters were typecast as hard-drinking, poorly dressed, ill-mannered parasites. Businesspeople were viewed as cigar-smoking, inconsiderate, patronizing money-grubbers. These were stereotypes, and like most generalizations, they left a wide margin for error.

There probably was a grain of truth here and there. The fact was that papers often put business news in the same league with country correspondence. It is reasonable to assume that at some papers, both jobs were done by the same person.

In other words, business news didn't amount to much in many newspapers in the '50s, and that suited both business and the newspapers just fine.

But time passed, and times were not so good anymore.

The stereotypes persisted and got worse. A common business view was that reporters had become self-important, setting themselves up as prosecutor, judge, and jury for all of the real or imagined sins of business, writing stories irresponsibly, without regard for either truth or consequences.

The press, on the other hand, often saw business as even more sinister than before, pursuing huge profits at the expense of the public, without oversight or accountability.

Sensitive to his audience, Burl chose a pertinent topic both to illustrate and to challenge the status quo.

For example, information is of central importance to both business and the press. But not at all in the same way. As a businessperson, such information as market strategy and sales figures may be most valuable to you if you have it and your competition doesn't. The best thing you can do with information is keep it secret.

For an editor, information is most valuable when it can be published. The best thing we can do with information is to *not* keep it secret.

He concluded the speech by saying, "We do you no service by letting puffery masquerade as news," and adding:

I would also respectfully suggest that business might help by trying to be a bit more open, a bit more direct. There is a middle ground of disclosure that can permit a company to be forthright without giving away trade secrets. I would ask that you not assume that every reporter is your enemy seeking to do you harm.

• • •

American Airlines had just moved its headquarters to Dallas. CEO Robert Crandall called Burl, saying he felt that American was being treated badly by *The News* and he wanted to discuss it with Burl over dinner.

It turned out Crandall was actually complaining about coverage that had appeared in the *Times Herald*. After that, every six months or so Crandall would host a dinner, and then Burl would host. *The News*' Hall, then a senior business writer, always attended and usually helped arrange the dinners. Five people attended the first; over time, the group grew to about twenty.

"We started meeting with a lot of companies," remembered Hall. "It was brilliant on Burl's part. It was kind of no-holds-barred. We would be saying, 'Here's where we're having trouble with you,' or they would say, 'We need better coverage.' This was a really good thing, very smart of Burl to do this."

Mong remembered one dinner at which Crandall arrived very upset. "He came into the restaurant's private room, where we were to be seated at a long table. At each place was a copy of the business section of the paper. Crandall just swept his arm across the table, and all the papers went shooting down the table and landed at the other end. Burl was not happy about it. He told Crandall, 'Now, that's not appropriate.' Crandall cooled down."

Burl's displeasure could go both ways. Hall remembered a time when she assigned a reporter of hers to write a profile of the new CEO of Neiman Marcus. "The story starts off with this anecdote. I asked the reporter, 'When did you interview him for this?' The reporter says to me that he hasn't interviewed him, but the anecdote he tells is something he envisions the CEO thinking. So I told Burl, we're not going to be running the story, and I told him why. And Burl said to me, 'If you had run that story, you wouldn't have needed an elevator for me to get up here to your office.'"

25

EXTRA! EXTRA!

In an announcement about Burl's taking the job as the executive editor "of that large Dallas newspaper" printed in the *Bluefield Daily Telegraph* in early January 1981, Currence wrote: "Buckskin came to Bluefield as a young fellow to work for the AP and his rise up the ladder was fast. That was certainly no surprise to us because it has been my opinion that no national news service that circulates in this state has ever had a better reporter in West Virginia than Burl Osborne. I doubt if any person ever went higher in a shorter time with the world's largest news gathering agency than Burl Osborne. And we'll brag a bit— we told you so, often."

• • •

Morning News Projects Reporter Howard Swindle, who was there when Burl arrived, said, "Burl established a presence in the newsroom that, quite frankly, scared the hell out of a lot of complacent journalists, and he let it be known very quickly that an average job was an unacceptable job, and we must perform to the best of our abilities. This was a very critical point in the turnaround of the paper."

Mong likewise recalled, "He was ultra-competitive and very demanding. Some people, behind his back, called him the 'Little General.' He would say, 'We are going to win more than we're going to lose. We're going to out-think and out-smart the competition.' And he was so smart to do this. He got great work out of people. I was so determined to do well that I was working about seventy hours a week. Burl noticed this and came to me and said, 'This isn't sustainable. You've got to get more rest.' So I cut it down to about sixty hours a week."

A detail guy, Burl also had some very particular new rules about seemingly insignificant issues. Within his first few months on the paper, for example, he instituted a policy of referring to individuals in stories as "Mr." or "Mrs." as opposed to using their surname only, much in the same way *The New York Times* does. When asked why, he said, "It's polite."

Burl also issued an edict about the word "posh." Iconoclastic reporters had used "posh" in a derisive way to describe homes, restaurants, and even a prison camp. "Don't call a house 'posh,'" Burl said. "Tell us how much it's valued for on the tax rolls. Give us a few words of description." He didn't like the word and wanted never to see it in *The News*.

• • •

Decherd and the senior executives were stalwart supporters of Burl's every move in his first months at *The News*. The support was invaluable as Burl disrupted what he considered a paternalistic and complacent status quo at the newspaper.

He recalled:

> I detected that there was a degree of lethargy. And so it seemed important to us to change it. I'm a change agent, and some people were displaced. An extraordinary number of people had the ability to get with it and excel. There were not many people who couldn't cut it. We found jewels hidden in unlikely places throughout the company, and we tried to identify those people and give them visibility and give them a chance. Many of them blossomed.
>
> There were terrible disparities and omissions in pay. A lot of the news department salaries were not competitive, and—worse—they were not equitable. A copy editor in this department with five years gets this, and the same level over here gets something else. So one of the first things we tried to do was to equalize or make equitable the pay scales, which you could only do by increasing at one side; we didn't cut anybody's pay. And, secondly, raising the "jump-bar"—the performance expectation—big time. And I guess the day everybody figured it out, finally, was in the spring of 1981.

On March 30, 1981, at 2:27 p.m. Eastern Standard Time (which was an hour earlier in Dallas), John Hinkley Jr. fired bullets at President Ronald Reagan as he left the Washington Hilton Hotel. Hinkley happened to be a former resident of Highland Park, an affluent town surrounded by the city of Dallas, giving the story a local angle.

That day's edition had already been printed, but Burl pounced on the Reagan story. He knew the paper had run comprehensive coverage of the Kennedy assassination the day after it happened, complete with first-person accounts from reporters on the scene and in the president's motorcade, but it had failed to run an extra edition on the day of the assassination. That hung like an albatross around the newspaper's neck. Other papers—from the *Fort Worth Star-Telegram* to *The Washington Post*—had managed to print extra editions without the hometown advantage enjoyed by *The News*.

Moments after he learned of the assassination attempt, Burl called Decherd to say he wanted to put out an extra edition of the paper. Decherd didn't hesitate. "I just said, 'Let's go!'"

There was only one problem. No one at the paper could remember how to do it.

With the advent of first radio, then television, extras had become rare in America. Staffers had no idea what it entailed. Were there enough reporters on deck to write the stories? Were the press operators still in the building to print it? How and where would it be distributed? But Burl didn't care how unusual it was or how difficult the logistics were. He hurriedly gathered the paper's circulation, production, marketing, and newsroom managers to discuss not *whether* but rather *how quickly* it could be done.

The newsroom filled with nervous laughter as reporters and editors, hearing that an extra might be in the works, whispered among themselves: "He can't be serious, can he?" and "Does he think he's still at the AP?"

Yet, by 3:00 p.m. Dallas time—a mere ninety-three minutes after the bullets were fired in Washington—reporters and editors had cobbled together a bold twenty-four-page extra edition that included staff-written stories, wire service dispatches, and compelling photographs. It was an up-to-the-minute report on the day's extraordinary events. "PRESIDENT SHOT," read the 120-point-type headline.

Before 4:00 p.m. in Dallas, *The News* had printed 27,500 copies of the extra edition and had resorted to giving them away at the entrance to the Dallas North Tollway and distributing them in downtown Dallas, at convenience stores, in hotels and motels, and in newspaper racks. And, yes, at some of the outdoor locations, the people distributing the papers did call out, "Extra! Extra! Read all about it!"

It was no accident that one of the places the extra appeared was at Joe Miller's, one of the popular bars where both *News'* and *Herald*'s reporters and editors hung out. The *Times Herald* had managed to get a small picture and brief story of the shooting into the final 20,000 copies they printed that afternoon. Their reporters arrogantly swaggered into the bar that afternoon to celebrate "kicking *The Morning News'* ass," as Burl later described it. How surprised they were when they saw *The News'* extra in the boxes outside.

"If there were any skeptics left," said Decherd, "I think they decided that day that this was for real."

Burl also pointed to the extra as a turning point for the paper's reputation and its employees' belief in themselves:

> It's rare that you can find the actual defining moment in a change, but I think that was the day everybody figured out, "God, we can." We did. We did it to the other guys. It's an example of how you can be responsive. It probably cost us a fortune, and to his eternal credit, Robert never pointed that out to me.
>
> You put out an extra, and you find out who's up to the challenge. What kind of people you want to build upon.
>
> What we saw was an almost overnight change in attitude and responsiveness and in assertiveness, and to this day, the bell has never gone off when our group did not respond with all the engines. It literally changed the behavior of the news department and changed the perception of us down the street [at the *Herald*]. I guess the first time out they thought, well, that's a fluke, but it started happening a lot. And, suddenly, everything changed, and success breeds success. Once we as a group knew that we could do things, that we could excel, that it didn't matter how big the

Times Herald company was if we did it better and first. And we began to believe in ourselves, and as we built on that, it just kept getting better and better.

• • •

Currence, who had never doubted what Burl could achieve and had been his most ardent supporter, died the day after the attempt on President Reagan's life. In the coming years, however, Currence's successors honored him—and Burl— by faithfully commenting on Buckskin's every advancement and award.

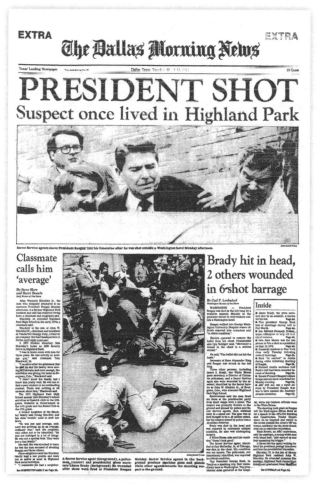

EXTRA! EXTRA!

26

Get a Bigger Dog

The primary market in which *The News* competes is the Dallas–Fort Worth Standard Metropolitan Statistical Area in north central Texas. According to the Census Bureau, the entire area grew by more than 25 percent—to a population of 2,975,000—during the 1970s.

In fact, the area was among the fastest growing in the nation, which was both good and bad for those who called themselves "native" Texans. They complained of clogged freeways and Yankee attitudes, yet most industries in Dallas had to admit they prospered: stores from more shoppers, restaurants from more diners, and newspapers from more readers. Among the newcomers, upwardly mobile workers were more likely to pick up *The News*, while blue-collar workers chose the *Times Herald*.

The biggest advantage *The News* held over the *Herald* was this: it was a morning paper, and by 1980, the majority of readers in Dallas—mirroring the trend nationwide—did not want an afternoon paper.

Because Dallas and its citizens were completely new to Burl, he relied heavily in his first months on the survey of the Dallas marketplace that the paper had recently commissioned.

"It was helpful to me to be able to read that data," he explained. "Not to figure out what to do exactly but to figure out who was here. What is this place, what are the various pieces of it, what are the demographic strata, and what do they care about?" Burl's top priority was "to listen and listen hard" to the good people of Dallas.

Most compelling was the study's suggestion that *The News* focus intensely on "cosmopolites," which it defined as "young, upwardly mobile, better demographic people in the market."

Burl thought one way to reach more cosmopolites was to include the paper's midweek fashion section more than once a week. Ellen Kampinsky, who was then in charge of the "Today" features section, had an even better idea. What about a new high-end section on the weekend—something like a combination of *Interview*, *W*, and *People* magazines—to complement the weekly fashion section? Burl liked the idea, and the glitzy new Sunday "High Profile" was born and introduced to the public in September 1981. "We wanted to put out a Sunday product with pizazz that was sort of 'in the know,'" Kampinsky said. "I think Dallas people are pretty glamorous, and we've got enough people in Dallas who are interesting and make good profiles."

Produced on heavier stock than the rest of the paper, the cover of each "High Profile" bore a half-page color photo of a local or a national personality with a connection to Texas. "High Profile" was an instant hit with the city's business and social leaders, who found themselves not just reading it but also vying to become the next face on its cover. Inside, the section—which often ran to thirty pages—included shorter profiles of big-name Dallasites as well as page after page of color photographs of Dallas' "Fête Set" at charity events.

Attractive local and national advertisements for top jewelers, clothes designers, and luxury boutiques filled out the pages. Burl knew the importance of advertising—which often accounted for 80 or 90 percent of a paper's revenue—as well as its appeal to readers. "Though some journalists don't like to admit it," he said, "advertising is news, too, for many people. In every readership survey, some people will tell you they read only the ads."

Burl realized that society news had always been big in Dallas and that readers still had a big appetite for it. As much as ever, Texans wanted to know what certain socialites wore to this luncheon or that black-tie event. Despite the society column's disappearance from the majority of large newspapers, it was afforded plenty of space and prominence in each "High Profile." Readers loved it.

Recalled one *Morning News* manager: "The *Times Herald* people thought 'High Profile' was bullshit. They knocked it and mocked it until they realized that people loved it. Then they launched their own answer to 'High Profile,' which wasn't very good. What they didn't understand is that they thought we were cutting feature space to put out 'High Profile,' when we were, in fact, adding space."

Burl often liked to include this anecdote in his speeches: "A retired *Dallas Morning News* circulation director recalled getting a complaint one day from a woman who said the paper had gotten too big. She had a small dog, and the paper had gotten so large the poor little fella couldn't drag it into the house anymore. A case, perhaps, of our tales dragging the dog. Anyway, the director says he responded to the woman saying, 'Lady, get a bigger dog.'"

Nikki Finke Greenberg, one of the main writers in "High Profile," was a Wellesley graduate who had worked at the AP bureaus in Moscow and London before Burl brought her to *The News*. Finke had the talent and brains, as well as the looks and style, to be a star, which is what Burl made her. "Burl liked me. He thought I was bright, and he liked smart women," she said. Finke became a household name in Dallas. "People couldn't get enough of Nikki," said Julia Sweeney, who ran a Dallas public relations firm at the time. "Everyone wanted to write like her and receive her cover of 'High Profile' assignments. She was very talented." Some jealousy from reporters in other sections of *The News* was directed toward Finke.

Decherd and Burl were unperturbed by the critics. In his book *Fresh Ink*, David Gelsanliter quoted Decherd on the subject:

> Burl looked at the data and said, "If we have a group of readers
> with such demographic characteristics and certain buying
> habits and social interests and they would respond to a news
> section that talks about their world, what's wrong with that?"
> Many editors would have backed off. They would have said, "I
> don't want to do that because I'm not comfortable in that world,"
> or, "I don't think that's a serious world." Well, this is Dallas, Texas,
> and to fail to acknowledge that world is to fail to recognize a part
> of our city.

Another key feature of Burl's plans as change agent was securing his old friend from Dayton, Ralph Langer, as managing editor for *The News*. The former photojournalist was then managing editor of *The Daily Herald* in Everett, Washington. His recollection was that "Burl said to me, 'I'm interested in hiring you as managing editor. Can you be here by 4:00 today to discuss it?'"

Langer didn't make it that afternoon, but he did fly to Dallas a few days later. "He said he wanted me to run the newsroom on a day-to-day basis, that I'd be in charge of hiring and firing." As Judith Garrett Segura wrote in her book, *Belo: From Newspapers to New Media*, "Ralph was the perfect foil for Burl. Burl had the foresight and imagination to know what needed to be done; Ralph had the equanimity and the insight to accomplish the task, day by day and step by step. The combination was powerful."

In Burl's own words, "If Ralph didn't exist, it would have been necessary to invent him."

Not long after his arrival on June 1, 1981, the six-foot-two Langer and the elfin Burl started being referred to as Mutt and Jeff behind their backs. They also had opposite temperaments. "I'm always the calmest person in the room" says Langer. No one would say that about Burl.

Langer recalled being at *The News* as exhilarating. "In those early days we were coming up with ideas and implementing them from dawn to dusk. Some days, when everyone else had left the office, Burl and I would call our wives and have them meet us for dinner somewhere, and the work conversation would continue late into the night. We were very tired, working very long hours. Burl had triple the competitiveness of a normal person."

Langer's friend John Brewer, with the AP's Seattle bureau, viewed hiring Langer as shrewd. "Ralph was a guy who was just as insightful as Burl but really knew how to do it on a day-to-day basis. The Burl I dealt with would throw out ideas, but you had to know how to implement them. Ralph could figure out how to do it. When I heard that Ralph was going to Dallas, it seemed like the perfect fit. Burl and Ralph were very different people, but they worked perfectly together."

Langer thought the paper was old-fashioned looking. One of his earliest jobs was to transform the morning daily into something graphically exciting. His goal: To wake up *The News*' readers with a jolt at least as strong as the coffee they drank while they read it.

Brewer said that one of Langer's strongest suits was his eye for aesthetics. "Ralph had modernized the heck out of the Everett *Herald*. He was one of the few editors I dealt with who really appreciated photos. He was using color. He knew how to use pictures. He was always ahead of the curve on photos and graphics. He knew how to do it and do it in a way that the staff loved him for it."

Under Langer's leadership, the art department made a concentrated effort to increase the use of maps, charts, diagrams, and sketches—as well as photographs—in order to both simplify and amplify the presentation of the news in the paper. This technique led to the presentation of significantly greater amounts of information in the same space, and it was more appealing to the eye.

Burl also had honed a critical eye for visuals as well as for words over the course of his career with the AP. One example of how passionate he was on the subject was his obsession with the newspaper's nameplate, or the flag—"*The Dallas Morning News*"—that appears across the top of each edition's front page. "Burl thought the flag could have looked neater," said Ed Kohorst, a design editor at *The News*. "He thought it looked messy." Consequently, Burl paid an outside artist $10,000 to adjust the letters ever so slightly—about a sixteenth of an inch—to rectify the imbalance. "The average reader never would have known the difference. But a visual artist in the business would have noticed it. And *Burl* noticed."

• • •

It didn't take Langer long to recognize the advantage of having the paper's owners on site, unlike at the *Times Herald*, whose owners were in Los Angeles. "If we needed more money for something, we were able to get an okay for it by 5:00 p.m." Langer said he and Burl were not constrained by a budget the first few years. "Certainly, in those first few years, I don't think there was anything we really wanted to do that we couldn't."

In fact, the editorial department did have a budget, acknowledged Decherd, but it speaks volumes that Langer's perception today is that there wasn't one.

One day soon after arriving in Dallas, Langer went with columnists Bob St. John and John Anders to Louie's bar on Lower Greenville Avenue, which was another popular watering hole among journalists. Langer was shocked at what he saw. "There was a table with *Morning News'* and *Herald's* people, and they were all interlocked, all talking freely about the stories they were working on. One reporter would say to the other, 'Oh, I just had a meeting with so-and-so,' or another person would say, 'I'm going to Chicago tomorrow to cover this that's happening.'" Langer listened and watched, incredulous that *News'* reporters shared their stories with the competition.

The next day at the paper, he called a meeting of reporters. "I told them, 'You can't do this! We're in a newspaper war! The *Times Herald*'s people are your competitors! When this war is over, there's going to be one dominant paper!'"

27

Sports Day

On May 27, 1981, *The Dallas Morning News* ran the announcement, "News editor Burl Osborne elected VP." In addition to his duties directing all news-gathering functions as the paper's executive editor, Burl had new responsibilities as one of the newspaper's seven officers.

The next month, in came Smith, who would put in motion the ideas for a revamped sports section that he, Burl, and Decherd had discussed the previous fall.

"It is a fact. Sports will build circulation and advertising. Therefore, we should have the best sports section we can have to make a profit. The sports editor is the most crucial position in the newsroom," Burl said. And, unlike American business, which was centered in New York, or politics, centered in Washington, sports were not confined to one locale. "Sports isn't locked in like the others. If you have a mix of professional sports, good college programs, high school sports, and the rest, you can be anywhere and compete to be the best." Dallas had all of those and then some.

Smith jumped into a seeming hornet's nest straightaway. The paper's top columnist was Skip Bayless, hired by *The News* in 1977 to cover sports. In recounting the backstory, Burl said, "We felt we could build an identity for Skip— create a star, so to speak." That "star-building," as Dwight Chapin would later write in "Some Sportswriters Make Bucks As Well As Waves" (*San Francisco Examiner*, May 7, 1982), included "billboards and bus ads of Bayless moving around Big D in his jogging suit." (No stranger to weight rooms or the omnipresent paparazzi, the photogenic Bayless was tailor made for the role.) "But he helped himself more by his writing style, which included some irreverent looks at America's (and Dallas') team, the Cowboys." The National Sportscasters and Sportswriters Association voted Bayless Texas Sportswriter of the Year in 1979.

"When Bayless' readership figures began approaching those of *Times Herald* 23-year-veteran sports columnist Blackie Sherrod, the *Times Herald* offered him a Texas-sized contract to jump teams," wrote Chapin. "Which he did, after sundry offers and counteroffers and items Bayless said he'd 'like to get' (such as a car, country-club membership and stock options) had been tossed around."

To replace Bayless, Smith promoted two first-rate in-house writers to become full-time columnists: Randy Galloway and David Casstevens. As Vince Doria, who succeeded Smith at *The Boston Globe*, told *D Magazine*, "With Dave, it's the product more than the people."

There wasn't major turnover, but Smith did move forward quickly to hire the best sportswriters he could find from across the country. "Good was no longer acceptable. We wanted the best out of our staff. Our feeling was either you show that you can perform at a much higher level or we will find people who can."

In his first months at *The News*, Smith also instigated "doubling coverage of high school sports, Southwestern Conference football, and hunting and fishing," wrote Gelsanliter in *Fresh Ink*. "And he started giving year-round coverage to local golf tournaments, bowling, horse racing, rodeo, and cycling events."

Smith was full of ideas for the section and often ran them by Burl, who basically gave him carte blanche.

> There were probably a couple of situations where he thought that something I suggested might not work, but most of the time he'd just say, "Okay, let's go ahead and try it."
>
> Very seldom did he say, "Pare down the budget." When I presented him with my budget—as long as I could make a case for it—he never hassled me. Burl's greatest strength was that he could get whatever resources we needed to do the job. To be the best, you had to pay money to get the best, and we did.
>
> Burl's visions were not limited. He was a risk taker. He was also a great leader, one of those generals you serve under whom you're happy to be serving under.

On July 16, 1981, *The Dallas Morning News* launched "Sports Day." Burl was so excited the first day it featured in the paper that he stood by in the pressroom as the sports pages came off the presses.

Burl's love of sports was both professional and personal. Both Burl and his son, Jonathan, were "fans of the Dallas Cowboys, always," Betty said. And Jonathan and Burl spent many hours shooting hoops in front of the garage. "I can still see Burl in his dress shirt and shoes shooting hoops with Jonathan," Betty recalled. "Burl would pull into the garage after work and immediately join Jonathan without changing his clothes. They would shoot and I would cook."

In Smith's first year, "Sports Day" developed into an editorial mix of news, feature stories, commentary, statistics, and trivia, enough to "fix any sports junkie," wrote *Adweek*. His approach to grabbing die-hard as well as casual readers was to pack the "Sports Day" section with articles ranging from how many points a high school neighbor scored—in basketball, baseball, football, soccer—to world records broken by downhill skiers in France.

But even the enthusiasm of sports fanatics has its limits. "How many papers we sold on Monday during Cowboys season had to do with how well the Cowboys did," Smith said. "If the Cowboys won on Sunday, we'd sell 10,000 to 20,000 more newspapers on Monday. If the Cowboys lost, there were very few extra sales. People didn't want to read about them losing."

Burl's commitment to building a great sports department never wavered, and he firmly believed it would yield dividends for other parts of the newspaper. Smith ultimately oversaw thirty writers, five editors, and fifteen copy desk staff.

Burl introduced yet another initiative that maximized the popularity of sports and the riveting photographs of the professional athletes who played them. As his first anniversary at *The News* approached, he began to drill the idea of creating a special Sunday edition—known in the industry as the "bulldog edition"—into the heads of staffers.

The first part of the allotted Sunday print run would go on sale in the city's stores and kiosks at noon on the preceding Saturday. One of the bulldog's attractions was its larger photos. Those would give way to words for the A, metro, state, and sports sections that were updated for the remainder of the print run that was available early Sunday morning. (The *Times Herald* would copy this strategy and introduce their bulldog edition four years later.)

"Burl basically wore everyone out mentally and physically with the prototype project and finally getting it out," Swindle, a projects reporter, said. "Some enterprising editor printed up a whole bunch of T-shirts with a likeness of Burl, but it had bulldog ears and a bulldog body. On the maiden voyage, all staff members showed up wearing the shirts. This had a good morale effect on the staff. It made us feel like here was an imaginative, creative editor who was going to bring something to *The News* no one had thought of or suggested before."

Thereafter, staff affectionately referred to their boss as "Burldog" (when they weren't still—albeit rarely—calling him Little General out of frustration or pique).

"Burldog" t-shirt (Credit: 1981 *Morning News'* staff, photo David Woo)

• • •

The hotly contested tug-of-war between *The Dallas Morning News* and the *Dallas Times Herald* became a national curiosity over the summer months.

The June 1, 1981, issue of *Newsweek* featured "The Battle of Dallas," coauthored by satirist Lewis Grossberger and then–Houston Bureau Chief Stryker McGuire. They viewed the competition as something good for both papers. "In Texas, where men are men and newspapers are awful, it is a refreshing spectacle."

After describing at length Burl's arrival at *The News* and Editor Ken Johnson's at the *Times Herald*, the story concluded: "But winning the battle of Dallas is not enough for either paper. Not even dominating that state is enough. . . . As Johnson puts it, 'There is no regional voice in the Southwest now. Our goal is to become that regional newspaper.'"

Just a few months later, the September 7, 1981, issue of *Time* included an article headlined "Shootout in the Big D" by the weekly's Senior Writer Janice Castro: "Few American cities nowadays can boast two thriving newspapers. As a result, old-fashioned journalistic competition is practically a thing of the past. Gone are the days when rival dailies would scramble to beat one another on every story, raid newsrooms across the land for talent, open new out-of-town bureaus like bottles of beer, and in the process keep getting livelier and better. Dallas is a notable exception to that woeful rule. "

It was generally believed at both *The News* and the *Times Herald* that the paper with more bureaus in important cities would have the edge—certainly in terms of image and prestige, if not coverage. The competition to open first was tough. For example, the *Times Herald* announced that it would place reporters in New York City, a Central American city, Toronto, and seven additional Texas cities. Its theater critic would begin to review the arts from all over the nation, and its top local columnist would become a roving national reporter. At its height, the *Times Herald* intended to have eighteen bureaus and two roving correspondents.

The News, in a counterstroke, began opening its own bureaus nationwide. Eventually, those bureaus would include, among others, Washington; several new ones in Texas' cities (Tyler, for instance); more coverage in Mexico City, Central America, Houston, and Austin; new ones in Toronto, New York, Oklahoma City (to cover stories for Texas' residents from Oklahoma), Tel Aviv, and San Antonio; and budget commitments for bureaus in El Paso and eastern Texas. *The News* would even eventually open a bureau in Cuba, joining only three other such papers to do so.

Once, in a speech to news editors, Burl showed slides on a large screen of the places where *The News* had opened bureaus. Then he showed a slide of a tall chest of drawers, and quipped, "This is the *Times Herald*'s bureau."

• • •

One day when he passed Langer's desk, Burl noticed a letter from popular advice columnist Ann Landers. Burl inquired about the letter, and Langer explained that he had met her in Dayton and the two of them had instantly hit it off. "She liked me, and she said, 'I'm going to keep an eye on you.' So she wrote me letters from time to time." Burl asked Langer to call her and see whether she'd be willing to move from the *Times Herald*—which published both the syndicated "Ask Ann Landers" and her twin sister's "Dear Abby" columns. Langer called Landers, she called the syndicate, and the next thing fans knew, their favorite agony aunt had moved to *The News. The News'* marketing staff, of course, wasted no time in publishing their own clever ad to proclaim, "Someone gave Ann Landers some great advice."

• • •

Burl leaned on his past experience in that first year, implementing his plan to reshape the paper, to move it from dull to compelling:

> We have tried to take a newspaper that was quite good to begin with and create a reader's newspaper. We have tried to organize the newspaper to make the sections and various features easier to find and easier to read. We have packaged foreign and national and state and regional news and anchored more features. We have cleaned up the look of the newspaper, but the greater part of our energy has been spent on content.
>
> Basically, we simply put into practice the principles I learned over my twenty years with the AP. The news product must be fair, accurate, balanced, and straightforward, presented as objectively as can be managed. The quality of the content is the foundation for everything else that happens.

28

The Soul of Dallas

The Dallas Morning News had developed a deeper understanding of Dallas than the *Times Herald* had. Burl in particular, *Adweek* wrote, "had a more sensitive finger on the pulse of the city." Burl's strategy was to build on that insight as well as on the paper's historical ties to the community, as he outlined to the Dallas Chamber of Commerce in the spring of 1982:

> It would be very difficult to separate *The Dallas Morning News* from the soul of Dallas.
>
> We certainly watch over and report on the institutions of Dallas. At the same time, *The News is* a Dallas institution. The A. H. Belo Corporation, which publishes *The News*, is the oldest business in Texas. *The News* is, to borrow from a TV commercial, "the National Newspaper of Texas."
>
> That is a fine reputation, and we're glad to have it. But that kind of tradition imposes on us . . . the responsibility to look out for the interests of the entire community as well as our own narrow business interests.

• • •

The principles Burl carried with him from the AP were unimpeachable, but some of the rules he clung to from his time there made crafting more dynamic and compelling stories difficult to achieve. Nothing was more annoying to the staff, for instance, than his edict that everything written must be attributed.

"It was hard to make your story flow when you had to end every sentence with the words 'he said' or 'she said,'" recalled Jeannette Keton, a City Desk reporter at *The News*, in the early 1980s. "At *The News* every single thing had to be attributed to a source, and it got in the way of creative writing. The editors were real sticklers for that. If you didn't do it, the editors would call you out on it." That was much less the case at the *Times Herald*, where many stories appeared in the paper exactly as the reporters wrote them, often with very little attribution.

Related to the attribution rule was Burl's insistence that the simple, definitive verb "said" was always preferable to an equivocal or judgmental one such as "claimed" or "insisted" or "admitted."

With neither time nor mandate as executive editor to oversee their day-to-day copy, Burl asked Langer to hire a writing coach. After all, Burl reasoned, along his own career path with the AP he had learned from the writing experts they employed; why shouldn't *The News* have at least one?

Langer's first hire to reverse the unevenness and inconsistency Burl observed in the reporters' styles was Paula LaRocque. She joined *The News* as assistant managing editor and writing coach in the fall of 1981. For the ten years prior, she had taught technical communication at Western Michigan University's School of Engineering and journalism at Texas A&M, Southern Methodist, and Texas Christian. Smart, funny, and talented, she nonetheless faced a formidable challenge. "A lot of people turned up their noses at the mere idea of a writing coach," said a former *News* reporter. "The feeling was that if you were good enough to be hired by *The News*, a major metropolitan daily, you didn't need a lot of coaching on your writing. There also was the problem of tight deadlines. If you had time to run something by Paula before your deadline, then good for you, but most reporters didn't have that luxury."

In time, LaRocque not only implemented the AP style manual but also helped to localize and expand it. Now and again she put out an entertaining newsletter called "F.Y.I." in which she critiqued reporters' stories and headlines and gave advice on both how to write a catchy lead and how to avoid clichés. As Gelsanliter wrote in *Fresh Ink*, LaRocque's dictums were far flung and far reaching. Among the many warnings she issued were:

- Avoid writing sentences longer than twenty-three words, max.
- Ask for a graphic or a bar chart to complement a story that cites numbers or statistics.

- Keep it simple; if you can't boil down your explanation of a term/subject (as in "credit crunch"), don't write about it.
- Guard against the elevated tone that's often generated in telling big stories.
- Expunge clichés from your copy, as with "firestorm of criticism," "window of opportunity," "critical mass," and "laundry list."
- Eschew judgmental verbs such as "concede," "contend," and "vow."
- Never use words in headlines that present stereotypes or are sensational. (The examples Gelsanliter cited were priceless: "AA member charged in traffic deaths," "High school dropout held in sexual abuse case," "Ex-Marine goes on shooting spree," and "Baptist slays family, self.")

LaRoque also set up an in-house cross-fertilization program whereby veteran reporters and columnists mentored others who wanted or needed to add to their writer's notebooks of tips and tricks of the trade.

As Langer told Gelsanliter, "We have been long accused of being too colorless or boring because of a policy of avoiding pejoratives or stereotyping adjectives. Yet if anything has brought us as far as we've come, it's the perception that we're neutral, that we don't choose up sides, that we don't have a smartass, patronizing attitude. A reporter doesn't have to be weird to be creative."

Eventually, the newsroom staff did start knocking on LaRocque's door, and they continued to do so for twenty years.

Bill Cox, who was *The News'* senior vice president of operations and administration, observed that Burl inherited a news staff that was, on a scale of one to ten, about a five. "Over a period of about a year and a half, he recruited top-notch talent so that the staff became a nine or ten on a zero-to-ten scale. He also applied his common sense rule that every replacement result in an upgrading of every position.

"He had an unusual talent in mixing journalism with a business plan. A lot of journalists have tunnel vision, and money isn't on their radar. But that wasn't the case with Burl. He was always focused on journalism, but he also knew that he needed the resources."

"A good newspaper is also a good business," Burl said. "It needs to make a profit, and it needs to be solvent. It needs to be a going business concern, or else it will not have the resources to carry out its public service responsibilities. . . News is where the newspaper begins. Advertising pays the bills."

Cox valued one of Burl's managerial tactics in particular. "Burl would meet every day at 10:00 a.m. with the company's officers: the ad guy, the circulation person, news, and marketing. This meeting every single day was one of the practices by Burl that paid a great dividend. We were all on the same page."

A few years later, Burl elaborated on the value of that meeting.

> Everyone who is going to have a role in executing whatever strategy we agree upon, number one, must understand it, number two, subscribe to it, and, number three, participate enthusiastically in executing it. That requires that we talk to each other. We have to know each other quite well. One of the ways that we attempt to do that is to require attendance at an officers' meeting every day for those who are in town. And we meet maybe for five minutes if nothing much is happening. It may be for five hours if we have a major issue to decide or discuss. And we try to tell each other what we're up to.
>
> So, for example, if there is a production problem that caused circulation to be late the previous night, everyone understands that and understands why the phones are ringing. If the news department has a major project that it proposes to publish the next morning, then circulation can be aware of that to order extra newspapers, promotion can be aware of it in order to make the proper arrangements for perhaps radio or other promotion.

Leubsdorf said: "He had a lot of good ideas, but he needed someone by his side to say, 'I'm not sure that's a good idea.' At times he would call me up and say, 'Someone here at the paper wants such and such,' and I could tell immediately who that someone was. It was Burl. My standing was good enough that I could say no to him."

After Congress passed President Reagan's first budget cuts and tax cuts, the president delivered a second speech to Congress calling for a second round of tax cuts. In a column analyzing that speech, Leubsdorf predicted that financial markets would not react well. Burl immediately called *The News'* bureau chief in Washington and asked whether he thought he had gone too far in his prediction.

"I told him the markets were down about two hundred points, which was a lot in those days," Leubsdorf said. "Never again did he call me about a story."

29

War of the Words

Burl and Betty were invited to a state dinner at the White House on May 21, 1981, in honor of German Chancellor Helmut Schmidt. This would be the first state dinner following the assassination attempt on President Reagan's life.

"Burl and I were so excited to be going, but we were a bit nervous," Betty said. The protocol classes the couple had taken in their D.C. days would finally be useful. Burl requested an advance copy of the dinner's guest list, which he and Betty studied carefully. "We wanted to know who would be there so we could brush up on current events."

Seated next to movie producer Armand Deutsch, a longtime friend of Ronald and Nancy Reagan, Betty remembered momentarily being intimidated—not by her dinner companion but by the elaborate place setting in front of her. "There were so many pieces of silverware, at least six on each side of the dinner plate." Deutsch, noting Betty's uncertainty, put his hand on the table, looked her in the eye, looked back down at the silverware, and exclaimed, "Sweetheart, we can handle this!"

"After that," recalled Betty, "I completely relaxed and had a great time. After all, I was a graduate of Helen Williams' 'class class.'"

Also at Betty's table was Lawrence Eagleburger, a career diplomat who later briefly served as Secretary of State under George H. W. Bush. Betty wanted to keep her place card and menu as mementos and struggled to fit them into her small evening bag. Eagleburger slid them inside his tuxedo jacket and promised, "I will mail them to you," which he did.

Seated next to Betty for the after-dinner entertainment was actor Efrem Zimbalist Jr., looking like he'd just walked off the set of *The F.B.I.* At the end of the performance by the Juilliard String Quartet, Zimbalist grabbed her by the shoulders and exclaimed, "Doesn't this make you proud to be an American!" Betty found the entire evening "unforgettable."

• • •

Burl's "hire the best at any cost" approach to securing top-notch talent for *The News* got yet another boost in January 1982 when a Dallas native, Bill DeOre, signed on with the paper as a political cartoonist. Burl described DeOre as having "an incisive wit" and being "one of the finest young editorial cartoonists in the country today."

The self-taught political satirist read five newspapers every day, plus all the news magazines, for what he called "a well-rounded flow of information." DeOre's goal was—to him—plain and simple. "I just like to kick holes in just about anything I think is wrong."

That attitude offended Burl's sensibilities somewhat, and he preferred when DeOre's cartoons didn't "cut or bite or hurt someone." As he pounded into the heads of news writers and editors alike, "When we're trying to be reflective of the total community, we don't contribute anything by screaming and shouting. It's hard to persuade someone who is thoroughly pissed off at you." Nonetheless, Burl gave DeOre free rein as long as he kept his images or captions from being "bawdy."

• • •

In an April issue of *Texas Monthly* headlined "War of the Words," Peter Applebome wrote about the rivalry between *The News* and the *Times Herald*. He quoted Rone Tempest, a former metropolitan editor at the *Times Herald*. "I know both papers, especially the *Herald*, used to feel they could just go in there and wipe the other guys out. I don't think anyone realized what a protracted war this was going to be."

Decherd was pleased with the direction the paper was headed. As Thanksgiving approached, he promoted Burl again, to senior vice president and editor.

Decherd wrote to Burl, "It has been a thrill to watch you meet every challenge successfully and earn the greater responsibilities which have been given to you. I know this will not be the last congratulatory letter I write. We are counting on you."

Along with their boss, a healthy mix of the talent Burl recruited or retained were promoted too:

- Managing Editor Ralph Langer would become executive editor;
- Sports Editor Dave Smith would oversee not just sports but all art and photography;
- Washington D.C. Bureau Chief Carl Leubsdorf would assume additional news department management and planning duties as an assistant managing editor; and
- Projects Editor Bob Mong would oversee the state, metropolitan, and business sections.

30

Are You Trying to Destroy Each Other?

On March 18, 1983, Burl and *Dallas Times Herald* chairman and CEO Lee Guittar appeared together on *Good Morning America*, hosted by David Hartman.

As the face of *The Dallas Morning News* to the public in general and reporters in particular, Burl did not shy away from publicity. On the contrary, he encouraged it. He would do just about anything that would sell papers.

DAVID HARTMAN: Lee, besides doing things like reducing ad rates, maybe trying to take reporters away, or having the other paper do that to you, has there been anything this paper, *The Morning News*, has done that has really griped you?

LEE GUITTAR: Well, David, I think the easy way to say it is that until General Osborne got there some years ago, we kinda had the turf. We were the ones who were innovating and moving out to improve, and they were kind of copying us. Since Burl has been there, he's done some things, and we've had to move to counter him. But nothing that gripes me. The rhetoric in this so-called war sometimes outstrips the battle. One thing I will say: I think there will be two papers in Dallas for a long, long time . . . ten years. Beyond that, I'd be hard pressed to predict what will happen.

HARTMAN: What are you trying to do? Are you trying to destroy each other, honestly? Trying to knock the other paper off?

BURL OSBORNE: Absolutely not. We're not trying to run anybody out of town. We're trying to serve the people who live in Dallas, the people who are coming there, the 50,000 or so a year who move to the Dallas–Fort Worth area. Everything we do is designed to align our newspaper with the needs and interests of the people who live there. If that gives us supremacy and we believe we are the dominant newspaper, we think there are objective measures to show that—so be it. But our objective is not to run somebody off.

• • •

In the mid-1980s, at a time when the overwhelming majority of editorial pages at major daily newspapers in America were run by men, Burl promoted Rena Pederson to editorial page editor of *The News*. At the time, there were only men's rooms on the editorial floor. Burl immediately had one converted to a ladies' room.

"Burl was progressive for his era, and being married to a strong woman probably contributed to that," said Pederson. Prior to becoming editorial page editor, she had covered the federal beat and city hall and been both a feature writer and the first woman writer for the editorial page.

"Being a woman, I was an anomaly running the page. Across the country, there was Meg Greenfield [at *The Washington Post*] and maybe one other woman on a large paper, and that was it," Pederson said.

Ever since George Dealey purchased the paper in 1926, his intention was "to ally the paper with the interest of the city," wrote Peter Elkind for *Texas Monthly*. "The advancement of Dallas is the advancement of *The News*. The one is inseparable from the other." The paper's opinion pieces and news columns had historically conveyed Dealey's campaigns for civic improvement, making *The News* the voice of the Dallas establishment. Notable among the developments he promoted for Dallas were that a city planner be hired; it be selected as a location for the Federal Reserve Bank; Southern Methodist University be built there; and it be home to the Texas state fairgrounds. One civic act stood above all others, though: Dealey was respected and remembered for his courageous fight against and crippling of the Ku Klux Klan in Texas.

Prior to Burl's arrival in Dallas, the editorial page had focused on national issues; by the mid-1980s, the page had increasingly returned to its roots and looked at state and local issues. "I think we did the most thorough job in the state on issues like school finance and water reform; we considered ourselves the state paper. That brought more readers because we became influential on state issues. People in the business community recognized that. If we had three editorials on the page, one was always local. That's what the business community wanted."

As to political leanings and cultural values, the editorial page changed quite a bit after Burl arrived, but it was done "very deliberately," said Pederson.

> It was an incremental effort to move the paper to a reasonable center, what I called pragmatic conservatism. There was an old dictum that said your paper should never be more than 20 percent ahead of your audience or 20 percent behind your audience. We moved very gradually. The page was still conservative, but we hoped to address things with a changed tone. We introduced new subjects like child abuse, and we did a big series on West Dallas, historically one of the poorest, most overlooked parts of the city. We went door to door and interviewed people in their homes. We would say, "We're editorial writers and we want to know about your lives." It was path breaking for its time.

Pederson was "almost" always grateful when Burl suggested a topic for the editorial page, and she "never" felt that he was imposing his opinions on the page. "He had a very good news sense. He was a very smart man. If he made a suggestion for the page, it was usually a helpful one, or one we appreciated."

As senior vice president and editor, Burl had oversight responsibility for the editorial page and the op-ed page, which *The News* called the viewpoint page. He described his views on editorials at some length during an interview in the late 1980s.

> If the news content of a newspaper is the body of the paper, I suppose the editorial page and the editorials represent the soul. The editorial page is where the institution is able to articulate its view of the world in which it lives. . . . I think it is fair to say that the editorial page of *The Morning News* is the most influential in the southwest in terms of the respect given it by leaders of government and business and the other institutions that make up the fabric of our society.
>
> For more than a century now, readers and leaders have come to expect us to take a reasoned, well-articulated, clearly

expressed view of the issues that are paramount at the time. That has reflected itself over the years in everything from the concept of city planning seventy-five years ago to the concept today of planning for the next millennium. And everyone in the newspaper is conscious of the opportunity to capitalize on that wonderful tradition but also the responsibility that goes with it to be extremely careful, to make sure that our positions are well thought out. And that they are articulated in a way that will not drive off more people than we are able to persuade through our point of view.

Although real estate, manufacturing, and health care had buoyed the Dallas economy through a nationwide recession in the early 1980s, it struggled in the latter part of the decade. Oil prices plunged, the real estate bubble burst, home prices collapsed, and a series of major banks—which had heavily invested in oil and real estate—went under. "By 1988, the toxicity of the depression had had time to settle deep into every square inch of dirt in the state," *D Magazine* wrote.

"Real estate, oil, and banks all toppled at the same time," Pederson recalled. Amid this economic downturn, Burl came up with a plan called Get Dallas Moving.

"He wanted us to come up with some ideas on how we can revive the city," Pederson said. "So we really worked on it and came up with the ideas for a new international center downtown, redoing Farmers Market, creating Dallas Area Rapid Transit, expanding community colleges, and completing the arts district downtown. There were a lot of things that could be done to get Dallas moving, and most of it got done."

When asked about Burl's politics, Pederson came as close as any of Burl's friends, family, or business associates to naming them. She had the feeling that "Burl wasn't heavily ideological, but he was moderate to left. But he knew where our audience was."

Most people, when asked for this book, seemed unsure and merely speculated. Longtime friend and Dallas entrepreneur Richard H. Collins, a libertarian with strong ties to the Republican Party, doesn't claim to know Burl's politics. "My guess is that he would have been center right. Growing up in coal country, he probably thought government could help people, but he was probably skeptical about whether government could do a good job. That's just my guess."

Either way, he was more liberal than the views expressed on the editorial page, said Pederson, and that was uncomfortable for him. "In 1988, he wanted the paper to endorse Dick Gephardt in the Democratic primary, and I think I said to him, 'If we do that, half of our subscription base will have a cardiac.'" She and Burl had a serious discussion about whether to endorse the liberal candidate. She was strongly against it. "We sat there for several minutes in silence, and then he said, 'Well, you're probably right.' I think we ended up endorsing Al Gore in the Democratic primary."

Pederson and Cheryl Hall were only two of many women whom Burl either promoted at *The News* or strongly admired in his daily life. Laurey Peat, who runs a successful Dallas public relations firm, became a good friend of Burl's in the 1980s and remained a close friend throughout his life. She appreciated Burl because he took her seriously in a way that not all successful men did.

"Burl loved smart women," Peat said. "He was always very respectful of women. His mother must have been a big influence in that area."

Charlotte St. Martin was an executive at the Anatole Hotel in the 1980s, with a long list of accomplishments (she would be featured on the cover of "High Profile"). She said Burl intuitively understood how to treat women executives, even though there were not that many women in business in those days. "He was particularly supportive of me and at the same time tough," St. Martin said. "We would talk business and politics and strategy. He never once said to me, 'Don't worry your pretty little head.' He was one of the most supportive men I've met in my career."

31

Put the Top Down and Go!

Six months after Burl's appearance on *Good Morning America*, *The News* announced that for the first time in its history, it had overtaken the *Times Herald* in Dallas County circulation. *The News* had a record total circulation of 335,000 daily and 417,000 on Sundays. This gave *The News* a total daily lead of 66,000 and a Sunday lead of 56,000—the largest leads, both daily and Sunday, in the paper's history.

Jeremy L. Halbreich, then *The News'* senior vice president, was quoted in the press release:

> Our ascendancy as the daily circulation leader in Dallas County will serve to reinforce the decision Dallas advertisers have already made to place the majority of their advertising in *The Dallas Morning News*.

As Burl saw it, "The fact is that improved results in advertising generate more advertising, which generates more readership, which generates more advertising."

On November 21, 1983, it was announced that beloved *Times Herald* sports columnist and editor Blackie Sherrod would join *The News* the following year.

The news of Sherrod's defection hit *Times Herald* staffers like a slap in the face. The "dean of sports columnists in Texas," he was a legend; he was the biggest star among a cast of star columnists at the paper. A longtime *Times Herald* reporter recalled just how low staff morale fell when he left. "Looking back, that was the first really, really bad sign for the *Herald*. When Blackie went to *The News*, you couldn't quantify what it meant in terms of newspapers sold, but that wasn't the point. What we all felt was the psychological impact.

We were getting beaten, and we were going to lose the war. Blackie's leaving represented something monumental, and it really depressed a lot of people."

His leaving caught the attention of the national press. A December article in *Newsweek* reported, "Sherrod's announcement last month that he was defecting to the rival *Dallas Morning News* for a five-year contract reportedly worth $750,000 sent a shock through the *Times Herald*'s already demoralized newsroom—a tremor felt as far away as Los Angeles, home of the parent Times Mirror Co."

• • •

Alan Peppard, who was *The News'* society columnist, remembered seeing Burl's Mercedes in *The News'* parking lot.

The company selected cars for *News* executives with certain specifications—it had to be four-door, an automatic, etc.—that Decherd dubbed "FBI cars," but Burl refused to drive his. "Belo gave out company cars that were on the level of a Ford Taurus. But Burl's preference was for street-legal race cars."

Burl decided to play a trick on Moroney. Burl borrowed a Rolls-Royce from a friend and had the newspaper's art department make a license plate that read "DMN – BO," which they attached to the front of the car. The staged car sitting in the executive parking lot brought all the laughs Burl expected. Besides, the car *did* fit many of the specifications. Nowhere did it say that the car *couldn't* be a Rolls-Royce.

"For Burl to challenge the deeply embedded culture at Belo in this way, well, he was openly defying the power structure," Peppard said.

"All of this made perfect sense the more you were with Burl," Decherd later said. "He wanted to live every day for all it had to give and be totally engaged in activities and relationships that mattered. His clothes said, 'Let's dial up the energy level.' His cars said, 'I never thought I could afford one of these, and I don't know how long I'll be around to drive it, so let's put down the top and go! And by the way, if you judge me for owning the car, you don't know me.'"

Burl took pains to be suitably attired at the wheel of his luxury convertible. He had cared about stylish clothes his entire adult life, not only wearing them but also shopping for them. Burl loved colorful striped Turnbull & Asser shirts with white collars and white French cuffs. How convenient that *The News'* building was just down the street from Neiman Marcus's downtown store. The salesclerks knew his size and preferences and would hold shirts for him they thought he would like.

Yet another interest Burl cultivated in Dallas was a taste for fine wine. In 1985, *The Dallas Morning News* held its first-ever national wine competition. Becky Murphy, a local sommelier and brainchild behind the competition, launched the event, which attracted 570 entries from nine states.

Murphy recalled, "It all started because I met Burl and he said, 'I think there might be somebody at *The News* who might be interested in sponsoring a wine competition.'" That somebody, of course, was Burl.

It wasn't long before the newspaper's wine competition "became Burl's baby," Murphy said. "It wouldn't have been what it was without Burl's help. *The News* got behind the competition in a big way." Burl "was always making suggestions about what we needed to make the competition better."

Burl not only had his own private wine collection but also loved going out to dinner and savoring new vintages. One of his favorite restaurants in the city was the Mansion on Turtle Creek, which he liked both for its extensive wine list and its chef, Dean Fearing, who became nationally known in the 1980s for his southwestern cuisine. Fearing recalled the night he came out from the kitchen to greet guests in the mansion's dining room and talked to Burl for the first time.

> Burl was there with people from *The Washington Post* or *The New York Times*, and he said to me, "Do you know where I'm from?" I didn't know, of course. And then he told me he was from Ashland. He had read in a profile about me that I was from Ashland.
>
> After that, Burl would bring bigwigs into the mansion, and I'd come out to say hello to him, and Burl would say to everyone at the table, "Dean and I are both from the spit town of Ashland, Kentucky." He loved saying that.

32

East Meets West

Burl began 1984 by taking a sabbatical of sorts, enrolling in Harvard University's Advanced Management Program. He would be away from *The News*, and Betty, for thirteen weeks.

Burl's time in Boston overlapped with their tenth wedding anniversary, so Betty flew to Boston to see him. He gave her a ring and a card with a snowy Christmas scene at Faneuil Hall on it, writing:

Dear Betty—This may be an unusual way to wish you a Happy Anniversary and Happy Valentine's Day.

It isn't the right day yet—this really isn't an Anniversary card—or a Valentine's Day card—and you haven't even seen the scene on the front. And it surely isn't Christmas time, as the Santa Claus would suggest.

But—I don't remember a Christmas where I waited as anxiously as I have for the past few days. It seems like Christmas Eve to me.

Betty, I want you to know that these have been the best ten (and a few more) years of my life—only because you made it so. Jonathan has only made my life better and fuller.

Despite the schedule here, there is time, late at night, to think about values other than business and career, I return to one, every night. That is simply this: I love you, and Jonathan, more than I thought possible. I'll do whatever I can, as imperfectly as I usually do things, to cause you to love me back.

Happy Anniversary
   with love
   Burl
   2-10-84

Burl relished the academic environment. He would later write to a friend, "I was off at Harvard for a three-month course on how to run a business. I went up there with the answers and came back with the questions." Unlike the AP, which declined to reimburse Burl for his studies at Long Island University, *The News* was more than happy to pick up the cost of tuition.

Shortly after completing the program, he would also finally earn his MBA. When he'd accepted the editorship at *The Dallas Morning News* in the fall of 1980, the directors of the MBA program at Long Island University at Mercy had worked out a distance-learning program for him to complete the fall semester class requirements, as they had for Betty. Burl had then enrolled at the University of Dallas in Irving, Texas, in their similar MBA program for working executives to complete the work, which he did over the next few years.

His master's thesis essentially described his philosophy for the newspaper as a whole:

> The tone of *The News* is by design, restrained, calm, informative, useful and . . . friendly. Extreme care for fairness and balance is required. *The News*, as a morning paper, frequently is in front of its readers before they have shed their pajamas or have that first cup of coffee. It is not a time to scream. Every article is subjected to a series of tests. Is it fair? Does anyone need or want to know this? Is it clear? Have we presented this information in the easiest-to-understand way? Is it balanced? Is there appropriate context, the paragraph that explains why this is important? Is it accurate in every detail?
>
> *The News* is a "reader's paper" . . . placing the needs and interests of both reporters and editors second to those of readers.

• • •

Burl joined the American Society of Newspaper Editors (ASNE) and enthusiastically got involved in association work. The more editors he met at other newspapers—and the more that people became familiar with *The News*—the more likely it was that *The News* would gain national recognition and prestige.

He participated in a first-of-its-kind exchange program between the ASNE and journalists from the Soviet Union. Eleven members from the U.S.S.R. Union of Journalists arrived in Washington, D.C., on June 25 to begin their ten-day itinerary, which included meetings with U.S. government officials and media representatives in Washington and New York City and a July Fourth one-day conference with a similar delegation from ASNE. The day before, Secretary of State George P. Shultz gave a speech indicating a "Soviet link" to international terrorism, saying, "The Soviets use terrorist groups for their own purposes." Claiming insult, the head of the Russian delegation canceled the meeting with Shultz and worked to publicize his complaint in the American media.

Burl wrote a column that captured those events, and it ran on *The News'* editorial page on July 7. Headlined "East Meets West," it concluded:

> The American editors suggested that, in similar circumstances, U.S. reporters would have kept the appointment and used it as an opportunity to ask further questions about the speech. They explained that, in America, reporters are supposed to report in a fair and balanced way on what the government does. The Russian journalists, noting they all were members of the Communist Party, suggested that they set their priorities otherwise; that their duty to advance the state's propaganda has a higher priority than any journalistic responsibility.
>
> The Americans did not accept the Russian notion of how news media ought to perform, or dismissal of the watchdog role traditionally performed by the U.S. press. The Soviet visitors did not accept the American concept. No minds were changed. The editors parted with slightly increased knowledge of each other; increased understanding will be an uphill but worthwhile struggle.

• • •

In 1984, Michael Jackson performed in nearby Irving, Texas, for more than 118,000 in the Dallas area as part of his Victory Tour. His latest album, *Thriller*, released in 1982, was a certified phenomenon, having sat at number one on the Billboard charts for thirty-seven weeks.

In Dallas, the tour would make news beyond the stage—and Burl and *The News* would be at the center of the story.

Jackson and his five brothers had checked in to the Loews Anatole Hotel. *Dallas Morning News* Reporter Donna O'Neal interviewed guests as well as hotel employees—including maids on the floor where the Jacksons were staying.

As she was leaving the floor, O'Neal said the hotel's head of security escorted her to the "Public Relations" office, where "a person asked to see my notebooks. He didn't identify himself . . . and I didn't know he was with the Jacksons' security. I felt they had been cooperative, and I was going to be cooperative with them. I tilted the notebook so he could see it, and he took it. Then he began ripping pages out." The security guard later said he thought O'Neal's presence and her notes "jeopardized the security of the Jackson tour."

Although the notes were returned by the Jacksons' manager about eight hours after the incident, Burl said *The News* considered it a theft nonetheless. "Our property was stolen. It was very clear from the manager of the Jacksons that they think they didn't do anything wrong. We do."

The AP picked up the story on July 12, 1984. "We decided to drop the charges," Langer was quoted saying. "The notes were returned, and, given that, we feel a point has been made."

And Burl said, "The point is the laws against theft and other constitutional guarantees were not suspended for the Jacksons."

• • •

Dallas hosted the Republican National Convention in the summer of 1984. Both *The News* and the *Times Herald* viewed it as a way to showcase their product to a national audience. Each had assigned a team of reporters to the story who had begun working on convention coverage more than a year before the event's opening gavel.

As one newspaper reported, "Although there would be no battle for the presidential nomination on the floor of the convention hall, there were symbols all-around of another battle taking place." The dueling papers each printed special sections, guides and supplements to the convention. *The News* weighed seven pounds on Sunday; the *Times Herald*, three pounds.

Burl was skeptical that the week's coverage would have an effect on regular readers, the people he cared about most. He even sounded irritated when he added: "I don't think the people who live here will make a decision based on a single week's worth of coverage. In the long term, the day-in, day-out coverage is what affects things like advertising and circulation."

• • •

Cable-Satellite Public Affairs Network—better known by its acronym, C-SPAN—set up temporary studios in Dallas' Sammons building across the plaza from City Hall. The public-affairs-focused network was only a few years old and had recently switched to a twenty-four-hour programming model. The Friday evening before the convention kicked off, Burl participated in a national TV call-in program.

Within the week, Burl began to hear from friends around the country who'd seen the segment. Kentucky friend James Wells wrote, "Words cannot express how pleased and surprised I was to see your smiling face beaming at me in my own living room. I was switching through the channels and said, 'Wait, I know that person. That's Burl Osborne.' Everyone else thought, 'Sure you do,' until your name was flashed across the screen. You really looked great and not much different from our old 'Corvette Days' in Ashland. As the Editor, you also are apparently doing well."

Burl's reply was incredulous. "It was a big surprise to hear a voice out of the past. Apparently, more people watch C-SPAN than I thought. I'm having a good time in Texas and have an eight-year-old son now. Don't get back to Ashland often, but maybe we'll run across each other there one of these days."

• • •

Soon after the convention ended, Burl and Betty packed their suitcases and left for a two-week tour in Russia.

The Soviet journalists in the cultural exchange had "suggested that the delegations discuss stabilizing U.S.-Soviet relations and what role the press should take in the matter." They had consequently invited twelve representatives of the ASNE to visit the Soviet Union in August, and Burl had been chosen to be a member of that delegation.

The ASNE's reciprocal visit with the U.S.S.R. Union of Journalists spanned late August and early September. The itinerary included formal and informal meetings, as well as sightseeing in Kiev, Moscow, and Leningrad (now St. Petersburg once more). Food was scarce, and Betty and Burl were sure their room was bugged.

"We were appalled at the conditions in the country," Betty said. "We were mostly served bread with meat that was not edible and a few vegetables. Fresh fruit could not be found. During some of the meetings, a bowl of small wormy green apples would grace the center of the table. We would take all we could and hide it in our pockets to take back to our rooms."

Burl wrote another column, published on *The News'* editorial page on October 2, to recount and reflect on his experiences amid the Soviet journalists, government officials, and everyday folks.

KIEV, U.S.S.R.—Bits and pieces of insight into Soviet life are about the most one can expect from the superficiality of a brief exchange visit.

Still, these glimpses, however fragmented, suggest that the Soviets may be thinking about more than the arguments with the United States they constantly talk about.

Among the examples were

- There are long lines at food stores, here in the Ukraine, in Leningrad, in Moscow, as people wait longer to choose from a more limited variety of foods.
- Housing is still a major concern in the Soviet Union.
- The Soviet Union is not about to become a computerized society.
- There is widespread interest in things Western, especially fashion.
- Reminders of the horror that World War II inflicted on the Soviet Union are everywhere.
- There is a great curiosity about Americans and American life.

• • •

The American visitor, perhaps naively optimistic, can find amidst the gloom some small hope for a better U.S.-Soviet relationship.

For one thing, the Soviets expressed clearly a desire to expand discussions with Americans. When people talk to each other more it is possible they will fight with each other less.

For another, if Americans and Soviets can find some common values and interests, such as trade and exchanges, then they may conclude, despite the rhetoric, that they have a tiny fraction less to fear from each other.

33

The Pit Bull

Throughout his time in Dallas, Burl often heard from professors at his alma mater, the W. Page Pitt School of Journalism at Marshall University, asking for his take on a particular aspect of the business. In 1984, Deryl R. Leaming, director of the journalism school, asked Burl about the ethical problems that journalists face. Burl had plenty to say on the subject.

Dear Deryl:

This list is not all-inclusive, nor does it attempt to prioritize ethical problems. But those on the list seem to crop up a lot in one form or another quite regularly.

For convenience, I have grouped them:

DAMN THE TORPEDOES
These are matters of ethical concern or conscience relating to a habit we have of not fully considering the consequences of our actions.

—The publication of gratuitous detail, needlessly damaging the victims, in stories of tragedy and violence.

—The television mike-in-face "How does it feel" ambush of grieving relatives and survivors.

—The tendency to greatly overplay stories about problems or minor wrongdoing, holding people up to unduly high levels of humiliation, simply because we got the story first and want to impress peers and contest juries.

NEWS AT ANY COST

Related to the list above, these involve getting stories at an ethical price not, in my view, worth paying.

—Stealing papers that may be incriminating but hardly threaten the national security.

—Sleeping with a source to gain competitive advantage.

—Promulgating one side of an issue in return for competitive advantage. A favorite lawyer's trick.

HIDDEN AGENDAS

—Accepting payment from a professional sports team you cover.

—Writing an "authorized" biography for—and simultaneously covering—the same public person, especially professional athletes.

—Freebies. There seem to be more junket offers than ever, and somebody's going.

—Self-interest. More and more "name" journalists are getting speaker fees from groups they may have to cover.

SACRED COWS

—Writing puff pieces for advertisers.

—Not covering newsworthy advertisers at all, for fear of offending them.

—Not covering newsworthy advertisers at all, for fear that peers will think the stories are puff pieces.

(Substitute any of the following for "advertisers" and repeat the sequence: community institutions, civic leaders, schools, our friends, etc.)

LOOSE CANNONS

Finally, this question: Is it ethical to permit reporters with near zero background to write as though they know about sensitive and important subjects such as medicine, health, economics, education and business, given the high level of

confusion and misunderstanding that frequently results from
this kind of coverage?

Editors at other publications appreciated Burl's insights as well. On November 25, the *Miami Herald* published "What's on editors' minds," written by its executive editor, Heath Meriwether.

Meriwether reached out to the more than five hundred top editors from across the nation to ask them what important and serious concerns were on their minds.

"There is more good work being done than ever before," Burl said, at the same time expressing his concerns about government officials abusing the Freedom of Information Act to avoid or delay releasing public information.

> Dallas' Osborne is worried about the money he spends on lawyers simply to win access to information he thinks the public has a right to anyway. "We've spent thousands and thousands of dollars trying to get documents from a federal agency: those guys have been told by people in Washington to make us work hard for everything we get. We weren't asking for the Pentagon papers. They were just making it tough on us," says Osborne. He believes the government's attitude about information comes back to the perception that newspapers are "uncaring, insensitive and unmindful of whether we get things right."
>
> "I think we are at risk of not being able to do our jobs because of the stifling of the flow of information. Are we going to be able to get the information that allows us to write fairly and completely about government?"

• • •

On December 27, 1984, *The News* announced that—effective January 1, 1985—Decherd, now thirty-three, would become president of the newspaper's parent company, the A. H. Belo Corporation, and that Burl, at forty-seven, would become president of *The Dallas Morning News*. In his new position, Burl was to "be in charge of the newspaper's daily functions and will continue to oversee news and editorial departments directly."

Gelsanliter described the mutually beneficial partnership of Decherd and Osborne in *Fresh Ink*: "If Decherd was rational and reserved, Osborne was street-smart and visceral. If Decherd was primarily interested in Dallas and Texas, Osborne had national as well as international experience. And if Decherd sometimes gave strangers the impression of being laid back, Osborne could act like a pit bull. It became the perfect fit."

34

They'll Be Back

The Dallas Morning News turned 100 in 1985. To kick off the centennial year of celebrations, Burl and the paper's Washington bureau chief, Leubsdorf, scored an exclusive sit-down interview with the president in the Oval Office on January 8. Ronald Reagan was newly reelected and remembered Burl from the 1981 state dinner at the White House. And he was long and well acquainted with Leubsdorf's work.

The discussion ranged from foreign policy issues, including U.S.-Soviet talks in Geneva and defense spending, to domestic issues like the federal budget, tax reform, and Social Security.

A platoon of aides hovered around, paying close attention to how the president responded to questions and making sure the session didn't last too long.

The atmosphere during their thirty-some minutes together was congenial as the president answered their questions candidly. Burl asked the president for his views on the media:

> BURL: I was going to ask, given the fairly widespread view, perception, that you don't think too highly of the media, however one defines it—I wonder if you would tell us what you do think of—not the media, but newspapers and television, specifically, and what their faults are, and what the—
>
> PRESIDENT REAGAN: I've never had any complaints about the paper you represent [*laughs*].
>
> BURL: Well, that's very kind.
>
> PRESIDENT REAGAN: I think inside the beltline here, in Washington, is kind of a company town. And the great search for leaks, and the premature billing of something as a fact when many times it isn't a fact, this

can become a problem. It can become a problem, for example, on the international scene. To take a leak, some information from someone who won't let their name be used, and take this as valid enough to print on the front page of a paper, and then leave us with having to mend fences with some friendly government that is offended by this misinformation—and there have been cases of that kind.

I guess all that I would like to say is I wish that the media that does so much of that, that portion of the media, I wish that they would have an ethic in which they would check that out with us to see whether it, in some way, might be harmful to our national security; and take our word for it if we said that it would be. And we'd be willing to explain why it would be. Then we might—we might not have so many incidents that cause us problems and set back sometimes programs that have been going forward.

BURL: Thank you, Mr. President.

The same year, *The News* moved into a $57-million state-of-the-art printing plant that marked a new era for the daily. The population of Dallas was approaching a million, and *The News*' daily circulation numbers topped 360,000. The new plant was designed to meet the needs of rapidly growing circulation and competition with television, magazines, and a second major local newspaper for readers and advertising dollars.

For decades, newspapers had been bought out of necessity; now, with the advent of CNN and other cable news channels, viewers could tune into the news at any point in the day or night. Newspapers were becoming an add-on to people's sources of information, not their core.

Newspapers had to do everything they could to compete. The capacity to print on the new high-speed offset presses was "the largest expansion of the newspaper's facilities since the construction of the downtown building in 1949" and meant *The News* could now produce newspapers at speeds up to 70,000 copies an hour.

In a *Wall Street Journal* article in May—"Dallas Times Herald Is Losing Its War With Morning News for Readers, Ads"—staff reporter Jonathan Dahl wrote:

It is becoming increasingly clear that the newspaper is losing its circulation and advertising war—one of the fiercest in the nation—to the Dallas Morning News. After trailing by only 41,000 papers in daily circulation three years ago, the Times Herald has now fallen 127,000 behind, based on March 31 figure—the widest gap ever. The Times Herald now sells 241,000 papers Monday through Saturday, compared with 368,000 for the Morning News. In addition, the Morning News now has a 55% market share of ads run in all editions.

That summer, Mark Fitzgerald, in his article "Newspaper war in Dallas is not over yet" for *Editor & Publisher*, quoted the A. H. Belo Corporation's CEO Jim Moroney. "I'd like to sit over here and say, 'Boy, we've knocked them down and they'll never come back. But that's not true. They're a big company, a strong company, and they'll be back. They may have made some mistakes, but they'll come back."

In reality, the leadership at *The News* smelled blood.

35

A Newspaper of Distinction

While Burl was a fervent believer in the freedom of the press, he also held that news organizations had an obligation to their respective communities to practice that freedom responsibly and, when appropriate, with restraint.

He crystalized his thoughts on the media's responsibility in response to a request from a former AP executive and now University of Georgia journalism professor, Conrad Fink, who was working on a book called *Media Ethics: In the Newsroom and Beyond* for McGraw-Hill.

Specifically, Fink asked Burl for "anecdotal examples how, as one of today's media leaders, you formulated the professional attitudes and sense of ethics you now hold. Toward that end, I would appreciate hearing about one or two most memorable ethical crises or problems of professional conscience that arose in your career and that, looking back, you now feel were most formative." Fink's main target was university upperclassmen and graduate students.

On December 12, 1985, Burl replied to Fink's request for the instructive material.

I have made a couple of false starts at responding to your September 23 letter but backed away each time because I realized that the examples I started to cite really didn't apply.

I now will try again, not responding directly to your question and using an unexciting but contemporary example that perhaps makes up in applicability what it lacks in trench coat glamour. Also, for what it's worth, I am enclosing a couple of other pieces that have some bearing on our view of the obligations of newspapers and, indirectly, upon ethical behavior. One is a copy of our house organ, Intercom, that happens to have on its cover what has been the closest thing we have to a written credo. It is taken from a 1906 speech by G. B. Dealey and is chiseled in granite on the front of our building. The other is a copy of a little talk I was asked to make before the Chamber of Commerce in Dallas last month. The talk isn't much but will give you a brief view of how we believe we fit into our community and perhaps some context for the example I will use.

This case is not so much a dilemma, because we were not in doubt about what to do. But matters of professional conscience did play a large role as we determined how to do what we knew we had to do.

The situation arose earlier this year when our City Desk received a tip that someone fairly high in the Salvation Army was appropriating to his own use substantial amounts of goods, including a car and boat and motorcycle, that had been donated to the army to be sold to carry on the agency's work. We made a thorough investigation and confirmed beyond doubt a number of the allegations.

For context, the local Salvation Army organization had an outstanding record for community and public service, was held in extremely high regard in the city, and had a board that was a "who's who" of local philanthropic, civic, and business leaders, including the president of our own parent company.

Once the reporting was done, the reporters took their information to officials of the army, laid the findings before them, and asked for comment or response.

The Salvation Army officials were extremely candid and totally open in return.

However, once they realized the seriousness of the problem, they pleaded that we not publish the story, citing the damage that would be done to an institution that was itself innocent (though one of its own had gone astray) and that had overall done an outstanding job in the community. They offered to open to our examination the internal examination they were conducting so that we might satisfy ourselves that the wrong had been righted.

We, of course, declined and explained that we had to publish; that not to publish would cause greater damage to the institution since rumors already were about and that, further, not to publish could be construed as vigilante journalism, with us in effect going around threatening people with exposure if they don't do what we say.

That decision was reached quickly. What was more difficult, at least for me, was deciding how to publish the story, doing what needed to be done, without unfairly painting an entire organization as tainted. There also were the standard forces working against that concern: reporters had invested a lot of time. That circumstance generally produced an overlong story and expectations of second-coming play, whether or not it is merited.

Here is what we did:

We ran the story on page one, with a very carefully written headline, not at the top of the page. We made certain that the army's response was high. We followed up with a story in the same place on the page when corrective action was announced. We wrote an editorial focused on the Salvation Army's value to the city and trying to ensure [that] the problem was viewed in context. And we undoubtedly will find a good Salvation Army Christmas story to tell.

This isn't a big-deal event to a newspaper. There is a common view that our responsibility is to get it and get it right. I am not sure our responsibility ends there.

This case was a big deal to the Salvation Army.

I believe that newspapers, as ubiquitous institutions within our communities, have obligations of care and compassion that even exceed those of many of our other institutions. Our obligations are greater because our power is greater, to strengthen, or weaken, the fabric of community life.

We should publish what is wrong, to be sure. A greater error would be to pull back and shy away from putting light on the problems and flaws within institutions.

But I do not believe newspapers, or their people, can just sit on the sidelines, immune from consequences of our actions, and throw stones willy-nilly at everyone else.

We should be concerned when we are about to publish stories that will be perceived as subverting the community, whether about the Salvation Army or the school board.

It is important, in addition to getting the story right, that we assess how readers—not our peers or contest juries—will perceive our actions. If the sum total of everything we do on a subject conveys exactly what we intend to convey, then fine. But if we think the story is mild, with little damage, and our readers perceive that we are trying to unravel the community, we may need to rethink how we are presenting what we have to say.

I believe that in the little case I cited, we came out okay. But it did require some careful thought.

I recognize that you asked for examples that helped to formulate the ethical standards by which we operate today. I had difficulty with that because most of the cases I could think of involved the application of whatever values already were in place at the time. There was learning and an extension of those values in each case, of course.

I remember one Saturday night in the middle of the Three Mile Island nuclear reactor accident, when a competitor filed a story suggesting strongly the imminent risk of a meltdown. As newspaper deadlines approached, we were under intense pressure to match the story. We did not believe the source cited for the report to be valid and could not otherwise substantiate the report. Our decision was easy; we did not file a matching report, although we could have found someone to say the same thing.

This was no ethical problem for us as it turned out. However, had we gone ahead, I think we would have had a serious one. The point is that our rules were so clear that it never became an issue. The framework for decision already was in place.

I'll stop here, with the hope that some of this may be of some value to you. If not, just toss it.

Meanwhile, I trust that all goes well and I will look forward to seeing the book.

• • •

As *The Dallas Morning News'* centennial drew to a close and former and current staff of *The News* reminisced about highlights from a hundred years of serving the citizens of Dallas, Burl silently thought back on how he had come to be in this place, at this time. How he had taken hold of the chance to be part of something that was lasting, important, and—as he described it—"maybe even spectacular, at least in our little world. It was a high mountain but with a very handsome reward, personally and professionally, if one can succeed."

Burl likely had more than an inkling that he was already nearing the summit of that high mountain. Using his own yardstick—results—it was evident that *The Dallas Morning News* was a paper of high quality, of integrity, of distinction.

36

A Faster Draw

On June 26, 1986, the Times Mirror Company announced that it was selling the *Times Herald*.

William Dean Singleton, a thirty-four-year-old Texas native whose New Jersey–based company, Media News Group, owned twenty-one daily newspapers and fifteen weeklies in six states, had agreed to buy the paper.

According to *D Magazine*, Singleton hatched the idea to buy the paper at the American Newspaper Publishers Association in San Francisco that April, after downing "cocktails at each of eight convention parties that day."

As Singleton tells the story—and he tells it often—he bid into the Dallas newspaper war in a moment of half-crazy impulse, a moment seasoned with camaraderie and lubricated by alcohol. It wasn't a thing he planned to do. He was simply showing off a little, bragging with the big boys. Somehow, though, he heard himself blurting it out, and a $110 million deal was born: "I'm going to buy the *Dallas Times Herald* and show you idiots how to run it."

As *The New York Times* wrote in its coverage: "The sale marks the Times Mirror Company's capitulation to A. H. Belo, the owner of the *Dallas Morning News*." In the 1980s, *The Morning News* had slightly more than 52 percent of the market share of advertising. By 1984 the figure was 55 percent and growing. And Burl confirmed that by 1986 *The Morning News* "now has about a 57 percent advertising market share, with about a 60 percent share in the profitable classified category."

The *Times* article concluded: "The company's substantial resources seemed to give it the upper hand in the newspaper war [in Dallas], but its efforts brought about an astonishing renewal at the A.H. Belo Company, a Dallas company that blossomed into a major communications concern under the prod of Times Mirror competition."

Texas Monthly Publisher Mike Levy saw it differently. "What happened was, when you placed Ken Johnson and Will Jarrett against Burl Osborne," he told the *Chicago Tribune*, "Osborne was just a faster draw. You put out a better magazine or newspaper and you get the readers and the rest follows."

For years, critics of the *Times Herald* both inside and outside the paper had claimed its greatest drawback was that its owners lived in Los Angeles, not Dallas. "To influence people in this town you have to be viewed as part of the ball club," Fred Meyer, chairman of the Dallas County Republican Party, told *The New York Times*. "The *Herald* was always seen as a Los Angeles paper. They didn't think like people in Texas. They didn't act like people in Texas. They were out of step. They were irrelevant."

Singleton agreed. He was quoted in the *Times Herald* as saying he bought the paper because it had recently been profitable and, more importantly, he believed that he could turn things around through local ownership. He pointed out that he'd been born in Graham, Texas, had once owned a Fort Worth newspaper, and planned to move his corporate office from New Jersey to Dallas.

"The paper at one time was referred to as the *Los Angeles Times Herald*," Singleton said. "We will now be the *Dallas Times Herald*."

Singleton said he was optimistic about the paper's financial future, pointing out that the *Times Herald* had the fourth-largest classified, the sixth-largest retail, and the eighth-largest overall amounts of advertising nationwide. Money, he said, can be made on those kinds of numbers.

Kohorst, who became editorial art director for *The News* in the mid-1980s, remembers something Burl told him years after leaving *The News*. "He said to me, prior to Singleton taking over the *Herald*, 'I had this fear that the Times Mirror Company would just write a check and buy *The News*. They would just buy us and it would all be over.' Burl was completely serious when he said this. Indeed, his fear was not far fetched. Times Mirror was capable of just writing a check for *The News*."

In the days following the sale, Burl received several dozen letters of congratulations. Some of those letters made it sound as though the newspaper war was over, but Burl was careful to respond that this was no time for *The News* to pull back even a little. His message was clear: "The sale was a big surprise to us here. Times Mirror had competed on a very high plane, and I think it made both newspapers better as a result. I hope that the next chapter will be conducted the same way. We are assuming the fight will be just as tough in the future as in the past, and we are making our plans accordingly."

• • •

Burl and Betty traveled to Davos, Switzerland, in 1986. Burl was part of a six-person delegation representing the "dynamic entrepreneurial character" of Dallas at the World Economic Forum, which drew nearly 1,000 men and women from the highest echelons of world business and politics.

The group traveled to Bonn, Germany, in advance of the symposium for high-level meetings with Chancellor Helmut Kohl, President Richard von Weizsäcker, the defense, economics, finance, and research and technology ministers, and several business and academic leaders.

Tragedy struck back home on their second night there.

Burl, who was chronicling the trip via dispatches in *The News*, wrote on January 30, 1986:

BONN—This capital of West Germany is 5,000 miles from Cape Canaveral and yet its people seem to have joined America in shared sorrow at the fireball death of space ship Challenger.

For a half dozen Dallas executives here for informal meetings with Chancellor Helmut Kohl and other leaders of German government and business, it was a poignant reminder of how inextricably bound together are the interests of West Germany and the United States.

Members of the Dallas group, aboard a train from Frankfurt during the afternoon, learned of the tragedy from U. S. Ambassador Richard Burt on the steps of his residence as they arrived for a dinner with American diplomats and German executives.

From that moment, the visitors encountered an extraordinary outpouring of sympathy, warmth and understanding from Germans at all levels.

A young waiter at the Hotel Steigenberger brought out a photograph of one of the astronauts who had visited Bonn, and offered his condolence.

The president of West Germany, Dr. Richard von Weizsacker, prefaced an hour-long meeting with the group by speaking of the courage required to cross the frontiers of space, and Germany's intention to stand by the United States in future endeavors.

Defense Minister Manfred Woerner talked of the price of the kind of progress space exploration has made possible.

Wednesday night, Walther Leisler Kiep, chairman of the Atlantic Bridge, a non-partisan organization dedicated to German-American friendship, said at a dinner meeting, "Your loss is our loss."

In Davos, about fifty executives from throughout the world came to hear the Dallas presentation and peppered them with questions about Texas. Jim Landers, covering the event for *The News*, wrote that even the topic of American football came up. An Australian businessman asked jokingly about the future prospects for the Dallas Cowboys. "Burl Osborne, president and editor of *The Dallas Morning News*, replied that better results were expected in the future," Landers wrote.

That evening, the Chamber of Commerce delegation hosted nearly six hundred dignitaries at a reception in the Hotel Bellevedere. Guests included Prince Philip, Duke of Edinburgh, and exiled Iranian Prince Sadruddin Aga Khan. "My friends in France and Italy tell me Dallas is an excellent city, dynamic, with a good quality of life and a good business atmosphere," Landers quoted the Aga Khan saying.

• • •

About a month later, Burl and Betty flew to Washington for another state dinner at the White House, this one for the prime minister of Canada and his wife. While Burl sat at President Reagan's table next to Donna Marella Agnelli, whose husband was the chairman of Fiat, Betty was seated at Vice President George H. W. Bush's table along with none other than Prince Aga Khan, who remembered the Osbornes from Davos.

"The Aga Khan, seated on my right, invited Burl and me to Switzerland as his guest to ski," recalled Betty. "Seated on my left was Utah Senator Jake Garn, who had recently donated a kidney to his daughter. We had much to discuss."

When Betty had a chance to speak a few words to the president, she commented on how lovely the evening had been and that she would also remember it for another reason: it was their son's tenth birthday.

President Reagan took Betty's program and wrote across it, "To Jonathan, Happy Birthday. Wish you were here. Ronald Reagan."

"Happy Birthday, Jonathan" from President Reagan, March 18, 1986

37

Make Sure It's Loaded

Morning News Reporter Steve Blow said of Burl:

> It seemed that no matter what shift I worked—days, nights,
> weekends—he was in the newsroom. He prodded us toward a
> more ambitious brand of journalism. We began to whisper a
> magical word—Pulitzer.

In April 1986, *The Dallas Morning News* won its first Pulitzer Prize. It was
awarded for National Reporting, to Reporters Craig Flournoy and George
Rodrigue, and to their editor, Howard Swindle, for their investigation into
subsidized housing across the United States. Titled "Separate and Unequal:
Subsidized Housing in America," the series uncovered patterns of racial
discrimination and segregation in public housing in East Texas and across the
country. The prize-winning series would eventually lead to significant public
housing reforms.

"To win the Pulitzer for national reporting for something like this said
that *The Morning News* had arrived as a player among big-time American
metropolitan newspapers," Flournoy said.

The Pulitzer was not only prestigious but also good for business. "One
day I'm on the elevator, and a lady gets on from the advertising department,"
Flournoy said. "She recognized me and told me that prior to the Pulitzer,
Neiman Marcus gave 55 percent of its advertising to *The Morning News* and
45 percent to the *Herald*. But she said that after the Pulitzer, Neiman Marcus
started giving 60 percent of its ad budget to *The Morning News*."

Flournoy said he and Burl sometimes had a contentious professional
relationship, often disagreeing on what the newspaper should focus on. "I think

it should be about comforting the afflicted and afflicting the comfortable," Flournoy said. As he saw it, "Burl saw nothing wrong with comforting the comfortable."

But Burl's stance was that the newspaper should act with what he called a "professional conscience," as he had when he'd made tough decisions during the investigation into the Salvation Army. The paper had to recognize the power it wielded over institutions and the community at large. This could mean holding a story until it was thoroughly reported or if the sources were questionable. "If you're going to fire the gun," he would say, "make sure the bullets are in the chamber."

Flournoy appreciated Burl's serious commitment to the multipart series on subsidized housing. "He gave us the time and the resources to do this story, so Burl gets a lot of the credit. I'm sure if you asked him what made a great newspaper, he would say a great sports section and a great business section. He never said investigative reporting. But if *The Morning News* was only interested in selling newspapers, they would not have run our stories."

Flournoy also admired Burl's journalistic instincts.

One day George and I were in Howard Swindle's office looking over the top of the day one main story. The day one main is always the most important story in a series because it effectively serves as the foundation and the entryway to the rest of the series. Given that we were about to publish an eight-day series, the day one main for "Separate and Unequal" was all the more important.

All of which means the lead paragraph had to be just right.

George, Howard, and I had been arguing for God knows how long about what the lead graph should say. Each of us was sure he was right, and, quite frankly, each of us wanted to put too much info in that first sentence.

Burl walked by Howard's office and, like anyone else who came within thirty feet, could hear us fighting like cats and dogs. He stepped inside and asked what the problem was. When we told him we could not agree on the lead for the day one main story, he sat down and in perhaps two minutes wrote essentially the lead we used. I say essentially because I cannot recall exactly what he wrote, but I damn well know it was very close to what we used: "Despite federal laws prohibiting racial discrimination, the nearly 10 million residents of federally assisted housing are mostly segregated by race, with whites faring much better than blacks and Hispanics."

That's our entire series. In twenty-nine words.

Just a few days after the paper won the Pulitzer, Burl flew to Spokane and gave a speech at the Spokane and Inland Empire Artificial Kidney Center, which had helped him with his home dialysis so many years earlier. Although the Pulitzer had nothing to do with dialysis or medicine of any kind, Burl apparently could not help but talk about the award he was so thrilled his paper had just received.

Since I am in the newspaper business, I hope you won't mind if I tell you a couple of stories about a couple of stories.

The first is a story about a newspaper story, one that might give you some idea of how a newspaper works and how it can serve the people who read it every day.

The second is a more personal story that reflects more on what I believe to be our good fortune, yours and mine, for having come to know the people who run this dialysis center.

(For many of us who are glad to be here—we are glad to be *anywhere* given our medical histories—we owe our lives to the people who played out this story.)

The story about the story started a couple of years ago in a tiny town in East Texas, Clarksville, where *The News* has many longtime readers.

A federal judge issued an order that twenty-five residents of an all-white federal housing project there had to swap apartments with twenty-five residents of an all-black federal housing project. The judge gave them two weeks to move, saying the housing developments, supported by tax money, were illegally segregated.

Our original intention was just to follow up this ruling and try to determine whether there really was segregation in East Texas.

We assigned two reporters ... to check. They spent three months studying the racial makeup of federal housing in forty-three counties of East Texas. ... The results of their study amazed the reporters and us. They studied 182 housing projects; 80 percent of them were segregated. In every case, the black-only projects were inferior to the others in location, condition, and services.

In the white housing developments there was new construction, central heating, air-conditioning, and libraries and recreation centers. In black developments there was substandard plumbing, no air-conditioning, torn screens, and muddy yards.

These findings raised more questions: What about the rest of Texas, and our own city of Dallas? And what about the rest of the country?

So what had started as a routine follow-up story in our own backyard turned into the largest national study our newspaper had ever attempted. And the project was not easy.

As the federal authorities became aware of the questions we were asking, they realized that they may be very embarrassed by the results. And so they became increasingly unhelpful. Finally, we had to use legal means—including invoking the Freedom of Information Act—to get information that normally would have been public all along. And even then, the housing people tried to stall.

The conclusion was that we found unequal treatment in federal housing throughout the country, in a system that provides housing for 10 million Americans.

We also learned that it was not true that black welfare mothers with six kids accounted for most of the housing. In fact, two-thirds of the federal housing is occupied by whites. And 45 percent of the apartments are occupied by the elderly.

And almost nine out of ten of the apartments were provided in the last twenty years, after Congress passed the Civil Rights Act of 1964 that prohibited discrimination in federal programs. Segregation and unequal treatment could not have existed without either the neglect or the tacit approval of the federal agency that was supposed to enforce the law.

Burl, who himself joined the Pulitzer board in 1986 and would have a hand in selecting the next year's winners, said, "I was first in line with the champagne when we won that first Pulitzer Prize—the industry's equivalent of an Oscar."

Ever the pragmatist, however, Burl didn't envision that a Pulitzer would entice more subscribers to *The Dallas Morning News*.

I'm trying to think of a polite way to say that . . . it's a bunch of us titillating each other about how wonderful we are, and patting ourselves on the back, when we're not the people who put the quarter or dollar in the machine and buy the newspaper. Those are the people who vote; that's where you find out where the prizes are. The prizes are the people you reach, not the people you impress.

People in this city who vote with their quarters . . . those are the votes I care most about. Our first, second, and third most important obligations are to our readers. If they are happy and engaged and interested, the rest will follow.

In the fall of 1986, shortly after taking ownership of the *Times Herald*, Singleton filed a lawsuit in a Chicago federal court against *The Dallas Morning News* and the Illinois-based Audit Bureau of Circulations (ABC). The suit accused *The News* of artificially inflating its circulation figures by using a variety of bookkeeping tricks and fraudulent circulation practices.

The News staunchly denied the charges and countersued. Lawyers would take hundreds of depositions before both papers ultimately dropped their suits in 1988.

One evening toward the end of 1987, Burl received a surprising phone call at his home from Singleton. Burl later testified about that call while on the witness stand in a different civil trial:

> [Singleton] said that he had bought *The Denver Post* and he had also bought *The Houston Post* and that he was having some trouble in Denver with the paper, getting it running the way he wanted it to, and that we had competitively been a problem in Dallas and he wondered whether I would consider going to Denver to run *The Denver Post* in return for what he said would be a satisfactory salary plus some ownership in his company.
>
> He said that he had not been as successful in Dallas as he'd hoped to be with the *Times Herald* and that he felt that the strength of *The Morning News* was part of that, and he indicated he thought that I was part of the reason for that.
>
> No is what I told him. I said that we were in the middle of a dispute that had been going on for about two years and that there was no way in the middle of that that I would even consider any offer from him.

• • •

John Rector Jr. retired as publisher of *The Dallas Morning News* in 1986. Burl wouldn't officially attain that title until 1991, but the paper's masthead retroactively acknowledges that he essentially took over the job upon Rector's leaving.

"So although I didn't have the title, I functioned that way," Burl said. "We call me different things but—and some things weren't in the title—but, functionally, that's what I did."

Burl liked to say that "newspapers are like battleships. It takes a long time to turn them around and even longer for anyone to notice." But people had, in fact, noticed in a very short time that *The News* was a substantially different paper with Burl at its helm.

Burl felt a weight lift off his shoulders. The newspaper war wasn't over, but things had improved markedly during his tenure.

"I loved juggling all these balls," Burl told Kohorst. "And then one day I realized two of these were mine."

The next year, Burl celebrated his fiftieth birthday and joined the A. H. Belo Board of Directors.

Happy fiftieth, Burl (Credit: *The Morning News* editorial department)

38

Funny Pages

Singleton quickly abandoned his turnaround project on June 7, 1988, announcing that he was selling the *Dallas Times Herald* to a group controlled by his former partner John Buzzetta. Although Buzzetta would not disclose the amount he paid for the paper, the AP reported that Singleton was negotiating to sell the *Times Herald* at a $140-million valuation and would keep an equity stake in the new entity.

Surprisingly to many media watchers, the new owner paid *more* for the paper than Singleton had when he purchased it from Times Mirror Company two years earlier. The thirty-eight-year-old Buzzetta said the paper was "healthier" and, therefore, worth more. But the notion that the *Times Herald* was healthy at all was a stretch. It was not the general feeling in Dallas or among newspaper analysts nationally. The truth was that the *Times Herald* was falling further and further behind *The News* in both advertising and circulation, and the ailing Dallas economy was not helping.

Buzzetta insisted that no editorial staff cuts were planned. In fact, he planned to expand business coverage. He also said he was convinced that the *Times Herald* could increase its market share of advertising. Buzzetta ended his press conference by admonishing his audience not to doubt his talents: he had advanced from reporter for a New Jersey daily with a circulation of 6,000 to major newspaper publisher in just sixteen years.

Two days after the sale, Burl wrote a letter to his staff, saying, "A number of you have asked about the most recent sale of the *Dallas Times Herald* and what effect that might have on the operation of *The Dallas Morning News*. The answer is that the sale will not cause any change in the philosophy or direction of *The Morning News*."

• • •

A big part of the *Times Herald*'s problem was turmoil in the newsroom, created by its ever-changing news management. There had been six executive editors in eight years, and leadership often rested with the managing editor, where turnover was even greater. "There was a revolving door of too many people who had too little understanding of Dallas," said Bode. "We brought in a lot of good people, but there was a tremendous amount of churn, which was very hurtful. There were good people on the business side, but they passed through there very quickly."

Halbreich of *The News*, agreed with Bode's assessment. "*Herald*'s executives were moving through Dallas in the hope of going somewhere better, while those of us at *The Morning News* were here because we wanted to be here. It was a totally different mindset, and we used it to our advantage."

The result of that massive turnover, Langer wrote in a memo to Burl, was "loss of institutional memory, immature news judgments, herky-jerky approaches and policies. Staff often doesn't know the significance of a breaking story or, in particular, obits."

"Another result of turnover and lack of strong editing has been embarrassing and visible blunders," Langer wrote. "Most notable recently was the [page one] story that [owner of the Dallas Cowboys] Jerry Jones was in financial trouble. Story was stripped across the front of the paper. The next day a six-column story was stripped in the same place saying that Jones was in great financial shape."

• • •

Bode was in his office at the *Times Herald* in early August 1989 when a salesman from the Universal Press Syndicate entered and dropped a bombshell.

"I have some bad news," he told Bode. "We have to cancel all of our contracts with you."

Universal provided many of the paper's best comic strips—among them: the popular cartoon strips *Doonesbury*, *Cathy*, *Calvin and Hobbes*, and *The Far Side*—and such staples of the lifestyles section as "Erma Bombeck" and "Dear Abby." Comics alone sold many papers. To lose so many comic strips all at once was unthinkable.

After almost two decades, Universal intended to cancel the *Herald's* year-to-year contract once it ended. They were forming a new joint venture with *The News'* parent company, the A. H. Belo. Corporation, and its ABC affiliate to produce television programs based on Universal's popular comic strips and columns.

As part of the deal, within a few months a collective package of twenty-six features would move to *The News*. The agreement, for which Belo would pay $1 million over five years, included a provision that gave *The News* exclusive first rights, meaning the *Times Herald* could pick over anything *The News* rejected. Burl had been instrumental in negotiating the deal. The venture would be called Belo Universal.

Bode was almost too shaken to speak. He told the salesman that he would do everything in his power to stop the cancellation of the *Times Herald's* contracts.

No one at the *Times Herald* believed that *The News* was really planning such a venture. They believed it was just a ruse to steal the comics.

In short order, the *Dallas Times Herald* filed suit against A. H. Belo, *The News*, and Universal, seeking $33 million in damages and demanding that the companies terminate the agreement.

Burl would later testify: "What we were trying to do is enter into a joint venture, and part of that was the ability to improve what we offer our customers. And to the extent that we were able to do that with this and with other improvements we have made, then it allowed us to perform better competitively against all our competitors, one of which is the *Dallas Times Herald*."

When asked whether it would upset *Herald's* readers to find their favorite features suddenly removed from the *Dallas Times Herald*, Burl replied: "Well, I had a reasonably good suspicion it would upset the managers of the *Dallas Times Herald*."

The *Times Herald* went to court, but a judge denied its request to stop Universal from removing the comics while the *Times Herald* pursued its lawsuit.

Bode wrote a letter, addressed "To Our Readers," which appeared on the *Times Herald's* front page. In its conclusion, he wrote:

We like competition.

Competition built Texas.

Competition has made Dallas a great American city.

Today, Dallas is a two-newspaper city and it can remain so. And Dallas can remain a world-class city with vigorous independent newspapers providing diverse news and editorial pages.

But to ensure that, the competition here must be conducted fairly.

For several weeks, the *Times Herald* ran blank spaces where their comics had once been. A note inside the blank space said: "This comic no longer appears because of a lawsuit [with] our competitor. We expect to have a replacement soon that will be just as good."

• • •

The News won a second Pulitzer Prize in 1989, this time for Explanatory Journalism. Reporter David Hanners, Photographer William Snyder, and Graphic Designer Karen Blessen won for their story "Anatomy of an Air Crash: The Final Flight of 50 Sierra Kilo." The twelve-page special section, published on February 7, 1988, analyzed a National Transportation Safety Board investigation into the crash of a twin-engine executive jet during a violent thunderstorm in East Texas. As *The News'* announcement proudly revealed, "At least four universities now use the Section in their air safety and engineering curriculums."

Part of what made the story jump off the page were the graphics. "This was the first time that a 'visual journalist'—in this case Blessen—had been included in a Pulitzer nomination," said editorial Kohorst, and it was Burl "who insisted" that Blessen be included. Kohorst continued:

The flight story won the Pulitzer and put *The Morning News* on the map in reporting visual news. Burl understood the power of graphics. He knew that if you had a story with a visual component, you could put that into a visual format and give the reader access to the information in an easy way.

Burl described the project as a "wonderful step forward" in public service by a newspaper.

> It takes a very complex subject that we hear a lot about but don't understand very well at all—and explains it in terms that anyone can understand. The public is able to make judgments about the performance of the institutions that are supposed to guarantee air safety. The award is the recognition of good work already done on a daily ongoing basis and confirmation from our peers around the country that we do very good work . . . The project merged the talents of three separate areas of work—words, pictures, and graphics—in a manner that I think will become the way newspapers tell stories in the future.

39

Hypothetically Speaking

Dennis Holder wrote in *D Magazine*:

It was the week before Thanksgiving, 1989, and word shot
through the *Times Herald* newsroom like a scourge. The time
had come. The paper was closing. More than 200 reporters and
editors, along with nearly 900 full timers who toiled each day to
produce a newspaper, would be pounding the streets. A meeting
Editor Roy Bode had set for that Friday afternoon would bring the
final blow.

With grim foreboding, they huddled around the city desk
at the appointed time. Sportswriters, columnists, copy editors,
news clerks waited with knotted stomachs for the guillotine
to descend. When Bode climbed atop a desk and grinned his
off-center Cheshire cat grin, more than one person in the room
murmured, "That callous bastard."

"We've all been hearing rumors for weeks that the *Dallas
Times Herald* is about to go out of business," Bode began. The staff
nodded in bleak agreement. "I've called this meeting to put those
rumors to rest once and for all."

Times Herald staffers barely heard the rest of what their
editor had to say. Most were so gripped with relief that they
couldn't even cheer. The eyes of some hard-bitten veterans
flooded with tears. They were not out of jobs after all. Bode
wheeled out cases of wine, beer and soft drinks, and production
on the Saturday and Sunday papers ground to a standstill as the
staff toasted the continued long life of the *Dallas Times Herald*.

That so many persons who earn their livings collecting, writing and editing the news so thoroughly misread the situation inside their own newspaper says something about the fallibility of journalists. But it also reveals a great deal about the strength and pervasiveness of the rumors that had plagued the *Times Herald* for a year or more. Throughout the city, advertisers, readers, journalists, and casual observers believed—and many continue to believe—that the paper's demise was just a matter of time.

News business editor Hall recalled: "Ralph Langer called the business section into his office and said, 'In a very short time the staff of one of these two newspapers is going to be lined up at the door of the other newspaper, and you'd better hope you're not in that line.'"

• • •

Linda Quick was in charge of advertising for the department store Sanger-Harris (later Foley's) when the store advertised equally in the *Times Herald* and *The News*. "We were the biggest advertiser in both papers," she said. "Fifty percent of our advertising went in *The News* and 50 percent in the *Herald*. It had always been done that way." But by the late 1980s, Quick wanted to know just how much return on investment the ads generated from each paper. She recalled:

> Audited information showed that *The Morning News* gave us a better return for our money and that our merchants no longer wanted to advertise in the *Times Herald*. At that point, I didn't have great confidence in the *Herald*. The product just wasn't as good. *The Morning News* had just become a better product.
>
> I called Burl and asked him to meet me for lunch, and I asked him, "Hypothetically speaking, what would you do if we gave you 100 percent of our advertising budget?"
>
> He said, "Hypothetically speaking, I don't know."

I said, "Well, hypothetically speaking, you should come up with an answer, and we should discuss it."

The Morning News came back to us and said that if we gave them 100 percent of our advertising, they'd give us a nice price break and a multiyear contract. This would save us millions and millions of dollars.

Quick suspected that if she did withdraw her ads from the *Times Herald*, other advertisers would follow her lead. "I guess you could say I saw a parade and got in at the front of it," she said.

• • •

In 1990, the ASNE elected Burl president. The *Bluefield Daily Telegraph*'s staff remained as enthusiastic about Burl's accomplishments—whether he wore an AP or a DMN ball cap—as their late Currence had been. "Osborne heads editors," read an April 15, 1990, item in the paper.

George H. W. Bush, now president of the United States, sent Burl a congratulatory note on stationery with the heading "Aboard Air Force One."

```
Dear Burl,
     Somehow, until today, I missed this news.
     Congrats! And good luck in this new challenge.
     Barbara joins me in sending our warmest best wishes.
```

Burl wrote back ten days later.

```
Dear Mr. President:
     Many thanks for your kind note about my selection as
president of the American Society of Newspaper Editors.
     The coming year is a special opportunity for all of us,
as we observe the bicentennial of the Bill of Rights. I hope
that we can focus attention during the next year or so on these
precious rights that we too often ignore or take for granted.
```

Burl and Ralph Langer (Credit: *The Dallas Morning News*)

Burl and Dave Smith (Credit: Osborne family collection)

(L–R) Mike Whitehead, Bill Evans, Ralph Langer, Burl, and others working on the first "bulldog edition" front page (Credit: *The Dallas Morning News*)

White House, May 21, 1981; (L–R) Mrs. Helmut Schmidt, Nancy Reagan, and Betty Osborne (Credit: Official White House photo)

Jim Moroney discovers Burl's new company car: a Rolls-Royce (Credit: *The Dallas Morning News*)

(L–R) David Woo (*Morning News* photographer), Burl, President Reagan, and Carl Leubsdorf January 8, 1985 (Credit: Official White House photo)

The Osbornes and Dr. Peter Ivanovich enjoying a ski vacation (Credit: Osborne family collection)

Burl (center), co-chair, 1995 Pulitzer Board (Credit: The Pulitzer Board)

Burl behind the scenes putting the final touches on his ASNE speech (Credit: Osborne family collection)

"Best of Texas" dinner NAA, Dallas, 1998; (L–R) Robert Decherd, Maureen Decherd, Burl, Barbara Bush, President Bush, and Betty Osborne (Credit: Kristina Bowman)

(L–R) Elaine Bock, Betty Osborne, Harry Bock, and Burl (Credit: Osborne family collection)

Bob Mong promoted editor of *The News* upon Burl's retirement (Credit: Michael Mulvey, *The Dallas Morning News*)

Burl, chairman, the Associated Press (Credit: AP)

Joy Starzel, Dr. Thomas Starzl, Burl, and Betty

Dr. Peter Ivanovich and Burl (Credit: Osborne family collection)

David and Juanita Osborne
(Credit: Betty Osborne)

(L–R) Studie Smith, Burl, Dave Smith, Kathy Langer, Ralph Langer, and Betty (Credit: Osborne Family Collection)

(L–R) Jonathan's wife, Brigette, Jonathan, Betty, and Burl Osborne (Credit: Osborne Family Collection)

(L–R) Burl, Brigette, Harry, and Jonathan Osborne celebrate Burl's seventy-fifth birthday, June 25, 2012. (Credit: Tracy Trahar)

Burl, Betty, and Robert Decherd (Credit: David Woo)

Jonathan, Harry, and Burl, June 25, 2012 (Credit: Tracy Trahar)

Burl's last ride in his Ferrari California, 2012 (Credit: Betty Osborne)

Fittingly, the 1991 ASNE convention will be held next
April in Boston and I will be writing a little later to ask
that you join us there in a renewal of our dedication to our
constitutional freedoms.

Meanwhile, we miss seeing you in Dallas.

Betty joins me in sending our best wishes. And our Springer,
Buckingham, sends his best to Millie.

• • •

That spring, Burl was focused in his new role on the chronic failure of
newspapers to make a breakthrough in assembling more diverse newsrooms.
He described the state of minority participation in newspapers as "progressing
and disappointing." *The News'* editorial staff at the time was 13.9 percent
minority, nearly twice the national average. But Burl admitted: "We need to do
better. We in newspapers have not done nearly enough, but I also think the issue
is more societal than we thought. It is not merely a matter of would newspapers
hire for diversity. We have thought of it in self-interested terms. But we should
be thinking of what we can do to make ourselves more attractive to minorities,
so when they get out of high school, they want to study print journalism and go
to work for us."

He added that newspapers must also begin hiring people from
nontraditional places. "I can see us going to think tanks in Washington to find
editorial writers, for example. I can see us going into institutions for people who
have great knowledge of that institution, teaching them the basics of journalism,
and putting them on the beat, rather than waiting until journalism schools crank
out news students."

Burl would go on to serve on the board of Paul Quinn College, a small
historically Black school in Dallas, for three years and worked to engender
interest in journalism among the student body.

40

The Witness Stand

By the time the comics case went to trial in Houston in April 1990, the question for jurors was whether *The News* was trying to put the *Times Herald* out of business. "Taking the comics away was a focus of the case, but it was not the big issue," said Harry Reasoner, a lawyer with Vinson & Elkins, the firm hired to represent the A. H. Belo Corporation. The *Times Herald* was accusing *The News* of trying to drive the paper out of business and have a monopoly over the news in violation of antitrust law.

The trial would take place in Houston because that's where the *Times Herald*'s law firm, Fulbright & Jaworski, was headquartered. Since both papers also sold copies in Houston, the venue was approved.

"We thought about moving it back to Dallas, but the more we thought about it, we thought at least a third of the jurors would be *Times Herald*'s readers," Bill Sims, the lead lawyer for *The News*, said. "We just decided to stay in Houston. I think that turned out to be a shrewd move. You didn't have the jurors being avid *Dallas Morning News* readers or avid *Times Herald* readers."

Before the trial even began, it was clear that Burl would play a major role in the proceedings. But on the eve of the trial, the lawyers expressed one concern about Burl. It had nothing to do with what he might say on the stand. It had to do with what he might wear.

"Burl was an impeccable dresser, and he wore Turnbull & Asser shirts, brightly colored shirts with white collars, and Hermès ties. We told him, 'You look great, but you're going to have to tone it down for the jury.'"

The flashy clothes, Sims worried, might lead the jurors to doubt Burl's "rags-to-riches" background, which he intended to emphasize:

While jurors don't like very successful people, they love to hear stories about people who started out moderately and became successful.

We suggested he go to Brooks Brothers and buy some plain white button-down shirts and striped ties. When we suggested this, Burl was astonished. He was like, *"Really?"* He couldn't believe we were asking him to do that.

Burl said, "I would never wear these shirts again." So since he was never going to wear those clothes again, he sent a bill to *The News* for the clothes, and it got to be a big joke within the company. He sent a bill to the company's president. He would ask, "Do you think I'm going to be reimbursed for these shirts?"

There was standing room only when the *Times Herald's* lawyers called Burl to the stand as an adverse witness. He was only the third person to give sworn testimony.

"They made a big mistake by calling Burl at the outset because he did a good job of explaining our side of the story," said *News* attorney Harry Reasoner. "I don't think they'd anticipated what a splendid witness he was going to be or they wouldn't have put him on. He was unflappable."

But he was concerned Burl could come across as argumentative. "Burl was so smart and knew the case so well that he would argue with the other side. When witnesses argue with lawyers, rather than just stating fact, juries don't like that. Burl was very good at argument, but that wasn't the time for him to be arguing. And *he didn't* argue."

Reasoner outlined the defense strategy of the case this way:

Our big argument was that the American antitrust laws are intended to permit hard competition. You want people to compete. And that's what *The News* was doing. Competing. On the comics themselves, we were able to show that [the *Herald*] deliberately had short-term contracts with Universal Press Syndicate. We showed that that made UPS eager to find someone who would give a longer contract and pay them more money.

If these comic strips had been so valuable, they would have entered into long-term contracts and paid them more.

[The *Herald*] claimed that this had cost them $30 million in damages, but we were able to show that the bankers who loaned the *Herald* money didn't take the fact they'd lost the comics into account at all. The bankers didn't think that losing the comics had hurt the *Herald*'s bottom line. And they couldn't prove they'd lost readers because of it.

What we were saying was that this is just competition. We could point to newspapers going out of business around the country, and it had nothing to do with comics. It's just the way the world was changing. Newspapers were hurting.

Sims said that Burl's life story was also instrumental.

The *Herald* tried to portray us as the big, bad bully, trying to crush the competition, and Burl was the face of the newspaper. The *Herald* needed to convince the jury that Burl was a guy who was a bully. But the jurors didn't see that. Instead, I think the jurors saw a lot of themselves in Burl. He had come from very humble beginnings and had risen through the ranks and become very successful. He personified the American dream. And the jurors appreciated the fact that Burl was in a very competitive environment.

What we were trying to show at trial is that moving the comic strips is not what was going to put them [the *Herald*] out of business. It was that Burl put out a better product. We were just arguing throughout that this was just hardball competition. "Hardball" is a word we used repeatedly. We argued that competition is what you want companies to do.

One of the points that the *Times Herald*'s lawyers repeatedly tried to make was that Belo Corporation was extraordinarily powerful because it owned both a newspaper and a television station in the same market, Dallas. Pursuing this point, the plaintiff's lead attorney, Wayne Fisher, questioned Burl about it in direct examination.

> Q. Are you aware of any instance in America where a television station owned by the same company that also owns the local—one of the local daily newspapers, where the newspaper and the television station have ever worked together—worked in concert as we've talked about, to help one another gain a competitive advantage in a business deal of that sort? Are you aware of any instance in America where that's occurred? To your knowledge?
>
> A. Well, I know of one.
>
> Q. Where?
>
> A. Dallas.
>
> Q. All right, sir. You're talking about the situation here?
>
> A. No, sir.
>
> Q. When was that?
>
> A. In about 1981, the *Times Herald* and the station its parent company then owned, which is KDFW, I think, worked together to hire away our lead sports columnist.
>
> Q. And did you feel that was proper conduct for them to do so at that point in time?
>
> A. I felt it was hardball competition. And we lived with it.

Burl caught the *Times Herald*'s lawyer completely off guard. Sims said that Fisher, a star litigator at the time, had been brought in late to the case and wasn't present during depositions where they discussed the topic of Skip Bayless jumping to the *Times Herald* nearly a decade earlier. And thus, Fisher walked right into it, said Sims.

"When Wayne asked him that question, Burl shot me a look that said, 'OK, here we go,'" Sims said. "And we were off to the races."

• • •

On May 8, 1990, after five days of deliberation, the jury found that *The Morning News* did not violate the law when it acquired the comics. The jury of eight women and four men rejected claims by the *Times Herald* that *The News* and its parent company, A. H. Belo, violated contract and antimonopoly laws.

Burl commented on the trial's outcome. "We're delighted. We have always felt that we did nothing wrong. We went out and competed . . . and we did it properly, and the jury has upheld that."

"A lot of my colleagues and I knew that it was time to start putting out our résumés, to start looking for jobs elsewhere," a former *Times Herald* city desk reporter said. "It wasn't that we thought losing the comics would push us under financially. It was that we were losing on so many fronts. This was just one more loss. It was a psychological loss as much as anything."

Shortly after the trial, Burl received another accolade. *Adweek* named him Newspaper Executive of the Year. The advertising industry magazine was concise in its praise: "One of the best; smart and tough, low-key, but ferociously competitive."

And after Burl's first decade at the paper, Decherd named him—officially this time—publisher of *The Dallas Morning News*. Decherd had predicted Burl's rise to publisher when he'd hired him and prevailed on the paper's executives to overlook his history with his kidneys.

"Although I have already expressed myself about your election as publisher of *The Dallas Morning News*," Decherd wrote in a note to Burl, "I could not let too many moons pass without writing to say how proud I am of your achievements and how much your contributions to Belo have meant to me personally. The past ten years have been pretty remarkable, and truly would not have been the same without you. Here's to another decade at least of challenge, success and friendship!"

Interestingly, Burl, while adding publisher to his business card, would also keep the title of editor. Decherd explained in 2019: "By modern times, it's unusual for someone to be both editor and publisher. We wanted to underscore the fact that Burl's proven judgment as editor remained the province of the publisher. We wanted to underscore that the chief executive of *The Morning News* also embodied the journalism of *The News*."

Burl's own image of himself was that of a coxswain seated in the bow of a rowing shell. "Blowing a whistle doesn't make the boat move," he said. "Rowing does. At the very most I sat up there and blew a whistle."

The man who took a chance on Burl went a few steps further. "If Burl's the cox," Decherd said, "he has handpicked the crew, bought new oars, and redeveloped the shell."

Admiral Osborne at the helm (Credit: Bill DeOre, *The Dallas Morning News* cartoonist)

41

Fairness, Accuracy, and Context

The ASNE traditionally asks its presidents to end their one-year term with a speech. As Burl's presidency drew to a close in April 1991, he delivered remarks about the First Amendment and the Bill of Rights to a packed auditorium of some seven hundred guests in Boston.

First, he addressed his ongoing efforts to increase diversity in the news. ASNE conducted annual surveys of diversity in newsrooms that consistently showed the largest papers had the most diversity and that among the nation's biggest newspapers, *The News* was one of the most diverse.

"*The News* became much more diverse than most big-city newsrooms," said Neil Foote, who started the Miami chapter of the National Association of Black Journalists. "This is something that Burl felt very strongly about—he wanted diversity at *The News*." Burl knew Foote through ASNE and brought him to *The News*, where he began working in an abbreviated executive management program. By the mid-1990s, four men of color would hold important news management positions at *The News*.

"Editors and publishers who demand diversity in hiring are likely to get it," Burl told his industry audience. "Editors and publishers who demand diversity at all levels of the newsroom, including management, also are likely to get it."

It had been a banner year for freedom of the press in the former communist countries of Eastern and Central Europe, as well as China and South Africa. But Burl said domestically he found an "uncomfortable atmosphere" in two major American institutions, the military and college campuses:

> I'd like to begin by reminding you of how Secretary of State Baker described the Persian Gulf War at this year's Gridiron dinner in Washington.

"The Gulf War was quite a victory," he said. "Who could not be moved by the sight of that poor, demoralized rabble— outwitted, outflanked, outmaneuvered by the U.S. military? But I think, given time, the press will bounce back." If Mr. Baker was kidding, he was kidding on the square. I hope that we *can* bounce back.

The fact is that on the battleground of public opinion, the press was clobbered in the Persian Gulf.

The fact is that the American people believed that strict controls on reporting, including censorship, were appropriate and necessary.

And the fact is that we, the press, failed to persuade people that timely, firsthand reporting will in the long run best serve the public interest and that we do understand the need for military security.

Many people believe the press didn't care about the safety of their sons and daughters and wives and husbands, that the press was arrogant (as usual) and ill prepared and out of touch with the values American soldiers fought to protect.

Most journalists are, in fact, neither arrogant nor uncaring nor out of touch, and we wonder how these opposite perceptions can exist.

For one thing, we have been heading for a train wreck with the military for a long time, since the experiences of Vietnam twenty years ago. The press quit trusting the military because it was not always truthful in Vietnam.

The military quit trusting the press because, some officers thought, journalists gave aid and comfort to the enemy.

There is a saying that generals always want to fight the last war. That didn't hold true for generals in the Gulf, in part because they didn't win the last war. What happened in the Gulf, I am afraid, is that journalists wanted to *cover* the last war.

The generals clearly learned from their experience as younger officers in Vietnam. You just heard one of them. It was no accident that General Schwartzkopf refused to talk about body counts or that the flow of information was strictly controlled. It was not the same as Vietnam.

So, despite our arguments, we got a different kind of system, with censorship and severe limits on access and rules that led to infighting among a gallon of reporters fighting for a quart of pool positions.

We also got a different kind of war. The U.S. entry into Vietnam was gradual, with ground combat from beginning to end. The allied entry into the Gulf War was lightning fast, mostly air- and seaborne, and the ground war, when it eventually came, lasted only one hundred hours.

These differences produced some limitations that it would be illogical to dispute. Fighter-bombers don't have extra seats for reporters. And ships can accommodate only so many reporters, assuming they can get to the ship in the first place...

The way television covered the war had a profound effect on how Americans perceived both the military and the press.

Television was present in Vietnam, but it was not so ubiquitous or so immediate. There were no portable satellite uplinks in the late '60s. Video material had to be ferried out to some relay point, and sometimes it reached our living rooms two or three days later. These delays dampened the sense of literal immediacy that exists today. These delays also allowed time to bring perspective and context to the video images— qualities that were often absent from the video verité atmosphere of the Gulf War. Quicker news did not always turn out to be quality news.

We didn't see broadcasts from behind enemy lines in Vietnam... Many people were troubled by the fact that Peter Arnett was broadcasting from Baghdad for CNN. I was not. As a result of his presence there, we will be better able to judge the war in our roles as citizens.

It is interesting to note that despite the heavy television viewing during the war, the demand for newspapers also increased sharply. This suggests that despite the fears we all have about erosion of readership, when we have news, we can sell newspapers.

Having said that, we must acknowledge television as a fact of life. The military thus far has adjusted to this better than we have.

Print reporters were largely invisible to the public when they covered the war in Vietnam. Any impressions they created at home were due entirely to the words they wrote.

Not so in the Gulf War. Print reporters found themselves with fifteen seconds of worldwide fame just by asking a question at the briefings . . . and all of us were judged on the basis of how they were perceived.

Most handled this challenge very well; a few did not. The few asked questions that reflected a lack of knowledge, or they seemed arrogant or their tone seemed to reflect bias. They weren't polite. Asinine has come to mind of a lot of people. It is these few examples that get played back time and again from those who watched us and judged us not on what we wrote but on what they saw.

The military briefers were, in contrast, straight out of central casting. They were in control, seemed evenhanded and straightforward, didn't lose their cool, and conveyed a sense of immediacy even when their information was old. Questions they didn't like were deflected, usually on the grounds of military security. We got no sympathy.

The only good news is that with the war now over, the issues of coverage restrictions are in suspension until the next time.

Burl then turned to the issue of speech on college campuses:

The core activities of a university, the competition of ideas and the pursuit of academic inquiry, can flourish only in the presence of the right to express any opinion or ask any question without regard to the correctness of the premise.

It is one thing to disagree with an opinion and defeat it with logic. To deny the mere expression of a bad idea is quite another. Now we find ourselves accepting intolerance of disagreeable or offensive speech in order to fight intolerance of other kinds... These concerns are especially important to journalists, because censorship on the campus today will be censorship in the newsroom tomorrow.

He concluded with a call for journalists to have "an introspective look at our own behavior." He wanted the public to see, as he did, that most reporters covered the news with fairness, accuracy, and context and tried "to give our readers the information they need to make their own judgments in a democratic system."

42

Nobody Beats *The Dallas Morning News*

in the Morning

On December 8, 1991, a gray and drizzly Sunday, the 112-year-old *Dallas Times Herald* called it quits. This time the paper did not have a new owner. It was closing forever.

After a year of private negotiations with *The News*, the *Times Herald* agreed to sell most of its assets—including presses and circulation lists as well as the land and the building it occupied on Pacific Avenue downtown—to *The News* for $55 million. In addition to the asset purchase agreement, *The News* agreed to pay the *Times Herald* $1.5 million to settle the antitrust comics lawsuit, which was up on appeal. Assured that Buzzetta could find no buyer other than *The News*, the Justice Department approved the sale, and a week later the early-December official announcement of the *Times Herald*'s shuttering became public knowledge.

On the A. H. Belo Corporation's side, only Burl and a handful of executives and attorneys knew about the transaction throughout most of the negotiations. The secrecy was important because Belo didn't want the news of a potential acquisition to affect its stock price and because the *Times Herald* could have lost readers and advertisers if word got out about a deal and that deal ultimately didn't close.

Bode was genuinely surprised when Buzzetta called him that dreary Sunday morning with news of the paper's demise. This was by design. "I purposely asked not to be included in discussions about a sale because I felt it would put me in conflict with my role as an editor," he said. "I would have been in a position to have to keep news out of the paper when it was my job to put news into it."

He immediately phoned his editors and reporters and asked them to meet him at the *Times Herald*. He wanted to talk with them face to face about the devastating news; plus, he needed their help in putting out one final edition—planned for the following day. All columnists, whether it was their day to write or not, were asked to file a final column for the Monday editions.

As staff trickled into the *Times Herald* that Sunday, most were in no shape emotionally to get to work. Computer terminals remained silent, chairs empty. "It felt like a punch to the solar plexus," wrote *Times Herald*'s Reporter Mark Potok.

While reporters at the *Times Herald* consoled one another, *The News* held a press conference. About a hundred reporters and editors, including dozens from both newspapers, crowded into *The News'* second-floor conference room to hear what Burl and Decherd had to say.

The two had decided together that they would not take the blame for beating the *Times Herald* to death—and that there would be no victory celebrations in the wake of the news. The way they handled the *Times Herald*'s closing would reflect on *The News* and its employees for decades to come. Besides, their first goal was to win over former *Times Herald* readers and advertisers, and they knew that neither would look kindly on a celebration of the *Times Herald*'s demise. Burl met with *News* reporters beforehand to emphasize that victory celebrations of any kind would reflect badly on the paper and were forbidden.

A somber Decherd opened the gathering. He discussed "the difficult economic environment all companies, including newspapers, are facing today, as well as the prevailing economies of the newspaper business."

He continued:

> The *Times Herald* and *The Morning News* were intense,
> legitimate rivals for news and information in the marketplace.
> This competitive spur served both papers and Dallas readers
> extraordinarily well for a long time. Unfortunately, the healthy
> and robust competition between the two newspapers—which
> produced great journalism for over one hundred years—
> is now over.

Burl, also somber, said: "The decision to close was made by the owners of the *Times Herald*. They decided they were going to close down. Then we [*The News*] decided that we would purchase the assets. The sequence is important... I don't think anybody envisioned until near the end that one of us would go away, would simply cease to exist." He later said:

> I recall driving to work, looking at the news racks on about every corner, and feeling a sad emptiness in my day. Tomorrow, I'm going to drive to work, and that box won't be there. I won't have to look and see what they did versus what we did. There was no inclination to gloat or to high-five, but an immediate sense that our newspaper had a greater obligation than before to serve everyone in the community.

"The feeling was just awful," said Peppard, then the paper's society columnist. "It was like, I've been arguing with my cousin for thirty years and now she's dead. It was not a good feeling. What it meant for *The Morning News* in terms of revenue and profit—good things perhaps for the owners—meant nothing at all to the people in the newsroom."

Former *News* Deputy Managing Editor Lennox Samuels recalled: "We had always relished the competition with the *Herald* and regretted that we would no longer have to look over our shoulders across town. We had enough sense to know that the *Herald* had helped make us better and worried that perhaps we might slip, become lazy, that some people might start cutting corners. Burl wasn't having any of that, of course, but it was a concern."

The one tangible item Burl wanted from the *Times Herald* was the silver nitrate used for developing photographs. A handful of *News* executives toured the *Herald*'s building following the press conference and retrieved it from the newspaper's photo lab. Burl took the silver to his good friend, local jeweler Harry Bock of Bachendorf's, and at Burl's instruction, one of Bock's master jewelers used the silver to make cufflinks engraved with: "NOBODY BEATS *THE DALLAS MORNING NEWS* IN THE MORNING."

Nobody Beats *The Dallas Morning News* in the Morning (Credit: Photo by David Woo)

• • •

A few weeks later, Burl delivered hand-engraved Montblanc pens to several *News* executives. The pens were inscribed "TDMN, 1991" with the executive's initials. This was another subtle way of memorializing the achievement of *The Dallas Morning News*.

With the *Times Herald* defunct, *The Dallas Morning News*' daily circulation grew to 520,000 and to 840,000 on Sundays. Advertising prices grew as well, to help cover the cost of increased circulation.

The News, then the "the biggest paper in Texas," was now also among the ten largest newspapers in the country, muscling veteran heavyweights such as the *Miami Herald* and *The Boston Globe* out of the way.

Jon Katz worked as managing editor of the *Times Herald* during the early 1980s and was a media critic and journalism professor at New York University in the '90s. He told *Adweek*: "Osborne is as good a newspaperman as there is, up there with the Ben Bradlees and Shelby Coffeys of American newspapering. If this had happened in New York or L.A., they would have named a journalism school for him. [He] was like a pit bull. Once he got the advantage he never let go."

Mong, *The News*' managing editor the day the *Times Herald* closed, perhaps said it best. "Burl just beat the hell out of them!"

ADWEEK article graphic (Credit: JWong 1990)

43

A Turtle on a Fence Post

The year 1991 also marked the twenty-fifth anniversary of Burl's kidney transplant surgery. Friends, family, and even some doctors were amazed that Burl's kidney had lasted as long as it had. In 1966, the average life expectancy of the recipient was four to five years, providing the kidney wasn't rejected immediately after transplantation. Burl's kidney had lasted an amazing five times that long.

Burl had not written about his kidney disease or transplant in years, but he was often asked to speak about his experience. In 1991, he gave the keynote address at Dallas' Methodist Medical Center's tenth anniversary of the first transplant at the center:

"Transplant recipients have an insight that some people never acquire. We understand, better than most people, the value of a single day. That trip into the operating room has a way of focusing the mind, of concentrating on what is really important and weeding out what is not. It changed my life, for much the better. Without that gift, I never would have known my wife and son, who are the center of my life. I am sure that many of you had similar experiences."

Burl reflected on the history of transplantation surgery in the United States and his role in its emergence.

> It has been twenty-five years since I got my new kidney. In some ways it seems like yesterday to me; in other ways it was a long, long time ago. I suspect that in 1966 some of the real doctors in this room were five or six years old and *playing* doctor with the girl or boy next door.
>
> In those days, a meeting like this could have been held in a telephone booth. And it wouldn't have been very crowded.

He described the difficult process he had endured on rudimentary home dialysis, then talked about the enormous strides that had been made since. "No one I know would choose transplantation over keeping the organs that Mother Nature provided in the first place. But despite all the problems and setbacks, we continue to make progress. I don't know how many transplants were done in 1966, but it wasn't very many. I have been told that in 1973, there were about 1,600. By 1985, there were more than 9,000, the great majority of which were kidneys. Last year, the number was over 15,000."

It was terribly important, he emphasized, to recognize doctors and other healthcare workers for their contributions and to help raise public awareness of the need for organ donors:

> They are like the pioneers who settled this country, the women and men who fought the deserts and mountains inch by inch to open up the frontier. The progress in transplantation has been won inch by inch as well, by those who do the research, by those who give long hours and make longer trips to procure donor organs, by those who use the scalpel and by those who assist, by those at the bedsides, by those who help the families through the ordeal. They press ahead, a little at a time, and they pay a price in their commitment, in time sacrificed from their families and their private lives. These are the heroes, the people who have made possible the success of this medical center and the better quality of the lives of its patients.
>
> The other thought I want to leave with you is that there is no free lunch. Those of us who have received the benefit of transplantation also have a price to pay. We owe something in return, to those who gave the gift to us, to those who follow us.
>
> We are obliged to give our own best efforts to overcome some of the obstacles that remain. Most of us can't help to find new drugs or new treatments or new ways to perform the surgery. We may not be able to solve some of the ethical riddles, like the current question of whether it is right to conceive a child in order that its bone marrow might save another child.

But we can improve the donation process within our hospitals, particularly the way the donation request is made of families. Although most Americans support the idea of donation, most families have not discussed it with each other. Still fewer have decided in advance what they would want done. If families are treated in a way that is sensitive to their needs at that difficult moment, they are most likely to give consent. However, if their emotional—and informational—needs are not well met, they are less likely to agree.

If more people understand donation, and make their decisions in advance, then more organs will become available. Transplant recipients are the best evidence of the good that can come from a tragedy, and that is where we can be of most help.

We can do something with the extra days and years that we have been given. We can try to leave for those who follow a place that is a little bit better than we found it. That is why we are here this evening.

Years later, Burl would contribute to the transplantation cause by serving on the board of the National Kidney Foundation and the Dallas-based Southwest Transplant Alliance, one of the largest organ procurement organizations in the country.

• • •

After a number of years in Dallas, Betty began seriously thinking about law school. She had wanted to be a lawyer since high school. "I was the only girl in a civics class when one day the teacher (the basketball coach) posed a question to our class about our goals and aspirations. When my turn came, I immediately said that I wanted to be a lawyer. All the boys in the class began to tease and laugh at me, saying that girls didn't become lawyers. I think that always stayed with me." Burl knew the story and encouraged her to apply.

Betty took the LSAT twice; she applied to Southern Methodist University Law School with an improved score and an excellent undergraduate record and was admitted. The campus was convenient to both home and Jonathan's school.

"I turned forty my first semester in law school," she said. Burl and Jonathan gave her the utmost support. "I tried to balance being the wife of a very busy man, a good mother to Jonathan, and as good a law student as my time allowed." Jonathan, she said, appreciated his independence "without mom always there hovering."

Jonathan had developed a love for tennis, participating in tournaments throughout the area, and he lettered in high school. He was a good student "and a good teenager, with a few minor blips," Betty said. He had worked on his middle school newspaper and became editor of the high school paper in his senior year. He was a good writer from an early age. "He says he had no choice because his dad was always editing him," Betty said.

• • •

To commemorate the anniversary of Burl's kidney transplant, Burl and Betty (Jonathan was away at summer camp) flew to Ashland, Kentucky, where Burl's brother David—who owns and operates successful engineering and construction companies—hosted 150 guests on July 27 at an outdoor party at his home in the country. There was a genuine pit barbeque, with a pig roasted over a wood fire buried in the ground, to celebrate Burl's tremendous success during those twenty-five years and honor his mother and kidney donor, Juanita. The family had lost Oliver Osborne to lung cancer in 1983.

Burl spoke informally to those gathered for the occasion, thanking all the guests for their support through the years. "Out in Texas," he chuckled, "when we find a turtle on a fence post, we say one thing: he had a lot of help." Insisting that he had had a great deal of help in his life, Burl began by thanking his mother. Still a lively, spirited woman, Juanita was as gracious as ever, saying, as she had before, that giving a kidney to her son when he was in need was something that a mother just naturally does. Then she pointed out that "it's not just a milestone in our family's background; it's a milestone in medical history. This sort of thing was almost experimental when Burl's was done." She ended her short speech by thanking the guests and suggesting, "Let's have a party!"

• • •

What Burl did not mention at the party was that his one and only kidney was beginning to show signs of tiring. Though Burl was fifty-four years old, his kidney was seventy. It still functioned, but not at an optimal level. At times he felt out of breath and listless, feelings his doctors attributed to a weakening kidney. And the urine test results, which revealed extensive information about his kidney's health, were beginning to cause his doctors concern.

In 1992, his friend and doctor, Peter Ivanovich introduced a new treatment. Twice weekly, Burl was to give himself an injection of ESA, or erythrocyte stimulating agent, a natural hormone produced by the kidneys. The nephrologist knew the product well, having done some of the earliest research on the drug for the pharmaceutical company Amgen. "Because Burl's transplanted kidney was losing function," Ivanovich said, "he was becoming anemic. I introduced the treatment to raise his hemoglobin and give a boost to his energy level."

Burl had been seeing Dr. Pedro Vergne-Marini, a highly regarded nephrologist who cofounded the transplant program at Dallas' Methodist Medical Center in the late 1970s. Dr. Vergne remembered that Burl had started to have "protein in the urine, which means that there's some damage to the kidney." Vergne performed a biopsy on Burl's kidney, "which showed what was in those days called transplant glomerulopathy, which basically says there is some damage that is associated with kidney transplant. It means there's been damage and you can expect progression of the damage. Nobody knew what caused the damage."

Vergne said that as kidney function decreases, patients tend to get more uremic, their blood counts drop, and they tend to lose energy. "His blood count was starting to drop. I told him that at some point he was going to need another transplant. Early on, he wasn't too keen on that. His brother, though, offered a kidney, and that started to change Burl's thinking."

At the time of Burl's 1966 transplant, doctors had determined that David— along with Juanita—was a particularly good candidate for donating a kidney. For years he had been waiting in the wings for his chance to help his older brother. "Ever since the first transplant, I knew that I was going to be giving a kidney one day," David said.

Betty knew of David's eagerness to help, so when she saw Burl's kidney faltering, "I just called David and said, very simply, 'It's time. His kidney is failing.'"

David called Burl to set up a time when they could have their joint operations. But "Burl kept finding an excuse to put it off. He said he had a number of other conflicts in his schedule." At times it seemed to David that he was more eager to have the operation than Burl was. "I finally said to him, 'You know, something could happen to either one of us. We've got to get this done.'"

Despite Burl's insistence that his schedule didn't allow time for a surgery, Betty knew what was really holding him back. "I was in my second year of law school at Southern Methodist University when we learned that Burl's kidney function had begun to decline. He wanted very much for me to finish. My graduation from law school was a big deal to him. He wanted no interruptions."

Betty also knew Burl was reluctant to go forward with the second transplant because he didn't want others to know about it. This was a complete reversal for the AP alum who had written extensively about his first transplant in the 1960s, but Burl worried that talking about his kidney disease could hinder his newspaper career and invitations to board memberships. After all, he had almost *not* been hired by *The News* because of questions about his health.

"He was involved with several organizations and on many committees and boards. He was afraid that he would have fewer opportunities if people knew about his health," Betty said. "If they knew he needed another transplant, people might assume that he wouldn't be healthy enough to do a good job or fulfill his commitment. He was very concerned about that." And, unlike when he first began to work at *The News*, the paper was now a publicly held company and he did not want his health to be an issue that could affect the stock price.

44

The Internet

The Dallas Morning News continued to grow and compete nationally in another significant way: it continued to rake in Pulitzer Prizes, every year from 1991 to 1994.

William Snyder won the 1991 Pulitzer for Feature Photography for his photographs of ill and orphaned children living in subhuman conditions in Romania.

Lorraine Adams and Dan Malone won the 1992 Pulitzer for Investigative Reporting for their article about Texas police charged with extensive misconduct and abuses of power.

Ken Geiger and William Snyder won the 1993 Pulitzer for Spot News Photography for their dramatic photographs of the 1992 Summer Olympics in Barcelona.

And *The Dallas Morning News'* team won the 1994 Pulitzer for International Reporting for a series that examined the epidemic of violence against women in many nations.

Buoyed by the success and recognition of its award-winning reporters, *The News* continued to devote significant resources to major investigative stories. According to Roy Reed in *American Journalism Review*,

> In late 1994, the paper assigned two top investigative reporters, Howard Swindle and Dan Malone, to one of the most ambitious projects it had undertaken in years. As assistant managing editor for projects, Swindle had supervised three Pulitzer-winning stories. Malone had been involved in some of the paper's best investigative stories, including the Pulitzer-winning effort on police abuse of authority.

The pair started a reporting project that the paper later
described as the first in-depth national survey of death row
inmates. The research staff and the writers, assisted by several
outside authorities on legal matters, drew up a survey of 75
questions. It was mailed to death row inmates in 35 states. It
was answered by 603 condemned people. More than 100 others
sent letters and other documents. The reporters interviewed
more than three dozen inmates. The resulting series appeared
in 1997, more than two years after research had begun, in four
installments. It was a revealing, intimate and chilling portrait of
the most violent Americans and the system that deals with them.

• • •

Neil Foote was working as assistant retail manager in the advertising
department when leadership tapped him to switch jobs and work on a new
concept: figuring out how *The News* could benefit from using the internet. "No
one knew what the internet was or what it could do," Foote said. "The newsroom
wasn't doing anything on the web, so we were really first. We put together
something called Cityview.com, which was a guide to Dallas." Foote was proud
of his work, but Burl couldn't get interested. "When we showed it to Burl, he was
looking at his watch the whole time, very unimpressed with what we had done.
Finally, he put a dollar on the table and said, 'As soon as you guys figure out how
to make a dollar out of this, you'll get my attention.' And then he left."

Two things happened that eventually pushed Burl to change his mind about
the internet. A *News* reporter had a scoop about American terrorist Timothy
McVeigh, who had been responsible for the 1995 Oklahoma City bombing. The
question at *The News* was whether to hold the scoop for the next day's paper or
put it on *The News'* website. "Burl said, 'We're putting it on the web,'" Foote said.

In 2021, Mong, then retired editor of *The News*, recalled Burl putting the
scoop on the website "way ahead of the print edition. While this is standard
today, it was shocking to many newspaper executives at the time. It was
impossibly difficult for many newspaper people to give up a print-first mentality."

The second breaking news story involved the arrest in 1996 of Dallas
Cowboys wide receiver Michael Irwin on alleged sexual assault charges.

"When the story was put on the website, there was so much traffic that the system crashed," Foote said.

"During this time, Burl asked, 'You mean I can break stories whenever I want, just like I did at the AP? And there are no space limitations?' Once Burl understood the internet, get out of his way!"

Decherd remembered that momentous period in the life of the daily. "*The Dallas Morning News* was the first newspaper in America to publish a story online before it was printed in the newspaper the next morning. That's a decision Burl Osborne made. He said, 'Look, this idea of a news cycle is kaput. We have to get used to the idea that our audiences are not going to wait for us to publish on our time table.'" Decherd instantly approved.

Burl "saw how vulnerable our classified employment advertising was to the digital web," Mong recalled. Employment and auto advertising "were huge sources of revenue for *The News*—more so than in most markets, because of its huge population growth, business and economic expansion, and a market far less dependent on mass transit and drawn to cars and trucks." Burl called the early internet a "better mouse trap" for classified ads and saw the daunting financial challenges it would pose in the future.

But "Burl was not afraid of the web," Mong said. "There is no question Burl completely understood that the web ultimately put the power in the hands of individuals and that this would eventually create huge disruptions not only in newspapers but also in most other businesses."

• • •

On November 9, 1995, *The News* announced that Burl would assume the additional responsibility as president of the publishing division of the A. H. Belo Corporation, the newspaper's parent company. This appointment put Burl in charge of Belo's DFW Suburban Newspapers Inc., publisher of eight community newspapers, Belo's "new media" initiatives in publishing, and any new newspapers that Belo might acquire in the future—all in addition to his role as captain of *The Dallas Morning News*.

A story announcing the promotion quoted Burl: "We do believe that there's an opportunity for us to make sensible acquisitions. I can't tell you when they will be. But, yes, we are interested in acquiring additional newspapers. One of the things I will do is pursue that."

During the next few years, Burl led the effort to buy six daily newspapers across the country. The largest and most prestigious of the acquisitions was *The Providence Journal*, the oldest continuously published daily in the United States, having begun in 1829, the year of President Andrew Jackson's first term in office. The five other purchases were *The Press-Enterprise* in Riverside, California; the *Messenger-Inquirer* in Owensboro, Kentucky; *The Gleaner* in Henderson, Kentucky; *The Eagle* in Bryan-College Station, Texas; and the *Record-Chronicle* in Denton, Texas. Each of those deals came about because of Burl's personal and professional relationship with the newspaper's owner. Each of those acquisitions fell squarely within Burl's core belief: "A good newspaper has a substantial need to provide public service. A good newspaper is also a good business."

He made a tradition of giving Montblanc pens to executives to mark every newspaper acquisition the Belo Corporation made.

Lee Dirks, founder and chairman of Dirks, Van Essen & Murray, the most active newspaper merger and acquisitions firm in the 1980s and 1990s, said of Burl as publisher:

> If someone asked me, "What's the single most important characteristic of Burl's?" I'd say exceptional vision. Burl was far more focused on where the industry was going and where his newspaper was going than the typical publisher or editor. When we'd go on a trip together, we'd wind up talking about where the industry was headed, and he was always looking at the big picture in the future. He was also conscious of the immediate, but much more so than any newspaper executive I ever encountered, he was looking to the future. I think he recognized that that was his role. An effective publisher is going to focus on the strategic future.

45

A Historic Operation

Although Betty could see that Burl was slowing down, several of Burl's friends and colleagues say today they never noticed a difference in his energy level. *Texas Monthly* founder and close friend Mike Levy put it this way: "Running out of steam for any mortal soul would mean slowing down, but Burl was working so much harder and faster and going at such a tremendously fast pace that I wouldn't have noticed if he slowed down. Nobody runs at the kind of pace he did."

Betty hadn't tried to get a job right away after graduating law school. She wanted to avoid the demanding hours of first-year lawyers at most firms, especially with Burl's need for a transplant in the near future. In time she went to work for their friend Harry Bock, the jeweler who owned Bachendorf's. Being an in-house lawyer for a small, closely held, family-owned company gave her great flexibility and allowed her to travel with Burl. She served as chief financial officer, human resource director, and compliance monitor over the retail store leases. "Whatever the need that day, that's the hat that I wore," she said. "Sometimes Mr. Bock would even have me try on jewelry for a customer."

Burl and Betty also tried to protect their son, Jonathan, from knowing too much about Burl's condition. Jonathan was still a teenager, and his parents thought that the less he knew, the less he would worry. But they were not always able to keep their concerns from him. "One evening Burl and I were talking about his recent urinalysis. We didn't know it, but Jonathan overheard us. Later, I went to Jonathan's room to say goodnight. He was crying, saying, 'I don't want my dad to die.'"

Recognizing Jonathan's fears, and after much foot dragging, Burl finally agreed to schedule the surgery. The date was set for October 31, 1994, at the University of Pittsburgh's Thomas E. Starzl Transplant Institute. Starzl, who had performed Burl's first kidney transplantation, had left Denver in 1981 and joined the University of Pittsburgh's School of Medicine. Although he himself would not perform the surgery, he would be in the operating room assisting Dr. Velma P. Scantlebury, one of his mentees, the United States' first Black female transplant surgeon. Joining them would be Burl's close friend Dr. Peter Ivanovich.

Burl bought four gifts at Bachendorf's before he and Betty left for Pittsburgh. He wanted to present Betty, Juanita, and David with their gifts in person, in the event he did not make it through the operation.

Two of the gifts were for Betty: one for her birthday, a few weeks away, and the other for Christmas. Her birthday gift was a pair of diamond earrings, and her Christmas present was a diamond ring to match the earrings. She wasn't to open either package, however, until the specified occasion.

Burl had beautiful gold watches for both Juanita and David. On the back of each were inscribed the words: "Thank you for my lifetime." Below the words were the dates of the transplants: 7-27-1966 on Juanita's watch and 10-31-1994 on David's.

Burl kept word about his second transplant so quiet that even his executive assistant, Amy Keepes, did not know about it until just a day or two before he went to Pittsburgh to have it performed. Keepes recalled: "He just said, 'I'm going,' and then he was off. That's about all he said."

David and Burl both flew to Pittsburgh for preoperative screenings. David assured a psychologist there that his decision to donate was completely voluntary, but "I told Burl that the kidney I was donating was just a loan."

As with Burl's kidney transplant in 1966, this operation would be historic. A complementary bone marrow procedure had been shown to help fuse the two immunological systems and dramatically reduce the need for antirejection drugs, so for the first time on record, doctors would perform a bone marrow transplant simultaneously with the organ transplantation between two living, related donors. (Dr. Scantlebury wrote in her book, *Beyond Every Wall*: "For many years it was clear that Dr. Starzl was opposed to living kidney donation ... With the increasing supply of deceased kidney donors, he explained, 'No life should be placed in danger by donating a kidney while alive.' He felt the risks were too great ... Dr. Starzl eventually embraced the use of living donors [however] ... It would be the start of a new era.")

The four-hour-long surgeries went as planned, and the surgical teams considered the operations a success. Burl's new kidney did begin to show signs of rejection, which had happened after his first transplant. Betty recalled: "Dr. Scantlebury assured us that it is common for the organ to be rejected at some time in the first week to ten days. Burl knew this from his first transplant. Yet he was still a little frightened when he had to reenter the hospital. They gave him high doses of prednisone to stop the rejection. After three days his chemistries improved. They released him from the hospital; however, we stayed in Pittsburgh for another three weeks. We went to the hospital every day for lab tests so that the doctors could monitor his kidney function."

Jonathan, who had just begun his first year at Washington and Lee University in Lexington, Virginia, flew to Pittsburgh a few days after the transplant surgery to see his dad. Levy also visited Burl shortly after Halloween. Reminiscing about that visit, he said: "I took one look at him and said, 'Geez, you look like shit.' Now, we never cracked a smile at what the other guy said, because that would have shown weakness. We were always trying to out-sardonic the other. You lost points if you ever smiled at what the other one of us said."

When doctors were certain Burl's new kidney was fully operational and he was in good enough shape to travel, they allowed him to go home. Back in Dallas, his regimen included taking a low-dose immunosuppressant drug, FK506, in pill form twice a week, as well as blood pressure and cholesterol medication. He would see his nephrologist in Dallas twice a year. As predicted in 1966, his brother David's kidney was a perfect match.

• • •

A month after the operation, Burl sent an engraved gold watch to Ivanovich with a letter that summed up his feelings about his "third" chance at life. He wrote:

```
Dear Peter,
    I don't want to get any farther away from the Halloween
miracle before trying, however inadequately, to express to you
how very much your friendship and caring has meant to Betty and
me and to all of my family. No one could have a more steadfast
friend, always there when needed at whatever the personal cost.
```

Very few people in this world are given a second chance at life. Now you have seen to it that I have a third, and I know that I must use it wisely.

I also have had an opportunity to reflect a bit on how today's state-of-the-art differs from that of twenty-eight years ago. The distance transplantation has come truly is enormous, to a point where the two experiences can't even be compared. The more I think about it, the luckier I realize that I am.

I hope that you will accept the enclosed token of our gratitude and admiration for your skill and caring, and for our friendship of three decades—which just gets better.

There is a little interesting history to the watch, which bears the name "Bachendorf" that you probably never heard of. One of our closest friends in Dallas is Harry Bock, who with his father escaped the Lithuanian concentration camps in World War II, found his way to Texas where he established a tiny, hole-in-the-wall jewelry store. It later became Bachendorf's and today is the preeminent jewelry retailer in North Texas. Now in his 60s, Harry never has forgotten his roots. A few years ago, he designed and made a small batch of 18K watches carrying his own logotype using the Eta movement, which is used in Patek Philippe and other Swiss watches; and he has made them available to friends. This is one of them, and I hope you enjoy it.

Please have a great holiday season. You already have made ours very, very special. With all best wishes.

Sincerely,

Although Burl came through the operation without incident, afterward in Dallas he began to feel sore all over. He no longer took the immunosuppressant that he had been taking. For the first time in twenty-eight years, his body was free of steroids; the result, however, was that everything—his muscles, his joints, everything—ached. Doctors explained that Burl was experiencing prednisone withdrawal and the pain could continue for as long as a year.

Despite that excruciating pain, Burl never complained and never missed a day of work.

To celebrate the transplant and bear witness to his "very active life," Burl purchased his dream car, a Ferrari Testarossa. Friend and former AP Washington bureau colleague Michael Putzel recalled visiting Burl in Dallas shortly thereafter.

> He knew I was a car freak. I wanted to take a ride in his Ferrari, and he wanted to take me on a ride. We got onto a highway in Dallas with several lanes. We were going 125 miles an hour. There was a curve in the road, and in a matter of seconds we closed in on a car that was doing about 70 or 80. I thought we were going to hit that car. If we had, it would have been a catastrophe. But Burl knew how to drive. He hit the brakes, and we swerved into another lane. It scared the hell out of me. He was pretty proud of himself when he got out of the car later. He'd shown me what he could do with that car.

Putzel is still amazed at how close he and Burl came to crashing. "I didn't go out to Dallas thinking we were going for a Sunday drive, but it was a whole lot closer to disaster than I expected to be. I don't think Burl was reckless, but he had a willingness to take risks that a lot of others wouldn't take, and it wasn't just driving a car. It was a risk for him to go to Dallas when not a lot of people took *The Dallas Morning News* seriously. It may have come from being a guy with just one kidney."

Get well card, 1994 kidney transplant (Credit: Bill DeOre and *Morning News'* staff)

PART III

Retirement

46

Publisher Emeritus

"Burl really wanted to build a new house," said Betty, "and the impetus for it was the AP annual meeting he knew would be held in Dallas that year in conjunction with the convention."

The Newspaper Association of America would hold its convention in the spring of 1998, and the AP was celebrating its 150th anniversary.[12] Burl "wanted to welcome his AP colleagues and board members to Dallas by having a special dinner for them in our home," Betty said. "He wanted to entertain them in a special way for this momentous occasion. Burl's motto has always been: 'All are welcome. The door is always open, and the light's on in the hall.'"

No one could doubt upon seeing their French-chateau-style home that Burl had come a long way from his humble beginnings. The home's main living area had a thirty-foot ceiling, which Burl liked to joke meant that he didn't have to worry about hitting his head.

Convention guests visited Texas Stadium, where they could take the field and try to placekick a football through the stadium's goal posts. And Burl and Betty hosted the AP's board of directors to dinner in their new home.

Burl, as convention chairman, put together a spectacular "Best of Texas" dinner at the Anatole Hotel. It was the highlight of the jubilant three-day weekend. A centerpiece of yellow roses graced each table, and the ballroom's many crystal chandeliers cast a golden glow over the guests. And, to salute the AP on its 150th year, Burl requested that the Anatole create a special dessert with a chocolate AP logo.

Burl assembled some one hundred Texas celebrities, including former President George H. W. Bush, Dallas Cowboys' owner Jerry Jones, and real estate developer Trammell Crow, pianist Van Cliburn, oil magnate T. Boone Pickens, and journalist and playwright Elizabeth Forsythe Hailey. Burl placed one Texas celebrity at each of the tables in the Anatole Hotel's ballroom so every member of the association could rub shoulders with one of Texas' best-known citizens.

Burl began the dinner by introducing the famous Texans and making a clever comment about each one. Asked later how he was able to get so many prominent Texans to come to the dinner, Burl said, "I invited them."

As the former president wrote to Burl in his thank-you note a few days after the weekend, "You sure put on a fantastic party. It was a grand evening and Barbara and I were very pleased to be a small part of it. I loved your idea of introducing the Texans to the visitors—a nice touch that made the evening extra special for all your guests, including the Bushes. We loved it!"

• • •

Every Saturday at his office in Dallas' Preston Center, Bock would host a lunch called the Saturday Wine Group. If you hadn't received an invitation from him by Thursday of that week, you were devastated. Burl was among the regular stag members, which included his close friend Dr. Ron Underwood, American Airlines executive Arnold Grossman, businessman Howard Meyers, attorney Dick Adams, and Dr. Paul Radman. They would cram into Bock's tiny kitchen off the executive suite beyond the showroom.

Bock always chose a special wine to accompany the bagels, lox, salami, and kosher side dishes that he ordered in from the Deli-News. Decadent chocolate, desserts, and Cuban cigars were plentiful too.

The lunches continued for twenty years, and the men always competed to see who could tell the funniest stories or jokes any given Saturday. A repeat invitation to the Saturday Wine Group spoke volumes about how amusing you had been the week before.

• • •

In May 2001, *The News* announced on the front of the business section that Burl had been elected vice chairman and chairman-elect of the AP, putting him in line for chairman the next year. Burl was quoted in the article: "The AP is the most credible and wide-reaching news organization in the world." He called his election "a great compliment to *The Dallas Morning News*."

Burl got a chuckle out of AP Hall of Famer Walter Mears' congratulatory "Letter to the Editor."

> As a friend and a fan, I have waited nearly 30 years to get this printed: Burl couldn't have done it without me. Had I not resigned as assistant chief of the AP Washington bureau in 1974 . . . Had I not returned within the year . . . he would have become chief of [that] bureau instead of managing editor of the AP. And even the wizards at *The Morning News* would have had trouble spotting him to become their editor in 1980 . . . There is something special about watching a good friend achieve the magnificent things he has accomplished. But don't forget that without my clumsy contribution in career planning, his golden years would not be nearly so golden.

The *Bluefield Daily Telegraph*'s Bill Archer, a columnist, was quick to place this announcement prominently in the May 6, 2001, edition: "Publisher Burl Osborne of the Dallas Morning News named VP and chairman elect of the AP. Bluefield was one of the early stops of his distinguished career."

Burl had come full circle from AP cub reporter in the Bluefield, West Virginia, "bureau" to chairman of the entire organization. Even for someone with all of Burl's success, this was a crowning achievement. The son of a father who had never learned to read or write, Burl was elected to run the world's largest news-gathering organization.

• • •

A few weeks later, on May 25, 2001, *The News* announced that Burl was stepping down as publisher and editor, effective June 15. He would retire as president of A. H. Belo's Publishing Division by the end of the year. He also planned to take on the title of "publisher emeritus," remain on Belo's board of directors until May 2002, and serve as chairman of the Belo Foundation. Mong was promoted to president and editor of *The News*.

Although Burl could have stayed another year at *The News*, James Moroney III was eager to take over the role of publisher, and Burl was ready to switch roles and begin working on the AP board.

He was also looking forward to devoting more time to other interests. Burl was president of the Southern Newspaper Publishers Association, and he served on the boards of the Newspaper Association of America and the Committee to Protect Journalists. He was a director and member of the executive committee of the World Association of Newspapers and served on the Advisory Committee for the Nieman Foundation at Harvard University.

"Frankly," Burl said, "I want to relax some." But he added, "I've loved every minute of it."

Word of Burl's plans spread quickly through journalism circles. When Burl retired, *News* columnist Peppard sent an email to Betty that he asked her to pass along to him. It poignantly expressed the feelings of many former and current staffers who had the privilege of working with and for Burl. In it, he recounted the beginning of *Lonesome Dove*:

> The two protagonists, Woodrow Call and Augustus McRae, have been stealing cattle and horses from the Mexican rancher Pedro Flores. On their way back across the Rio Grande, they find Pedro Flores' vaqueros stealing Texas horses and cattle and bringing them back the other direction into Mexico. Apparently, this game had been going on for years, Pedro steals their livestock and they steal Pedro's.
>
> Later on, they learn that Pedro Flores died suddenly. Call looks very sad to hear the news. He says, "I guess the fun's all over here for sure." That's when he gathers his herd together and sets out from the Rio Grande on a cattle drive to Montana.

He concluded, "When I heard that Burl was moving on from the publisher's office, I felt kind of sad, like Woodrow Call, and thought, 'I guess the fun's all over here for sure.'"

47

From Cub Reporter to Chairman

The early 2000s were a critical time in news, and the AP needed a leader like Burl to meet the challenge. The internet was beginning to disrupt the AP and the news business as a whole.

"All our money—which used to come from newspapers—was beginning to come from broadcasts," said Julie Inskeep, publisher of *The Journal Gazette* in Fort Wayne, Indiana, and member of the AP board.

Lissa Walls Cribb, who served on the AP board from 1997 to 2006, including as vice chair under Burl, likewise recalled the economic and philosophical challenges the AP and its member newspapers faced during that period.

> AP started seeing its traditional revenue sources decline, and it had to look at ways it could increase its revenue from nontraditional sources. And with technology it's always a bit of a gamble. AP was faced with big decisions that carried big risk. Burl was that calm voice and steady hand in the room when these decisions were being made. . . . Just as newspapers were adapting to the Internet, AP had to adapt also.

David Lord, head of Pioneer Newspapers Inc. in Seattle, joined the AP board the year that Burl became chairman. He admired Burl's political acumen:

> He'd call you up before the meeting and ask, "What are the things you're concerned about? Are there particular issues?" And when he did that, he'd also subtly lobby you to his issues. So that when something came up at a meeting that he wanted you to be in favor

of, he had already lined up your support in advance, and things ran very smoothly. He was really skilled at that.

Kathleen Carroll became executive editor of the AP the same year that Burl became its chairman of the board. She recalled: "What Burl was able to do was help unify the board to support AP's mission so that it could continue to thrive. What you need is a talented chair that can unify the people to a common mission, and that's what Burl was able to do."

Burl spoke candidly later on about two main issues the AP faced in those days: "the question of television and the question of what became online or internet or web businesses."

> The notion for the television business, when it developed, was a big deal for the AP. It involved borrowing money, it involved losing money for a period of time, and it involved the assumption that we could become at least one of the two most important players in international video. And it was at least the majority view of the board that we *had* to be in that business. And at the time we made that decision, I don't think we realized that we really had to be in that business not so much for television stations but for our own newspapers down the road when they, perhaps belatedly, discovered that a website without video is not going to be terribly successful.

> The other issue, which was even more argued on the board, was how, when, and whether the AP should be in the digital business arena. As time passed, the majority of the board agreed that the AP *had* to be in that arena. A small number of directors, but representing a large number of businesses, did not want the AP to sell anybody anything and felt that if Yahoo or Google or AOL or MSN wanted that content, they would have to go through us, the members. I think that was wrong. It's the only split vote I ever had as chairman. But it was debated and continues to be debated. I think the decision was an imperative; the AP might not exist today without that revenue.

. . .

Burl got to see his son follow him into journalism. While waiting for his then-girlfriend and eventual wife to graduate, Jonathan took a job in Washington, D.C., as a reporter for the Hill, then a scrappy upstart competing to cover the inside baseball of politics. He would eventually end up as a reporter then editor at the *Austin American-Statesman*. He was in the newsroom on the morning of September 11, 2001.

That morning, Burl and Betty were getting dressed and ready for work with the TV on. Burl always had the TV on in the morning to catch up on the news of the day. At 7:45 a.m. Texas time, she recalled, "We watched mesmerized when the first plane flew into the first building. We were stunned when it was realized that it was no accident. Burl continued watching for a few minutes before rushing to the office."

At a later AP board meeting in New York City, Betty and the other board spouses visited an apartment overlooking the site of the towers. This was the place some of the AP photographers had taken pictures that had gone on to become iconic symbols of 9/11, including those of people jumping from the building. "We were in the apartment, looking through the very windows where they were capturing those photos that awful day," Betty said.

. . .

Burl retired as chairman of the AP board in 2007. "I had been gradually handing stuff off at Belo and getting ready to really sort of find another phase to my life," reflected Burl after retiring from his chairmanship of the AP's board of directors.

> It was kind of interesting to have a relatively brief period where I could still be involved with the AP and, hopefully, could help. . .
>
> It was a great thrill. It's one of the nicest things that ever happened to me. It's very, very nice to be rewarded that way by your peers. Professionally, in terms of the industry, work, and other work, it was the nicest thing that ever happened to me.
>
> It is absolutely wonderful to be a part of something larger than oneself. I'm happy. That was a nice way to finish.

Once, when asked whether he enjoyed his time at the AP—both before and after his stellar years with *The Dallas Morning News*—Burl replied with a great laugh, "Can't you see the letters AP emblazoned across my forehead?"

Competition from the internet and the invention of smartphones had fundamentally changed the economics of the news business by this time. The "newspaper wars" of the past were now clearly only battles in a much larger conflict. Advertising was no longer a sustainable source of revenue for newspapers. The internet—like TV decades before it—was more immediately gratifying to consumers. As the internet became ever more accessible, news left the living room. There was less need to watch or read the news at home, because readers already consumed it throughout the day on their smartphone—and continued to do so when they got home.[13]

Burl looked to the future and saw the AP's role in it:

> The AP is constructed for the web. Nobody knew that 160-odd
> years ago, but it was built for today. It has been 24-7 forever. It's in
> the culture; it's in the DNA; it's in what the AP is and is all about.
> How that can best be monetized and how that can best be done
> to the benefit of the AP members is a different question that we
> could talk about, but nobody is or ever has been better suited to
> do this than the AP.

Throughout his retirement, Burl lent his management and editorial experience to a number of boards. Notable among them were Plano, Texas–based JCPenney; Andrews McMeel Universal, the comic and features syndicate at the center of the *Times Herald* case (and the publisher of this book); GateHouse Media, a newspaper acquisition company; and Freedom Communications Inc.—a media conglomerate that included *The Orange County Register* as well as a portfolio of other newspapers, television stations, websites, and mobile apps.

"I liked the way he thought," Alan Questrom, then–chairman and CEO of JCPenney, said. "Which is why I invited him on the board. I knew he had great management experience, in addition to his editorial experience. I thought it was very interesting—and unusual—that he was both editor and publisher of *The News* at the same time. I had not heard of that before. He had a terrific reputation."

Gerald Turner, the president of Southern Methodist University, served on Penney's board when Burl was asked to join. "One specific need was for someone in the communications area, who could advise the company on public strategies and who also had experience as a CEO of a communications company," Turner said. "With Burl's recent retirement from Belo and *The Dallas Morning News*, he was the perfect choice."

That same year, Freedom Communications sold a significant share of the company to two private equity firms, Blackstone Group and Providence Equity Partners. Private equity firms typically load up the companies they buy with debt in order to pay themselves dividends, and the transaction left Freedom with debt that would ultimately force the company into Chapter 11 bankruptcy reorganization in 2009.

The board tapped Burl as CEO to lead them through the tumultuous time. He loved the new challenge. The company emerged from bankruptcy the following April with new owners. Burl remained on the board.

48

No Pushover

Because of his long history with kidney disease and the two transplants, Burl had always been diligent about his medical appointments. Then, in February 2005, after his yearly colonoscopy, the doctor called him with the bad news that he had a cancerous tumor. As he had done with his second kidney transplant—and for the same reasons—Burl kept the news of his cancer quiet. Other than his doctors, only Betty, Ivanovich, and a few close friends knew.

Since those early days in Spokane, Ivanovich had always been with Burl during any major medical event. The colon cancer surgery was no exception. Burl's surgeon allowed Ivanovich to be in the operating room just as Starzl had done during the two transplant surgeries.

After a successful operation and recovery, Burl's oncologist recommended chemotherapy. While undergoing the treatments, Burl continued to fulfill his commitments. "He was tired. He wasn't himself at times, but all things considered, the chemotherapy wasn't too bad," recalled Betty. Burl jotted short notes in a personal diary he kept of his treatments. In typical Burl fashion, he wrote: "Understand that I need to maintain normal life. I intend to manage this and not let it manage me."

• • •

On January 22, 2009, Burl's eighty-eight-year-old mother, Juanita Smallwood Osborne, died of complications from pneumonia.

"Juanita's death devasted Burl," Betty said. "It was the saddest I ever saw him."

With a headline that read "Pioneering Kidney Transplant Donor Dies," hundreds of AP newspapers across the United States and around the globe, including *The Dallas Morning News*, carried her obituary, penned by Burl. In one article, Burl said that the risks were high in 1966 when his mother donated one of her kidneys to him. "The greatest fear I had was that something would happen to her remaining kidney." But after the life-saving transplantation surgery, Juanita never had trouble with her kidney. It was working "perfectly," she boasted, as she approached her nineties.

When Burl's mother died and Betty's mother became very ill, Betty told Harry Bock she'd need to stop working. She found and trained her replacement and continued consulting for Bock.

Within the first half of the following year, the personal sadness continued for the Osbornes. In Kentucky, Betty's mother and Burl's youngest brother, Rick, died. Both had been ill for several years. In Dallas, Harry Bock died suddenly. Burl wrote his and Betty's dear friend's obituary and gave the eulogy. Each of these events taxed the family emotionally.

• • •

In 2010, real estate investor Steven Roth and hedge fund manager Bill Ackman joined forces to buy up more than a quarter of JCPenney's stock and joined the board with a plan to transform the company.

In 2011, the board hired former Target executive and Apple retail guru Ron Johnson to implement a new vision. Johnson did so by ridding JCPenney of its discounting culture and redesigning its stores as town squares composed of boutiques for hip brands. As documented in numerous media reports, Burl suggested that Johnson test his ideas—standard practice in retail— at a few stores before implementing them throughout the chain. Johnson bristled at the idea, responding, "We didn't test at Apple."

Johnson would be ousted as CEO just seventeen months after being hired. JCPenney would never fully recover.

"Burl was first class in every way," said Mike Ullman, who served as Penney's chairman and CEO from 2004 to 2011 and then again from 2013 to 2015. "He was savvy and wise and smart. Burl said less than most people, but when he did speak, it was always profound and helpful. If something was being discussed or decided upon and he didn't think it was right, he would stand up and say so. He was no pushover."

• • •

Burl still found time in retirement to make new friends. Among them was Bruce Leadbetter, a colorful Dallas investor who started his career managing money for Lucille Ball and wound up working with Chicago scion Jay Pritzker for thirty years.

On a whim, the two decided to head out to the Middle East to explore a potential business venture.

> I took him to Abu Dhabi, Oman, and Qatar. He'd never been to the Middle East, and I'd been going since the 1960s. On the trip, Burl was like a big sponge. He wanted to talk to everyone and hear about their lives.
>
> Burl was so good at disarming people whom he wanted to talk to. His charm was that his questions were always offered in a way that didn't offend. For example, when we were in Dubai, Burl met the King of Dubai and asked him, "How do you keep from having terrorists in the Emirates?" The King said, "You want to know my secret? I have 300,000 spies, which is every citizen in the country."
>
> Pashmina scarves come out of Oman. When we were there, he met a pashmina maker on the street, and Burl talked to the guy about the whole detailed process of making the scarves. He talked to him for about an hour. He learned everything there was to know about the process. At another point during the trip, he talked to a Russian receptionist for a very long time. He was fascinated by her and all the changes she described having seen over the years.
>
> He tried to talk to everyone, everywhere we went. I found him absolutely charming, with an almost boyish charm about him with all of his questions.
>
> I've been going to the Middle East for decades, yet I learned things because Burl was along that I hadn't known before. Just because he was asking so many questions.

• • •

Even in retirement, Burl was in a hurry, always on the lookout for ways to parlay his experience into new but related opportunities to keep life interesting. Ever the optimist, he fantasized about owning a newspaper of his own.

"I keep looking at what point newspaper pricing is going to be so cheap that even I could run one successfully. I have a son who's thirty-two, a freshly minted MBA, with an interest in media. We're looking at a couple of things. It might be fun to do something entrepreneurial that way. But I'm kind of watching, waiting, hoping something will come along."

The realist side of him kept that notion in check; by 2012, he knew which direction the newspaper business was headed.

49

And He Lived

On Tuesday, August 14, 2012, Burl was again in a hurry. Behind the wheel of his second favorite car, a Mercedes-Benz C63 AMG, Burl—with Betty beside him—raced up Interstate 35 to Dallas from Austin.

They'd spent the weekend babysitting their grandson, Harry, while Jonathan and his wife, Brigette, went to California to celebrate a friend's fortieth birthday.

Eager to get home, Burl watched the clock. When he pulled the car into their driveway, he turned to Betty and said, "Record time: 3 hours and 1 minute." It was his fastest drive time yet between the two cities.

He was also in a hurry because his new Mercedes—an SL63 AMG—sat in the garage waiting for him. He wanted to put a few miles on it before he and Betty left for Tuscany in a couple of days. After they arrived in Florence, the first stop on their itinerary would be the nearby Prada Outlet Store to shop for his favorite shoes.

Early the next morning, though, Burl awoke feeling ill. A lethal bacteria, *Streptococcus pneumoniae*, raged through his body. This was a race he couldn't win.

He died that night of septic shock.

The man who made medical transplantation history in 1966 and again in 1994 died with a healthy kidney.

• • •

The morning after Burl died, Betty's first two phone calls were to their friend Robert Decherd and Gary Pruitt, president and CEO of the AP. Both men saw that obituaries were immediately put in the works, and Decherd offered to help Betty organize a memorial service in Dallas. Betty wanted Fearing, formerly the chef at the Mansion on Turtle Creek, to cater a celebration of Burl's life, so, she assumed, the service could be held at no other spot than the Ritz, where Dean's new restaurant was located.

"Burl and I always said we didn't want a solemn funeral occasion, that we'd rather have a party, a celebration of life," Betty said. She was making plans to have a celebration at the Ritz when she received a call from Mort Meyerson. He insisted that Betty hold the memorial service at the Morton H. Meyerson Symphony Center downtown. After it was determined that Dean could cater the affair at the Meyerson, he also agreed to play guitar and sing. Betty agreed and began planning the service.

Unlike many large memorials, at which many or most attendees have only the most tenuous connection to the deceased, everyone in the Meyerson symphony hall that Friday afternoon—whether they knew Burl personally or not—had walked down their front steps on countless mornings, picked up a dew-flecked *Morning News*, and unrolled the paper to read Burl's name on the masthead. All attendees had an intimate connection to the man that came from reading his newspaper day after day, year after year.

As hundreds of mourners entered the stunningly beautiful auditorium, they heard strains of "The Kentucky Waltz," played by a guitarist and a violinist. Once the approximately seven hundred guests were seated, Turner, the president of Southern Methodist University who had served for many years with Burl on JCPenney's board, opened the service with a brief prayer. Then Decherd asked the audience to rise and "sing with gusto," along with a member of the Dallas Symphony Chorus, "My Old Kentucky Home."

Frank Daniels, who was an AP board member and its chairman when Burl served on the board, was the first to speak. Daniels, a distinguished North Carolina publisher known by many as "Mr. North Carolina," spoke of Burl's legendary AP career.

Turner followed. Few people, he remarked, knew that Burl was a former chairman of the board of trustees of Paul Quinn College. "Burl also lectured at SMU and on many campuses and spent time at the University of Texas and other institutions helping to improve journalism and educate the leaders of schools of journalism. He was so sharp, witty, and experienced that students loved to have him regale them about the real world of newspaper publishing."

Ivanovich, who had flown to Dallas from his home in Chicago, spoke next. "Although I was honored to play a role as his physician, I was more honored to be the recipient of his friendship. We shared the vicissitudes of life over the past five decades, and Burl—a man of great character and loyalty—was there for me in my own times of difficulty. The joys and delights of life were relished together."

Suddenly overcome with grief, Ivanovich bowed his head and hesitated a moment before continuing, "Burl was as dear to me as a beloved brother." His voice cracked. Then, for a few moments, Ivanovich could not speak. Finally, he concluded, "And his death leaves a hole in my heart."

Jonathan had been sitting with Brigette and Betty in the front row of the auditorium, and after Ivanovich ended his remarks, Jonathan walked onto the stage and took his position behind the podium. Pulling back an unruly strand of dark hair from in front of his face and wrapping it behind an ear, Jonathan smiled brightly and began, "I'm going to borrow from my father's playbook today. Dad would always say that a good speech is a short speech.

"I'm going to tell you some things you may not know. I first met Burl Osborne shortly after midnight on March 18, 1976." The audience laughed all at once and loudly.

"I imagine he was as startled as I was. Dad left the hospital that night and returned the next day with hundreds of diapers and literally a ten-year supply of Johnson & Johnson baby shampoo." The audience again laughed loudly. "I'm convinced that through my birth, Burl discovered what would become a lifelong passion—buying in bulk. Whether it's razors, boxers, socks, wine, and, yes, shampoo, the man loved Costco." Jonathan had the audience in the palm of his hand.

Turning to face the other men on the stage, Jonathan remarked, "You guys didn't bring up Brownie the dog." Then, turning back to the audience, he said with a big grin, "Brownie was a dog that was trapped in a West Virginia coal mine for fifty-seven days, and it went out on the AP wire and captured the hearts and imaginations of people all over the country. My dad never thought he'd live that down because whenever he'd meet somebody, they'd mention Brownie the dog."

Jonathan referred to a line out of an obituary when he said, "I was surprised to read about my father's legendary temper." He paused a moment, then added, "I've actually never seen it, but I believe you."

He continued in an upbeat tone, "Dad was an optimist about everything in life except maybe the playoff hopes of the Dallas Cowboys . . . lately. Watching football games with him was an exercise in negativity. Regardless of what the lead was in the fourth quarter, he would too often rightly utter, 'They'll blow it.'"

Jonathan said his father was "a devout champion of my dreams. He was a mentor, a sounding board, a true friend. He was a great man but an even greater father. His love for my mother, Betty, was epic, as was hers for him, and his memories will live with and comfort her forever.

"My father approached life with a childlike joy. He was a risk-taker from an early age. He had to be. He was a great communicator and a true leader of men and women. He was witty, kind, caring, incredibly smart, just fun to be around, everything that everyone has said."

Slowing his delivery, Jonathan concluded, "Dad lived a wondrous and improbably long life." He paused before adding, "And he always told me, 'Strive to leave someplace better than you found it.' Well, Dad, the universe is certainly a better place because of Burl Osborne. So, well done. We love you, and we miss you."

When Jonathan ended his remarks, his wife, Brigette, read the Lord's Prayer. Betty, teary eyed but composed, dabbed her eyes and nose with tissues.

The last person to speak was Decherd:

Burl dedicated his life to the art of journalism. It was more than a profession to him—instead, a combination of seeking truth while holding high aspirations for our society and supporting good deeds for our community. Burl was intensely competitive. You don't get a nickname like "Burldog" by standing idly by.

Yet Burl's sense of balance and fair play, his perspective born of keen intellect and an immense capacity for general knowledge, endeared him to those he loved most as well as a legion of friends, his colleagues, and competitors. Do you know anyone more highly regarded by more people in more separate pursuits than Burl Osborne?

Acknowledgments

• • •

I am very grateful to Burl's widow, Betty Osborne, who spent countless hours with me being interviewed for this book. She provided great insight into the extraordinary man who was Burl Osborne. She also gave me full access to Burl's personal correspondence and email, private papers that included hundreds of letters and speeches, published and unpublished interviews, scrapbooks, and a lifetime of memorabilia, including clippings of stories he wrote dating back to his earliest days at *The Ashland Daily Independent* and The Associated Press, as well as detailed medical files on both of his kidney transplants, including data he collected as one of the first people in history to experiment with home kidney dialysis.

In addition, I am grateful to Burl and Betty's son, Jonathan, who was generous with his time and, as a former journalist himself, made sure that I had my facts correct.

During the year that I spent researching this book, I spoke with scores of Burl's friends, relatives, news associates, admirers, and competitors from throughout the United States, sometimes by phone and email and often in person. I am very grateful for information, which came in the form of interviews or observations, from the following:

Kathleen Andrews, Carolyn Barta, John Bassett, Lou Boccardi, Roy Bode, Ann Blackman, Steve Blow, John Brewer, Kathleen Carroll, Richard Collins, Bill Cox, Robert Crandall, Tom Curley, Frank Daniels, Robert Decherd, Lee Dirks, Karen Doran, Dave Easterly, Tom Engibus, Gregory Favre, Dean Fearing, Nikki Finke, Craig Flournoy, Neil Foote, Jeremy Halbreich, Cheryl Hall, Terry Hunt, Julie Inskeep, Peter Ivanovich, Bo Jones Jr., Gregg Jones, Amy Keepes, Tim Kelly, Jeannette Keton, Ed Kohorst, Ralph Langer, Bruce Leadbetter, Carl Leubsdorf, Mike Levy, Andy Lippman, David Lord, John Madigan, Stephanie May, Shelagh McElroy, Lisbeth McNabb, Joe McKnight, Morton Meyerson, Bob Mong, Becky Murphy, Richard Oppel, Bob Osborne, David Osborne, Laurey

Peat, Rena Pederson, Alan Peppard, Gary Pruitt, Michael Putzel, Orage Quarles III, Allen Questrom, Linda Quick, Harry Reasoner, Louella Reynolds, Lennox Samuels, Bobbie Seril, Mike Silverman, Dolph Simons, Bill Sims, Dean Singleton, Dave Smith, Paul Stevens, Charlotte St. Martin, Roby Terrill, Mark Thayer, Gerald Turner, Mike Ullman, Pedro Vergne, Lissa Walls, Stuart Wilk, Bill Winter, and David Woo.

I was also given access to Burl's large files (and those of the A. H. Belo Corporation) that are held at the DeGolyer Library at Southern Methodist University. I am especially grateful to librarian Ada Negraru for helping me find just what I was looking for—and then some!

Among the many books I read in researching this book, I found *Fresh Ink: Behind the Scenes at a Major Metropolitan Newspaper* by David Gelsanliter and *Belo: From Newspapers to New Media* by Judith Garrett Segura to be especially helpful. *The Puzzle People: Memoirs of a Transplant Surgeon* by Thomas E. Starzl and *Beyond Every Wall* by Velma P. Scantlebury, MD, were also very instructive.

Without the help of editor Linda O'Doughda, who assisted with incorporating into the manuscript a large chunk of Burl's newly discovered files during the Covid shutdown, the book may never have gotten published.

The Osbornes and I want to especially acknowledge and thank the AP, *The Dallas Morning News*, and the A. H. Belo Corporation.

Jane Wolfe

Publisher's Note
Andrews McMeel Publishing wants to acknowledge the outstanding work of developmental editor Evelyn M. Duffy and researchers Ben Gambuzza and Tyler Loveless of Open Boat Editing.

Notes

• • •

1. "Saying Goodbye to the Teletype," *Philadelphia Inquirer, 1986, via Poynter,* https://www.poynter.org/reporting-editing/2014/today-in-media-history-was-the-teletype-machine-the-twitter-of-the-20th-century/. (page 11)

2. Reporter Dave Wellman in a profile for a Marshall student publication. (page 12)

3. Jon G. Udell, *The Economics of the American Newspaper* (New York: Hastings House, 1978). (page 16)

4. Howard M. Leichter, "'Evil Habits' and 'Personal Choices': Assigning Responsibility for Health in the 20th Century," https://www.ncbi.nlm.nih.gov/pmc/articles/PMC2690243/. (page 32)

5. "Splits," in wire-service jargon, refer to the ten-minute state-level news breaks that occurred each hour in the AP's national broadcast report. These were allotted to "line bureaus such as Charleston, Louisville, Columbus—usually state capitals," according to Strat Douthat. (page 34)

6. An agate is a unit of typographical measure in the United States. It is 5.5 typographical points, or about 1/14 inch. It can refer to either the height of a line of type or a font that is 5.5 points. An agate font is commonly used to display statistical data or legal notices in newspapers. (page 61)

7. The author's family owned *The Columbus Dispatch* for generations. In 2015, the Wolfes sold the paper to GateHouse Media. (page 80)

8. Edgar Wolfe was author Jane Wolfe's cousin. (page 90)

9. The AP log was published weekly to report the in-house comings and goings—as well as the philosophy and policies—of the company. (page 101)

10. Donald Liebenson, "UPI R.I.P.," the *Chicago Tribune*, May 3, 2003, https://www.chicagotribune.com/news/ct-xpm-2003-05-04-0305040380-story.html. (page 110)

11. https://drive.google.com/file/d/1hkuXRJ3AXTs_dWwzzqFIkbpGdSaCVUve/view. (page 120)

12. The AP redated its origins to 1846 from 1848 according to newly discovered documents in 2006. (page 257)

13. John Dimmick, Angela Powers, Sam Mwangi, and Elizabeth Stoycheff, "The Fragmenting Mass Media Marketplace." In *Changing the News: The Forces Shaping Journalism in Uncertain Times*. Edited by Wilson Lowrey and Peter J. Gade, 181. New York: Routledge, 2011. (page 264)

Happy Trails

• • •

Burl was serious when it came to journalism. But he didn't take himself too seriously. In the summer of 1984, he received an invitation from Jim Lonergan, a Harte-Hanks newspaper group president and publisher of *City: Wichita Falls Magazine*. Burl and Jim became friends during Burl's Ohio AP days, where Jim worked for Horvitz Newspapers. Jim and Burl both arrived in Texas in 1980. Burl in Dallas and Jim in Wichita Falls.

The invitation allowed Burl an opportunity to let down his guard and share his quick wit and sense of humor. Jim asked Burl to write a "non-cowboy's view" of the city's Texas Ranch Roundup. The event, held annually in Wichita Falls—a town near the Oklahoma border, about 150 miles northwest of Dallas—bills itself as the "original" event "designed to replicate the big cattle roundups of the late 1800s and early 1900s."

The three-day event draws working ranches from across the state. The participants from the ranches come to compete in everything from chuckwagon cooking competitions to rodeo horse barrel races. Burl, having come to Texas via New York City, would make for the perfect "non-cowboy." And, it gave him a chance to get dust on the cowboy boots given to him by his AP colleagues when he left New York.

The story he wrote on June 13, 1985, which appeared in the August edition of the magazine, is included here to end Burl's story so that y'all can enjoy his sense of humor and come away with a chuckle. As he would have wanted.

Happy Trails, Burl ...

AN OUTSIDER'S VIEW OF THE RANCH ROUNDUP

Burl Osborne

June 13, 1985

Please understand that I want to see another Texas Ranch Roundup some day, but that I don't know the difference between a top hand and a backhand. I also don't know much about horses although once or twice I have been accused of acting like part of one.

I am doing this for only one reason: Jim Lonergan, the publisher of this newspaper, filled me full of chili and brisket and cornbread and cold beer and told me I had to write or ride. The quality of my writing may be open to question; the quality of my riding, unfortunately, is not. So here I am. Jim wanted a non-cowboy's view of the roundup. Here I am.

Not that I am entirely without knowledge. I learned something about ranch life in my childhood, when I never missed the Roy Rogers and Lone Ranger serials every Saturday at the Paramount Theater in Ashland, Kentucky. Those guys were real cowboys. They could ride and rope and shoot and sing and they never fell off their horses or got dirty and they always got the girl.

My best pal Jonathan is the handsomest and brightest kid
I ever saw, but he thinks Roy Rogers is a fast-food restaurant in
Washington, D.C. If you agree with him, you both may be correct but
you're not right; that isn't my Roy Rogers. What we may have is a
generation gap to bridge.

Now if you think of Trigger, and Dale Evans, as I do, we
understand each other just fine.

And if you think the Lone Ranger is a creature of television,
as my best pal Jonathan does, you need to understand that the real
silver bullets were fired on the silver screen. (If "silver screen"
is a foreign to you, we may as well quit now because we'll never
understand each other.)

All of this is just to say that I grew up as a broomstick
cowboy. My prairie was a hillside in Kentucky and the only steer
I ever roped was my grandfather's milk cow. (She stepped on the
rope, and my foot.) Got my first pair of boots five years ago, as a
probationary Texan, and they're just now broken in.

The imagined Texas of my childhood was a place where the bad
guys hid out and one riot called for one ranger. Ranches in the
movies were what the good guys fought to defend. And roundups were
when the bad guys tried to steal all the good guys' cattle. True
Texans wouldn't let them.

My pal Jonathan is a 9-year-old broomstick space jockey. I used
the broomstick for a horse; he uses it for a laser. His bad guys
hide in outer space and his favorite good-guy cowboys are Indiana

Jones and the Goonies. One of us is out of date. On the other hand, his good guys always get the girl, so all is not lost.

I do not wish to mislead you; I was not entirely without contemporary preparation for signing on as a watcher of the 1984 Texas Ranch Roundup.

For example, I learned from the television show, "Dallas," that Real Cowboys these days drive red Mercedes Benz convertibles, constantly fight with their in-laws and friends, lie, cheat and steal, and never go near a horse.

Just about every Sunday, I learned that Real Cowboys wear funny blue and silver shirts and pedal pushers, run up and down the cleanest pasture I've ever seen, hit on each other constantly, and never go near a horse.

And every Saturday night, guys they call cowboys ride up and down Greenville Avenue in Dallas in pickup trucks, preferably muddy ones, chasing girls and sometimes catching them, and they never go near a horse.

The purpose of reciting my education is not to bore you, although I suspect I have, but rather to explain my surprise at coming to Wichita Falls and finding cowboys who seem to like to be around horses, and to explain how I learned that my education was lacking.

Despite my predisposition to the contrary, I now am persuaded that these Ranch Roundup cowboys really are the Real Cowboys and True Texans, not the tintypes of my Saturday matinees or the TV Texans of our Saturday nights.

This revelation came gradually but it started early, even before we got inside the arena. The first thing I noticed was that everyone was parking their own cars. There wasn't a valet parker in sight. Then I noticed there was not a single Rolls Royce pulled up front. That isn't at all like the TV show.

The next thing that hit me was all those kids, even teenagers, who were with people who looked like their parents. Families fight on the TV show; they don't go around enjoying each other like that.

Then I saw a pickup truck drive up and a kid got out, wearing a blue and silver shirt with Number 11 on it and I thought I might have found a real Dallas cowboy. But he was wearing blue jeans instead of pedal pushers and he wasn't hitting anyone or chasing a girl; he was looking for his buddies to go check out the sack races. No Dallas cowboy, or Greenville Avenue cowboy, would be doing that.

By this time, my conviction was so shaken I got hungry and so I went off with my best pal Jonathan and my best friend Betty to find something to eat.

That's when I got the next big jolt. I was ready for a real Western cookout. I knew what to expect because my best friend Betty and I were invited once to a real Western cookout at Southfork. Well, not actually AT Southfork, but on the grass in the yard, under a big candy-striped tent with valet parkers and caterers and white wine and quiche, with people posing as Woody Allen and the Marlboro Man standing all around so we could notice them and then they could pretend they didn't notice us noticing them.

Well, at the roundup there was not a caterer anywhere, much less the rented chairs or white wine, and I never did see any cowboy quiche. I didn't notice anyone noticing us noticing them. They were too busy having a good time.

I also suspected right away that this was no ordinary Dallas cookout. The first taste of championship chile from the Waggoner Ranch, ladled out of a big black pot that got its crust in the line of duty, confirmed my suspicion because I knew what it was. And it surely did beat quiche.

We kept attacking my doubts with food for an hour or two, and then I remembered that I had forgotten whatever it was at the office that I had been worrying about. My best friend Betty and my best pal Jonathan told me I seemed relaxed and they held my hand. That's not bad duty.

After a little brisket here and some gumbo and beer over there, we got around to seeing the show. Notice I didn't call it a rodeo. Jim told me not to call it a rodeo because it's different, having something to do with the way you hold on. The only difference I could see right away was that these cowboys wore Levis; I think they wear Calvin Klein's at the big deal rodeos in places like Mesquite.

I never did quite get the hang of the penning contest. I kept squirming in my seat, trying to help nudge those steers into the pen. I didn't have any more luck than some of the cowboys. It was like parents explaining curfew to teenagers--the kids know what they are supposed to do but they just don't want to do it.

I didn't know what to think about the wild cow milking contest either. Nobody on Greenville Avenue, or television, ever milks a cow, certainly not a wild cow. I sort of figured out the objective, although I never did figure out how to keep score. I guess it's a nutritious kind of game.

I know from reading the paper afterward that Mickey Lowe led the Lewis Ranches to victory by riding a horse upon whose back he apparently was not welcome. It seemed to me that the horse should have gotten some kind of award, too, for shot putting Mr. Lowe end over end onto his Levi labels. This is the only sport I ever saw where the winner winds up on his backside, under the horse he just beat.

But there was one these people kept doing that gave them away as Real Cowboys and real ranchers. I knew this crowd was genuine, the TV show and Greenville Avenue crowd notwithstanding, because these people kept right on having fun, even when the television camera wasn't on them. No TV Texan would ever waste his time having fun without a play-by-play from Jim McKay.

I guess you get the idea about my experience.

Okay, I will concede a certain gap in my cowboy competence, but keep in mind that I never once, all weekend, got saddle sore. That's not all bad and I even got to keep the girl, who is still my best friend.

Did I have a good time?

Absolutely.

Would I do it again?

Absolutely.

Why not? My best pal Jonathan loved it. My best friend Betty loved it. So, as anyone with a son and a wife will know, it didn't matter much whether I liked it. But I did.

I'll bet you will too.